W9-AMX-077

Nigeria

THE SEEDS OF DISASTER

John Hatch

HENRY REGNERY COMPANY · CHICAGO

Published 1970 by Henry Regnery Company, 114 West Illinois Street, Chicago, Illinois 60610
Manufactured in the United States of America
Library of Congress Catalog Card Number: 78-126145

Preface

The object of this book is to assist those concerned with Africa to understand something of the depths of the problems that beset modern African societies. Unfortunately, the Nigerian civil war represents but one of the cancerous branches that spring from the central trunk of basic African dilemmas. To comprehend its significance—or the significance of any current African problem—one needs to examine the roots, which lie in the historical experience of the African peoples and their ancestors. I trust that this study will make some contribution to such understanding.

I first visited Nigeria in 1955; since then I have been in the country many times, the last occasion occurring a few days before the end of the civil war. During these visits I have been given the benefit of discussions with numerous Nigerians, all of whom have greatly contributed to my understanding of their country and peoples. The individuals themselves are far too numerous to list, and it would be invidious to select some and omit others. I therefore simply wish to thank them all for their time, patience, and help.

As in the case of my previous books, my main assistance has come from Gillian Hollings. Her industrious research and long hours of typing have been invaluable to the production of this book. I am deeply grateful for her support.

The opinions expressed in this book are, of course, mine alone.

JOHN HATCH

London
July, 1970

Contents

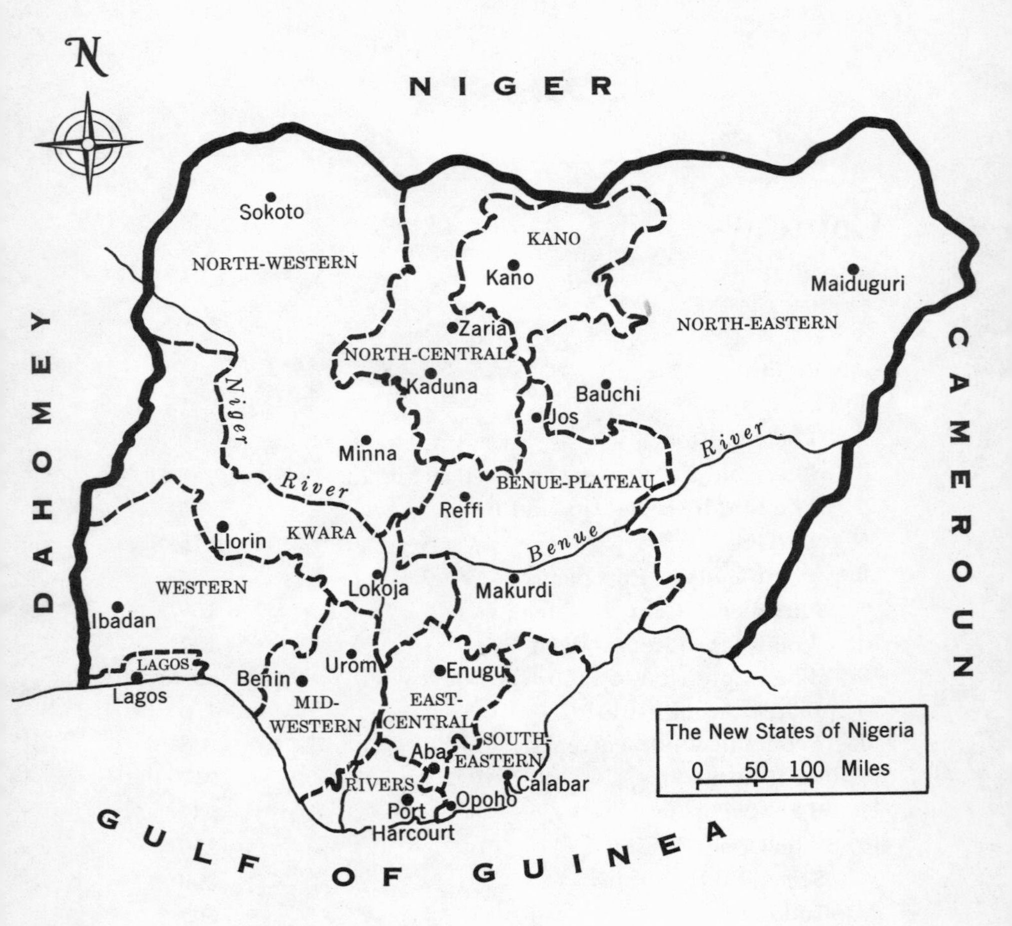
N
NIGER
DAHOMEY
CAMEROUN
GULF OF GUINEA
Sokoto
NORTH-WESTERN
KANO
Kano
Maiduguri
Zaria
NORTH-EASTERN
NORTH-CENTRAL
Kaduna
Bauchi
Jos
Niger
River
Minna
BENUE-PLATEAU
River
Reffi
Llorin
KWARA
Benue
WESTERN
Lokoja
Makurdi
Ibadan
LAGOS
Lagos
Urom
Benin
Enugu
MID-
WESTERN
EAST-
CENTRAL
SOUTH-
EASTERN
Aba
RIVERS
Calabar
Port
Harcourt
Opoho
The New States of Nigeria
0 50 100 Miles

1

PANORAMA

THE ROAD to the north runs between groups of thatched huts enclosed by screen walls of bamboo and rafia. It is paved in the center, but each time an approaching car is met, the dirt verges have to be used and a cloud of carroty dust hides the sky. Scrawny hens peck around the compounds; a dozen goats wander between them; around a well women and children take turns in hauling up pottery vessels of water; a pair of donkeys amble beside the road, their flanks bulging with bundles of firewood. From time to time one passes small groups of white-robed, dark-faced men, sitting beside the road on their sacks of groundnuts, waiting for a rickety bus or lurching truck to take them to town. Much of the land is thin scrub over visible sand, for the Sahara is just across the border with Niger, but occasionally one will pass a patch of green–cassava or guinea corn growing in a square field surrounded by a mud wall to keep out the goats. A flash of brilliant color reveals a horseman clad in scarlet and green, his face half hidden behind a white kerchief, his head encased in a snowy turban headdress, followed by two attendants on donkeys. Outside some of the compounds piles of dry bush branches laden with kernels await the nut pickers; beside others the gleam of a creamy globe indicates a growing calabash.

Such is the daily scene for nearly half the people of Nigeria. In the compound lives the family unit. A man and his several wives each have their own thatched-roof, mud-walled hut, normally containing a board bed and some blankets, mats, earthen-ware pots, and calabash gourds. The children usually live with their mothers until they move to a smaller hut, often just outside the compound. A few chickens and goats are attached to each family; guinea corn and cassava, grown in a nearby field, provide the staple family diet. A few families grow a little rice or cotton. Almost everyone cultivates the groundnut bush—which provides virtually the only means of cash exchange—to provide money to buy utensils or cloth, though occasional piles of cut wood, set at the roadside to attract the traveler from town, supplement this income. Water for cooking or drinking is drawn from the nearest well and carried back to the compound on the heads of women and children. The smoke of numerous wood fires rising in the short evening dusk indicates that the single daily meal is being cooked in the compound yard. The meal is almost certain to be a kind of corn pap, perhaps a little cassava, occasionally a piece of bush meat—rural subsistence life in a biblical setting.

Nearly forty miles from the city, where the road begins, stands the first village. Here many of the farmers from the countryside bring their groundnuts and buy the few utensils not made at home. One passes a long, low, whitewashed building surrounded by short grass and red soil; a few trees shade it from the burning sun. A painted sign at the gate indicates that this is the "Farm Institute," evidence of a desire to improve the centuries-old farming methods of the traditionalist-minded peasant families of the district. Here a handful of agricultural demonstrators learn about new seeds and plants that can produce larger yields, the use of fertilizers or manure, the value of modern—though they be no more complicated than the hoe—implements.

The second group of new buildings one meets is the village hospital, a group of single-story buildings also set in scrubby parkland. A dozen blue-and-white-clad nurses sit gossiping in the shade; a white-uniformed doctor hurries between buildings; some convalescent patients lie on bed-chairs under the trees. Everything looks clean, tidy, and peaceful; for this is a new hospital, built by the state government, further evidence of the gradual introduction of modern facilities into traditional society.

On the other side of the road a red laterite track leads up to the high school, another indication of the village's social importance. This is no village school; it is the only high school in the area. Few children in this district ever see the inside of any school, and a high school is especially uncommon. The school also is composed of single-story buildings—dormitories, classrooms, dining room, staff houses—surrounded by a few fields with soccer goal posts, a school garden, and well-kept, though thinly grassed, lawns. This is a boys' school, for the area is largely Muslim. Although social habits are slowly changing, the education of girls is still meager and coeducation not encouraged.

These are the modern trimmings of the village. Beyond a few rickety stores, a wooden "Travelers' Hotel," occasional gasoline or soft-drink hoardings, we reach the heart of village life. In the middle of the single tarred road, off which half a dozen dirt paths lead, a paved yard shows signs of unusual activity. On one side a dozen women, wearing long skirts of local patterned cloth, are shaking and winnowing large wicker baskets filled with groundnut husks, letting the husks fly in the breeze and depositing the nuts in piles on the ground. A one-armed crushing machine cuts off the shells, leaving more piles of kernels. On the other side, separated by an avenue of trees, a second yard is occupied by a collection of white-robed men, filling sacks with nuts, carrying them to a machine to be weighed and checked. Beside the road a pile of bags awaits the truck that will carry them into the city on the start of the long journey to the coast and then overseas to the world's oil factories. Life in the village, at least at harvest time, largely revolves around this groundnut focus, which provides the main social and economic attraction of the village for the peoples of surrounding areas.

The village is also an administrative headquarters. For centuries religion and government have been inextricably linked, with the emir providing the catalyst. He was, and remains, the religious leader, and until very recently he was also head of the governmental system. He formed the apex of an administrative pyramid that broadened down through his advisory council, regional, district, village, and hamlet representatives to the mass of the people (though confined at each level solely to male delegates). The emirs have now lost their political and administrative powers, but parts of the old administrative system survive. Thus certain villages, as area centers, are designated administrative headquarters.

The villages gain some prestige and a little economic benefit from the council buildings and the meetings that take place in their midst. Yet behind the façade displayed on the main road life continues very much as it has over the past thousand years. Goats gather beside the red-clay walls of family compounds; the roads are composed of laterite, hard rutted in the dry seasons, liquid mud with deep gullies in the wet. Boys in ankle-length white habits play in the roads, tend their goats, or drive their donkeys. The few visible women and girls all seem to be carrying pots of water or bowls of cassava on their heads; many are veiled, covered from head to foot in black. No one hurries, for the sun burns all day and it is still close to the biblical age.

At the other end of the road is the town or city: Kaduna, Katsina, Sokoto, Bauchi, or Kano. Kaduna became the capital of the northern region and, in addition to the attention it attracted as a political and administrative center, has been favored by many new industries. Katsina, too, developed rapidly in the eighteenth century, becoming the greatest trading entrepot of Hausaland. Yet it is Kano that still retains the aura of its great past. Here are blended the ancient, scarcely changing traditions and many of Nigeria's contemporary human difficulties. In the old walled city the respectful, even reverential life of medieval Muslim Africa is largely preserved; yet the new town of Yoruba and Ibo merchants was the scene of dreadful massacres in 1953 and 1966.

Kano was famous for its market as early as the twelfth century. In the fourteenth century Islam arrived. Early in the sixteenth the famous Moor, Leo Africanus, traveler, historian, geographer, and master of several other professions, described the inhabitants of Kano as "rich merchants and most civil people." (In a more misanthropic or perhaps more socially perceptive mood, he noted that the people of Katsina "dwell in most forlorn and base cottages . . . and beside their base estate they are mightily oppressed with famine.")

Kano is the central collecting place for groundnuts. In the railway freight yards stand huge pyramids of sacks. In factories nuts are crushed for oil, the scent of which hangs heavy around the city. Kano's market, four centuries old, still forms an entrepot for the wandering traders from wide stretches of the neighboring desert; indeed, the market's reputation dates from long before the groundnut age. Nor was it achieved simply because of the city's position at the crossroads of the trans-Saharan trade routes. Kano's inhabitants produced their own wares, acquiring a manufacturing fame to add to their skills at exchange.

One mid-nineteenth century traveler, Heinrich Barth, described Kano's activities most perceptively:

> The principal commerce of Kano consists in native produce, namely, the cotton cloth woven and dyed here or in the neighboring towns. The great advantage of Kano is, that commerce and manufactures go hand in hand, and that almost every family has its share in them. There is really something grand in this kind of industry, which spreads to the north as far as Murzuk, Ghat, and even Tripoli; to the west, not only to Timbuktu, but in some degrees even as far as the shores of the Atlantic, the very inhabitants of Arguin dressing in the cloth woven and dyed in Kano; to the east, all over Bornu . . . to the south . . . towards the south-east. . . . In taking a general view of the subject, I think myself justified in estimating the whole produce of this manufacture, as far as it is sold abroad, at the very least at about three hundred million kurdi [about $60,000].

Barth's writing suggests that he, like many nineteenth-century European explorers and administrators alienated from Europe's industrial revolutions, was attracted to the simpler structure of African life, and this emotional attachment may have led him to some exaggeration and hyperbole, though he did also admit that the slave trade flourished. Nevertheless, his witness to the commercial-manufacturing activities of Kano stands undisputed.

Kano today is two towns. Within its medieval red-clay walls narrow, dark alleyways run between turreted mud houses; donkeys, mules, and an occasional camel amble down the streets, urged on by the shrill cries of young boys; the men are almost all clad in long white gowns, some of the women in the all-black enveloping Muslim veiled dress, though increasing numbers of them display brightly patterned local cloths. In the center stands the emir's palace, spired, high mud-walled, courtyard leading to courtyard like a repeating mirror. Within the innermost hall the emir, clad in gorgeous robes, a dazzling white headdress, and beautifully patterned sandals, sits on a scarlet velvet woolsack, a quiet, thoughtful, gentle man, still the spiritual leader of his people. Near the palace rises the huge, domed, turreted central mosque, guardian of the community's social values, linking it with the wide Muslim world. As the sun sinks and the muezzin calls, thousands of white-clad figures in serried ranks prostrate themselves toward the east; from every roof rows of buzzards peer down at the humans.

This simple scene is interrupted by masses of bicycles, every bell tinkling, and scores of trucks and cars, each horn blaring. Yet the cacophony of modern commercial life within these ancient walls is mild compared to that outside. There, in the second town, marketing, bargaining, shouting, arguing rise to a frenzy, while a conglomeration of trucks, wagons, cars, cycles, carts, and donkeys add their contribution to the animated confusion. This is the *sabon gari,* the "new town" or "stranger quarter," built mainly by Ibo and Yoruba traders, with stores, street markets, residential houses, an odd club or cinema. The new town is constantly expanding, with small industries, warehouses, and workshops growing rapidly. The habits of the new town represent modern Nigeria, in sharp contrast to the time-aged, quieter, more dignified, traditional customs of the ancient city. The dichotomy can bring resentment and conflict; it was in the *sabon gari* that the tragedies of the Ibo massacres in 1953 and 1966 occurred.

Ibadan is an amazing city. It lies about ninety miles north of Lagos, in the western region. It has been built on the folds of several hills, so that when one approaches it, one looks down on a vast urban panorama. Wave upon wave of russet corrugated-iron roofs fill the scene; in Ibadan about 1.5 million people live in the largest African city outside Egypt.

Ibadan has no ancient history such as that of Kano. It has grown as a center for the Yoruba peoples since the first half of the nineteenth century. The Yoruba communities have a long experience of intercommunal warfare, and Ibadan has been both a military base and a haven for refugees. But its growth has been occasioned by the individualistic, commercialist outlook of the Yoruba. The Yoruba prefer to live in towns—there are seven large Yoruba towns beside Ibadan—and their total urban population is some 3 million, with many more living in villages, small and large. The urban atmosphere offers the Yoruba peoples their best opportunities to indulge their favorite activities: bargaining, marketing, political disputation, and reading.

Ibadan reflects all these characteristics. The tower of its great Cocoa House skyscraper rises amid the most appalling slums. The luxury Premier Hotel, with its air conditioning, swimming pool, numerous bars and restaurants, the center of many business deals, political intrigues, and academic discussions among the Yoruba upper class, looks over the city from its own hill; in the city thousands of small stores, workshops, and markets are crammed together. Trucks and transport wagons—"mammy wagons," painted with philosophical or biblical slogans—compete with every variety of private car and taxis for the inadequate road space of the city's narrow, winding streets. The traffic jams are incredible, without a vestige of control; horns hoot ceaselessly, every driver seeking his own advantage. On the outskirts of the city modern housing estates have been built beside the villas of the rich; in the city center tall office blocks and spacious public buildings overlook tin and straw shanties in the midst of glutinous mud.

Ibadan must possess more bookshops than any other city in the world. Every possible type of book is offered in their fly-blown windows, from obscure religious texts to the latest pornographic American paperback. The luxuriously appointed university just outside the city boasts what is perhaps the best bookshop in Africa, a vast, well-organized store where a wide variety of academic and intellectual fare is offered.

The university itself provides another contrast. In 1970 it

is a little more than twenty years old, the first of the African universities to be built in the postwar flush of British colonial academic concern. Its buildings are white or pale pink, built in open-work stone to a variety of architectural designs. Modern laboratories, lecture rooms, dormitories, even a theater for the drama department run by the world-famous dramatist Wole Soyinka cover the broad campus. The contrast between the ease of life for students and faculty here and conditions in town could hardly be sharper; yet this is not a Yoruba university: it serves the whole of Nigeria and forms an international community with many overseas residents. Before the civil war its vice-chancellor was Kenneth Dike, an internationally renowned historian and an Ibo. Although Dike decided that it would be prudent to resign and has been succeeded by a Yoruba, the first Nigerian psychiatrist, Dr. Lambo, the students and staff have continued to be drawn from all parts of the country.

The road north from Lagos branches near Shagamu. Continuing north, it reaches Ibadan and proceeds to Ilorin and the northern towns; the right-hand fork takes one along the new motor road toward Benin. Generally well paved, the road is narrow, and when an approaching vehicle is met one or other has to take to the dirt verge. Frequent wrecks bear silent testimony to the outcome of an encounter between two stubborn drivers.

Along the Benin road one first passes through the well-spaced trees of rubber plantations, among them a large one owned by Chief Awolowo, one of Nigeria's principal political figures for the past quarter century. Then one is in the rain forest, dense, brilliant green foliage of interlaced leaves and grotesquely twisting branches. Everything grows in the steamy, humid swelter, but little can be cultivated.

The road crosses numerous small rivers by narrow, single-lane bridges. Below the bridge women are washing clothes, laying them on the bank to dry; men, women, and children are bathing; a fishing canoe is slowly paddled down the stream. One passes through a score of tiny, straggling villages: mud-brick huts, thatched or roofed with corrugated iron. Beside the road one meets women and children, answering the always urgent demand for firewood, walking toward their villages carrying huge tree branches on their heads; others bear enamel bowls filled with cassava root or miniature pyramids of gari, the cream-colored cassava flour that forms the staple diet. At the roadside piles of plantain, looking like giant bananas, invite the bargaining traveler; bush-meat carcasses of grasscutter hang like bats from bamboo frames, for sale at a quarter the price demanded in town. In the villages and on their outskirts churches and the low buildings of mission schools reveal the widespread activities of Christianity; most of them belong to the Roman Catholic Church, its proportion rising the farther east one travels. Every village has its focal market, rambling rows of wooden stalls, a riot of brilliant colored cloths on women with purchases on their heads, a babble of animated talk and disputation.

The first considerable town is Ore, which saw the limit of the Biafran advance in 1967. Its few stucco houses and occasional brick-built office mark the change from village life. In the long main street a dozen wooden-slatted trucks stand beside the road. The trucks are crammed with humanity—vari-dressed men, women, and children packed like sardines, some clinging to the tailgate—for this is the only form of public transport. Along both sides of the street tables and benches are loaded with every conceivable kind of goods, from cotton reels to heavy-duty tires, from sofas to washing powders; other goods lie on the ground itself. Two or three gas stations, a "traveler's inn," one or two open workshops, and a church complete the streetscape. In five minutes one is past the town proper, passing through another wooden-villa suburb and out again into the bush.

There is an oral tradition that the people of Benin came from Egypt, pausing briefly on their way in the Sudan and in Ile-Ife in present-day western Nigeria. However that may be, the city of Benin was the focus of a kingdom of considerable wealth and power from medieval times. The Portuguese reached Benin in 1486 and quickly found its pepper crop greatly esteemed in Europe. The king of Benin was so friendly to his Portuguese visitors that he sent an ambassador to the king of Portugal, "a Negro, one of his captains, from a harboring place by the sea because he desired to learn more about these lands, the arrival of people from them in his country being regarded as an unusual novelty." The Portuguese showed equal friendship and feted the Benin ambassador:

> The ambassador was a man of good speech and natural wisdom. Great feasts were held in his honour, and he was shown many of the good things of these kingdoms. He returned to his land in a ship of the king's, who at his departure made him a gift of rich clothes for himself and his wife.

Before long the Portuguese persuaded the king of Benin to allow the teaching of Christianity in his kingdom; the monarch was so impressed that he "gave his son and some of his noblemen—the greatest in his kingdom—so that they might become Christians; and also he ordered a church to be built in Benin." By that time, 1516, the Portuguese were also helping Benin in its wars with its neighbors, and in the Benin museum a drum captured from the Idah in 1515 is displayed.

By the middle of the sixteenth century the English also were in Benin. Thomas Wyndham went there in 1553. Some of his merchants, together with his Portuguese captain, Pinteado, were taken to the Benin court

> to the presence of the king, who being a blacke Moor (although not so blacke as the rest) sate in a great huge hall, long

> and wide, the walls made of earth without windowes, the roof of thin boards, open in sundry places like unto lovers [probably louvres: ventilators] to let in the air.

Benin has, of course, become world famous for its brass sculpture. According to one Nigerian historian, Chief Jacob Egharevba, the curator of the museum in Benin,

> Oba Oguola wished to introduce brass-casting into Benin so as to produce works of art similar to those sent him from Ife. He therefore sent to the Oni of Ife for a brass-smith, and Iguegha was sent to him. Iguegha was very clever and left many designs to his successors, and was in consequence deified, and is worshipped to this day by brass-smiths. The practice of making brass-castings for the preservation of the records of events was originated during the reign of Oguola.

Tradition has it that Oguola reigned in the late thirteenth century; it is thought by some, however, that brass work only began in Benin about the end of the fourteenth century. Certainly, the art of brass-cutting was brought from Ife.

Today, Benin, once the capital of the mid-west region and now the seat of government for the new mid-west state, shows little sign of its past splendors. Some of its approaches are pleasantly flower-clad, but the city itself is dusty, rather drab, and badly in need of paint. Most of its buildings are wooden and somewhat ramshackle, though the hospital and parliament buildings have style. The store-lined streets collect dirt and refuse; there is little evidence of planning; and even the government ministries, scattered haphazardly around the town, are housed in shabby wooden buildings. The military occupation Benin has experienced since the early days of the civil war has not helped the city's development, either.

The eighty-seven miles from Benin to Asaba on the Niger are much more interesting than Benin itself. At first one is among Benin-speaking peoples; before one passes the halfway mark, though, one passes into Ibo-speaking country. The road is stringed with villages, all with their markets, mud houses, laden women—many with infants strapped to their backs—scores of children, and even more goats. Mission schools and churches abound in the area, almost all the people being Christian—many in the Catholic Church—or pagan. Some of the missionary secondary schools form extremely attractive pictures, long, low buildings set in grassland parks, usually with the goal posts of a soccer field in the center, often surrounded by brightly colored flower beds. The road itself is often pleasant, the heavy leaves of numerous trees sometimes meeting overhead to form a shady avenue. The only substantial town along the road, Agbor, is nondescript, yet the view down over it from the approaching hill provides soft contours and a pleasing aspect of animated humanity.

Through the straggling, quiet town of Asaba, dominated by its large, towered, gray-stone Catholic church, the road runs down to the Niger, one of Africa's great rivers, cousin to the Nile, the Congo, the Zambesi. The Niger has been the scene of many historical dramas, from the ancient empires of its upper reaches to the brutal days of slaving, and the focus of the expeditions of Mungo Park, the Lander Brothers, Macgregor Laird, Dr. Baikie, Bishop Crowther, George Goldie. Just across the river lies Onitsha, shelled for three days in 1879 by a British warship, an action calculated at the time to have a "most salutary effect up and down the Niger." Downstream at one of the river's many mouths in the delta is Bonny, described by an English ship's captain at the end of the eighteenth century as the "wholesale market for slaves, since not fewer than 20,000 are sold here every year. Of these, 16,000 come from one nation, called the Ibos, so that this single nation has exported over the last twenty years, not fewer than 320,000 of its people."

Unconcerned with past scenes of endurance or brutality, the mighty river sluggishly wends its way between sandbanks and islands toward the Bight of Biafra some hundred miles to the south. It has flowed in a wide arc from the borders of Guinea and Sierra Leone, though Guinea, Mali, and Niger, and along the frontier with Dahomey into northwest Nigeria. Something over a hundred miles north of Onitsha it was joined by the Benue at Lokoja, another town with historic nineteenth-century memories.

The Niger is a mile broad at Onitsha, and from the other side the glittering white tower of the famous three-thousand-stall market and the spire of the cathedral can be seen. For centuries the broad river has separated the people on the west bank from those on the east, although both are Ibo. Now, however, a shimmering latticed steel bridge, completed in 1965 at a cost of $15.6 million, links the two regions to each other and the east with Nigeria's capital, Lagos. When completed, the bridge at Onitsha was a noble span, functional more than beautiful, perhaps, but still conveying the aesthetic satisfaction of a well-proportioned edifice filling a valuable human need. In 1967 this vital link in the communications chain binding the communities of Nigeria suffered a cruel blow: its eastern end was blown up by retreating Biafran forces. The wounded giant, a limb amputated, lay helpless, all traffic halted for another two years. It was a melancholy sight, the road simply ending in midair a hundred yards from the eastern shore; below lay a mass of tangled metal, the constructive work of years destroyed in seconds.

Besides Onitsha, the east boasts two other large towns of well over one hundred thousand inhabitants. Port Harcourt owes its eminence and growing population to the wealth of oil in its environs. Port Harcourt originally was an Ijaw town, but the shrewd, thrusting Ibo soon saw the opportunities arising from oil production and came to dominate the town. Oil installations and port facilities characterize the town; an attending industrial complex keeps pace. As a result of the war almost all Ibo left Port Harcourt and the employment of the oil companies, leaving the minority communities to take their place in the new Rivers State.

Enugu was largely the creation of Lord Lugard, who planned it as a main administrative center. It became the capital of the eastern region. As befits its purpose, Enugu is a quiet town, planned on spacious lines, set in the folds of a number of hills. Two coal mines nearby provide the main industrial wealth of the whole area, which, until the discovery of oil, was the least naturally endowed of the four Nigerian regions.

Lagos, the capital of Nigeria, has been left to the end of this pictorial review, for it does not blend with any other part of the country. To a degree one can find an underlying unified pattern in the other areas. Basically, Nigeria is a land of subsistence farmers, living either in homesteads or in villages. Not much more than 10 percent of the population lives in towns, though there are, of course, many variations. Whereas the general picture in the north—at least in the large Muslim areas—is one of enclosed family compounds, with man, wives, children, and often other relatives living within a clearly defined unit, in the pagan and Christian districts the huts or houses are separate, usually housing a nuclear family. Food habits differ, too: in one area the staple will be cassava or gari; in another rice or guinea corn. Yet in a rough sort of way the country hangs together: two people from one area can usually find a common subject of conversation with those of another—always provided they understand a common tongue. In any case, travel around the country is not yet so frequent that most people venture beyond an area in which interests are common.

Lagos is an exception to all this. Geographically and, to some extent, metaphorically, it is an excrescence. The city is composed of a set of islands joined to an ever widening mainland area. It has no unity of pattern; nor have its inhabitants any homogeneity. Like all large cities, Lagos attracts people from all over the country. Often the immigrants tend to form communal pockets, although those who rise in social stature usually move into the more mixed middle-class areas.

Most observers recall the fine race course in the heart of Lagos, Independence Building skyscraper, the striking lines of the Supreme Court, the elegance of the parliament house, and King's College, the exclusive boys' school. The beaches of Victoria Island, the lawns, flower beds, and hedges of residential Ikoyi, the shipping lane alongside the marina—all claim frequent notice. But for me Lagos presents two different and distinct characteristics: slums and commerce.

For one side of Lagos go anywhere behind the main streets —to Musin on the mainland, on the side road just across the water on the way to Apapa, behind the bus station, in parts of Yaba—and the scene is always the same: slimy mud for streets, open drains (usually blocked up), naked infants crawling around the gutters, flies, excreta, urine, garbage surrounding the tin-and-lath shanties, old stucco houses left from some past era crammed with a score of families. Listen to these people and the unquenchable human spirit shines out. I once talked with a group of children in the foul stench of Musin; one lad of eleven told me that his ambition was to go to England to learn to be a doctor so that he could look after all his sick friends.

The other side of Lagos is its pervading commercial atmosphere. From the young girls who hold a tray of matches or endlessly peel oranges on the sidewalks to the open stores alongside many of its streets, gay with bright cloths, piles of fruits, pots, pans, shoes, clothes, to the air-conditioned offices of large import-export firms, the whole city seems to be constantly selling and buying. Even at night candles or torches light the peddlers' stands and the open stalls. On the sea roads ships are always lined up awaiting a berth; the trucks line up along the approaches to Apapa docks, for there are too many cargoes to handle; merchants haggle at street corners or enact more dignified business in elegant restaurants. Lagos has been an entrepot ever since the days when it served Benin as a slave market; it has always attracted a cosmopolitan collection of inhabitants and visitors; in the steamy, humid heat the city has grown out of mangrove swamps, with money-seeking pervading every fetid alley.

It would be quite unfair to suggest that Lagos is making no effort to improve itself. There is an impressive amount of excellent construction work in progress, although the very improvement often creates even worse confusion. Housing estates—Surulere, for one—have begun to appear in suburbs; the road-bridge intersection across to Apapa rivals any U.S. highway system, even down to the green and white indicator signs; on the way to Apapa, too, an impressive elevated road is being built to cross the railway that causes so many delays. But drive over old Carter Bridge, among the press of cars, trucks, cycles, and pedestrians, and along the fourteen miles to Ikeja airport: the sheer mass of humanity and vehicles will impress my point. There are over 1 million inhabitants in Lagos, and they all seem to be on the streets at once—yet still they pour in from the rest of the country. They have to find relatives or friends to give them shelter; existing services simply cannot cope, and there is little chance of their being expanded quickly enough to keep up with increasing pressures.

In Lagos I am haunted by the specter of Calcutta.

2

THE ANCESTORS

THE ORIGINS of the human race have been long and passionately debated. No doubt the debates will continue for many generations, with new research and discoveries adding to both the proponents' data and their fervor. When we attempt to answer the query as to who were the ancestors of twentieth-century west Africans, therefore, we necessarily enter the realm of speculation and conjecture. Probably the story we can hazard today will have to be amended as new evidence is revealed. Nevertheless, some attempt to answer the question based on extant knowledge is of value, for a coherent, if shadowy, story can be told.

The continuous story of man's emergence and evolution is especially apposite to Africa, for in that continent a series of modern discoveries seems to have provided certain vital links. South Africa, Tanzania, and the Chad area have supplied the twentieth century with remains from which it is now possible to chart the outlines of human evolution, although, it must be repeated, certainty may not yet be claimed.

It is suggested by some archaeologists that about seven hundred and fifty thousand years ago early man spread from Africa into Asia and Europe, though others might contest the assertion that this prehistoric evolution occurred only in the African continent. For our purpose what is more important is to note the divergence in cultural patterns that we know did take place in Africa. From about 50,000 B.C. the kinds of tools that seem to have been used in the wooded areas were different from those employed in the open plains. In the former, implements were clearly devised for use on wood and in digging up root foods: chisels, for instance, have been found in such areas, and heavy stones for pounding roots. In the open country the tools were smaller, finer, and pointed for the purpose of hunting.

It would seem that round about 10,000 B.C. man's development reached the stage at which differentiation into the ancestors of modern African people can be discerned. It is thought that by this time most of the inhabitants of Africa resembled the bushmen who today live in the southwest of the continent. They are thought to have been larger and so are called "big bushmen" by archaeologists. Remains of such men have been found both in the Nile valley and in west Africa. It would seem from current evidence that this type of man is the true ancestor of the negroid peoples who have predominated among African populations ever since.

The early populations of Africa were not entirely composed of Negroes, however. Caucasoid peoples lived in the north and northeast. In particular, the area now covered by the Sahara desert provided an opportunity for the intermingling of negroid and caucasoid peoples. Until about 2000 B.C. the Sahara region was fertile, bearing trees and pasture, crossed by rivers, sustaining animals. From the stone and bone tools and the rock drawings found in the Sahara it is clear that it was well populated. There was, therefore, no barrier between northern—Mediterranean—Africa and west

Africa. The peoples of the two areas mixed freely and exchanged goods with each other. It was only as the Sahara began to desiccate that families and communities had to move either northward or southward. In general, the caucasoid peoples went north and the negroid south, but naturally each had physical and intellectual effects on the other. Nor did contact between the two peoples ever cease. Even after the desiccation process had formed the desert we know today, routes between scattered oases were kept open and in constant use for trade or war.

The growth of the desert had, of course, profound effects on the development of African society. To a considerable, if never complete, extent the desert severed most African peoples from other than occasional contact with the communities of the Mediterranean, the Middle East, and Europe, where new ideas proliferated through international exchange. To a high degree Africans had to work out the techniques of social life in an isolation that was broken only by interchange among their own varied societies and a few ideas gleaned from intrepid desert travelers.

It may have been partly the effects of desert growth that also led to a separation between eastern and western negroid peoples. Differences in ecology induced contrasting ways of life. The communities based on the upper Nile valley, even more influenced by caucasoid neighbors, tended to concentrate on the pastoral activities connected with cattle and became largely nomadic; the higher rainfall and greater fertility in parts of the west led to greater agricultural development and consequently to a more sedentary life. There were exceptions, such as the Fulani in the west—who were probably influenced by nomadic Tuareg in the desert—who are a cattle-oriented community. Nor was the separation of east and west ever complete. Not only were a few trade routes preserved, there is evidence of some migration, especially from east to west. Many west African communities maintain folk traditions about ancestors coming from the east, but actual evidence to support the traditions is too weak yet to confirm or deny them. As we shall see, some peoples from the west greatly contributed through migration to the populations of the east, center, and south of the continent.

A knowledge of the effects of the growth of the Sahara is crucial to an understanding of subsequent African developments. It has become a stereotypical assertion of believers in the theory of racial "superiority" and "inferiority" that the "colored races," and particularly the Negroes, developed more slowly than the caucasoid peoples, for example, never inventing "anything." Much of this ignorant theorizing has now been exposed, largely by archaeological research, for the sophistry it is, though the prejudiced have tried to sustain their bias by claiming that the achievements of Africans—in building and government, for example—should be attributed to caucasoid "Hamites."

No serious historian any longer gives credence to such dogma. Nevertheless, it remains a fact that, because of the Sahara, much of Africa did not share in the urban revolution that developed in Asia, Europe, and north Africa as soon as sufficient food supplies and wealth accumulation made division of labor possible. This revolution in social life, assisted by metallurgical discoveries leading to the use of copper and bronze and by the invention of writing, allowed people to settle permanently in large cities for the first time. And it was the close proximity of men, which made easier the transmission and exchange of ideas, that induced most of the political, social, economic, and technological inventions that have frequently been the agents that have transformed society. The formation of the Sahara desert—together with the barrier formed by the Nile sudd and by the strength and self-sufficiency of Egyptian society—isolated Africans living south of the desert from those centers in which new ideas were being conceived. The desert was never as complete a barrier as the Atlantic, which isolated the Americas even more thoroughly, but it ensured that African societies remained much more localized and prescientific than those of Europe and Asia. (Of course, these disadvantages may have been partially compensated for by the Africans' greater concentration on human relations and the absence of large-scale warfare.)

This comparative isolation in a vast continent, bounded by the Sahara and the oceans, and one without any easy means of penetration from the coast into the interior, also left the tasks of exploration, of the exchange of ideas and goods, and of social settlement almost solely to Africans themselves. Arabs, Indians, and a few Chinese were frequent visitors to the east coast, but few of them penetrated into the interior before the nineteenth century. The Portuguese arrived on the west coast in the fifteenth century and on the east a few years later and were followed in the west by slave-merchants from most of the west European nations, but, again, few such travelers strayed far inland. The Dutch, who made the greatest impact on the African interior from their seventeenth-century settlement at the Cape, did not leave the peninsula in any numbers until the mid-eighteenth century.

When these visitors from other continents began to travel inland, Africans had already reached an advanced stage in the exploration and settlement of their continent. Not only had they discovered those areas capable of supporting human and animal life—a difficult task in view of the number of dangerous pests and infertile regions—but they had learned how to adapt their agricultural methods and crops to the differing environments found in the continent. They had also discovered a number of minerals valuable to the outside world—among them, gold, copper, and iron—together with such luxuries as ivory and animal skins, and were exporting them to the lands of Asia or exchanging them in the Sahara. African societies had also experimented with a variety of social and political structures, discovering which best fitted their widely differing communities, localities, and domestic needs.

When we also remember that many millions of Africans were transported to the Americas and the Caribbean, there to contribute to the human mastery of new environments, it is clear that the expansion of the negroid peoples was on an enormous scale. It continued up to, through, and after the European penetration and occupation of the continent; indeed, it still continues, for even today many parts of the African continent still need to be made capable of sustaining human society.

During this long process of colonization the Africans were assisted by one important element from outside their continent: through diffusion, first from Asia and later from the Americas, they were able to add to their indigenous food crops. Early men had to eat what they could find growing locally; they hunted wild animals, speared or trapped fish, took eggs from nests, and collected fruits or vegetables from trees, plants, and the ground. The evolution to agriculture, or deliberate planting and harvesting, was only possible where crops originally grew wild, that is, where man could exert his developing ingenuity to collect their seeds and plan their planting and harvesting. The history of much of this evolution is still obscure, and speculation abounds.

We know that several strains of millet grew in the savannah regions of Africa. It is suggested that one kind of rice was cultivated in west Africa, but the botanists are not sure about this. It is probable that yams were indigenous to Africa, but they were also imported from Asia. We have evidence that it was in north Africa that donkeys were first tamed and used for domestic purposes. Yet some of the most useful crops and animals came from outside the continent. Goats, sheep, camels, cattle seem to have come from western Asia; mangoes, coconut palms, sugar cane, bananas, taro, and rice came from the lands of the Indian Ocean; maize and cassava were introduced from the Americas; the sweet potato came first from either Asia or America. These crops and animals were then adapted and new varieties bred to suit the conditions of particular African areas, often by crossbreeding with local plants, and original means of using them also were discovered.

To what extent agriculture developed indigenously in Africa or was diffused from outside the continent is still a matter of argument. It seems probable that modern agriculture first developed in the Middle East, but it was being practiced in the Nile valley about 4000 B.C. It seems to have been easier to develop in the savannah plainlands and so appeared in such areas before it was adopted in the rain forest that covers much of southern west Africa. No one knows whether it evolved spontaneously in different parts of the continent or spread from one region to another, starting from the Nile area. Even the time scales are vague. It has been suggested by one writer, G. P. Murdock, that agriculture was being practiced in the area of the upper Niger between 5000 and 4000 B.C., and that it had developed there spontaneously; yet it seems most likely that cultivation only became common in most of west Africa during the last millennium before the birth of Christ.

During the period that saw the development of agriculture the use of iron became known in the region, providing a material that was to create another revolution in social life. Iron was much more plentiful than gold or bronze, and, once the technique of smelting the ore at temperatures higher than that required for gold or copper was mastered, it was available to many more people. The use of gold, copper, and bronze originally was largely confined to a small elite, providing them with a privileged position in society and thus control over the mass of people unable to employ the metals, as a glance at the Egyptian dynasties makes clear. But iron ore was obtainable over wide areas and once knowledge of its production had spread, the metal affected a much wider section of society. Iron offered the common man new opportunities to grow food and hunt animals and therefore enabled a greater number of people to be fed and to live longer lives.

In addition, however, its more widespread distribution also offered new opportunities for conquest, to some extent counteracting the equalizing effects of its use. Communal warfare was now practical, and war and the threat of war necessitated forms of hierarchical government and authority to organize defense and attack.

Iron seems to have been developed first in Turkey around 1500 B.C. Nearly a thousand years passed before its use spread to Africa, where the peoples of the Nile valley, north and northeast Africa, first made use of it. Later still, perhaps between 300 and 200 B.C., knowledge of iron smelting and of the use of metal appeared in west Africa. Opinions differ as to whether this knowledge came from Meroe, the capital of the powerful kingdom to the south of Egypt and an important iron-working center, or from Carthage, where the Phoenicians introduced their iron techniques. As traders from Carthage almost certainly made contact with the gold-producing areas of west Africa, it may be that they passed on their knowledge of iron-working to those from whom they received gold.

Certainly, iron soon became of special value to west Africans. It enabled them to begin to tame some of their toughest natural barriers, in particular, the rain forests. They could hew new paths and thus move about to a greater extent; as iron weapons provided them with better defenses against wild animals, their expeditions became safer. Indeed, once the techniques of iron implement production were mastered, west African peoples began to search for new lands, crucially influencing the history of the whole continent, as we shall see later. The military power induced by iron weapons also allowed the stronger communities—those that had first secured the knowledge, often keeping it secret for as long as possible—to dominate the weaker.

With larger populations, military adventures, and increased trade and migration, the need for new forms of government arose. The growth of the west African states and empires that were to form a vital factor in the history of their people for over a thousand years date from the time when iron techniques had been assimilated. Forms of political organization varied greatly: some gave rise to powerful kings and chiefs, others to simpler systems of kinship, clans, and family groupings. The structure depended on the local environment and the problems that had to be met in it. Of particular importance was the relationship to trading routes. As in other continents, crossroads on such routes, market centers, and convenient places for exchange became the focus of urban growth, sometimes leading to the establishment of centralized states or empires. Areas far from the early trade routes remained much more localized in their needs and outlook; these devised their own patterns of authority according to their particular circumstances.

The major division between the northern and southern regions was to have a crucial and continuing effect on west Africa. In general, the north is characterized by open savannah lands, where grain grew easily, cattle could be raised away from the tsetse pest, and cotton could be produced to supply hand looms. With the introduction of iron, greater food production provided that essential surplus needed for the introduction of some degree of specialization, allowing small sections of the community to spend most of their time weaving, at the smithy, or in making implements, clothes, or weapons. And it was therefore in the north that the earliest foundations were laid for the future states and empires.

In the south, in contrast, much of the land was covered by forest. The population still had to depend on roots, fruits, and a few domesticated animals. Clothes were rudimentary, for weavers had to use whatever materials were naturally available; the struggle to obtain sufficient food occupied almost everyone's daylight hours, and the only crafts that could be practiced were the molding of pottery and a little wood carving. Consequently, communities remained small and local; although the introduction of iron allowed a gradual development of techniques capable of clearing more of the forest than had previously been possible, expansion was a slow, painful task.

This division between the regions was never absolute. In one area especially it was bridged. Between the east of modern Ghana and the west of Nigeria, an area today partly covered by Togoland and Dahomey, the grasslands of the north penetrate the forest belt, reaching almost to the coast. It may well have been that this exceptional area formed the most important route of diffusion for northern techniques to the south.

One particular area has supplied us with evidence of life in remote times in this region. From the large number of stone axes found throughout the region, in the forest lands of the south as well as in the northern savannah, we know that many people lived in west Africa during the stone age. And at least one set of peoples were making beautiful statues at a time when a knowledge of iron entered the region.

In 1936, in the alluvial deposits near Jos, which were being worked for tin, a small monkey's head made from terra cotta or baked clay was discovered. Subsequently, other excavations were explored, with the result that many other figures and figurines were discovered. Human heads are the commonest figures recovered, but there are also many animals, including monkeys and elephants. The heads vary in size from about two-thirds life to about three inches. Many of them are adorned with ornaments—necklaces and bracelets—while various beads made from tin or quartz have been discovered independently. It seems probable that these figures were made to be placed in shrines for some form of cult worship or early religious rites.

Of equal importance in fitting together the pieces of our story is the discovery in the same place of various iron objects, including pipes used with bellows in iron smelting. Since many stone axes have been found beside the iron, it seems reasonable to suppose that this statue-making culture developed at the time when the transformation from stone to iron was just taking place.

According to modern methods of dating, the society that produced these objects lived on the Jos plateau from about 500 B.C. to about 200 A.D. Covering an area three hundred by one hundred miles, the culture has been named the Nok culture, after the name of the village where the first discovery was made. According to the tentative speculations of archaeologists, the Nok figures reveal strong similarities to later art forms in west Africa, in particular to the art of the Yoruba people, and discoveries of similar terra cottas to those of Nok have since been made not far from Ife, the ancient center of Yoruba cultural life. Nok established the fact that objects of intrinsic artistic beauty were created by the ancient west African peoples and provided us with vital clues in the construction of their history.

It seems probable that the discovery of the use of iron, combined perhaps with the diffusion of the new Asian food crops, provided the stimulus that led to the great Bantu migration that formed the most important population movement in African history. Much still remains to be learned of the migration and settlement of the Bantu peoples, but we do know that groups of these people moved into east and central Africa during the first millennium after the birth of Christ. There are various theories as to the core area from which the Bantu migration began, each of them somewhat short on evidence and all subject to further investigation. One of the most widely held theories is that it was from the plateau district south and east of the Benue River in Nigeria that the movement started. In any case, it seems virtually certain that the Bantu peoples were originally in one single community, large or small, for although Bantu languages vary and are now spread throughout the continent, linguists have established that all Bantu languages are related and have developed from a common origin. Moreover, it appears that the Bantu languages have a direct relation to certain west African languages.

It seems likely that this massive movement of peoples was occasioned by a comparatively sudden population increase and consequent pressure on land and food supplies. This change in population could easily be equated with the use of iron and perhaps the invasion of peoples from the north into the Nigerian plateau. However this may be, the Bantu (properly called the "Bantu-speaking peoples," but the simpler form is used here) took with them their agricultural techniques and so helped the communities they encountered to develop their own social life.

In the east, for example, the Bantu met the Nilotes and southern Nilotes, who were generally more concerned with cattle herding than with food growing. A wide variety of mergings took place, sometimes with a greater Bantu influence, at other times with Nilotic customs predominating. Some Bantu groups who moved into central Africa took a cattle-herding culture with them. Later they penetrated even farther south, into what is now South Africa and Southwest Africa—or Namibia—though this process was not completed by the nineteenth century. Indeed, the movement of Bantu peoples has been deliberately halted by the white South Africans, first in the eighteenth century when expanding European settlement tried to contain the Bantu at the Fish River, then by the wars of the nineteenth century, which attempted to keep them to certain reserved areas, and finally in the twentieth century, through the mass of apartheid legislation imposing restrictions on travel, residence, and employment. The Cape peninsula itself, the original settlement of

Europeans, had scarcely been penetrated by Bantu peoples until after World War II, and one of the objectives of the apartheid policy has been to turn the tide back.

It has been the Bantu, therefore, who have been the main explorers, colonizers, and settlers of the African continent south of the Sahara. Their migrations occupied two thousand years, although the most crucial expeditions took place in the first millennium after the birth of Christ. During their journeys they probably pushed the more primitive peoples—bushmen, pygmies, and hottentots—into the small areas of their modern habitat—the Congo forests, Botswana, and Namibia. It is probably during this period, too, that fragmentation took place in many communities, forming the clans, subtribes, and tribal communities known in recent African history. Perhaps most important of all the factors in this Bantu migration was the quality of assimilation displayed by them. They merged with other communities, absorbed some, were absorbed by others; they added parts of their language to those they encountered and received new words or phrases in return. It was from this mixture and mingling of peoples, with their varied racial heritage, their differing customs and beliefs, their variety of techniques, that modern African societies have evolved.

3

STATES AND EMPIRES IN THE WESTERN SUDAN

THE ARABS called the savannah grasslands immediately to the south of the Sahara "Bildad as-Sudan," "land of the blacks." As a result, the whole area from the Nile valley to the Atlantic Ocean has been referred to as the "Sudan" (not to be confused with the modern state of the same name). It was in this area that the four great empires of medieval times were built: Ghana, Mali, Songhai, and Kanem-Bornu. Their frontiers did not coincide; in places they overlapped. Their location was in the west and center of the Sudan, and each had communications stretching in three directions: north, east, and south.

The origins of the four empires remain somewhat obscure. We do not even know with certainty the period of their first appearance, though it seems fairly certain that Ghana was the first to be established, slightly antedating Kanem. Ghana was already in existence at the beginning of the eighth century; the community held traditionally to be mainly responsible for building the empire of Kanem is thought to have reached its Lake Chad home during the same century, though the empire itself was probably created a little later.

The pillars upon which these Sudanese empires rested were identical. Indeed, Songhai, Mali, and Ghana succeeded each other in power, each largely inheriting the functions of its predecessor. The grasslands offered greater opportunities than the forest for movement, contact, and diffusion of techniques, commodities, and ideas. Thus there was constant travel by at least a small section of the inhabitants. Certainly, Berbers and Arabs were frequent visitors, giving some credence to the racist theory that the empires were the product of "white" effort; one hypothesis has it that some of the more famous Sudanese rulers were connected with the Middle East. Yet, although there was certainly some intermarriage between these visitors and the indigenous population, and although invasion from the north was at times an important factor in imperial developments, all the evidence points to the dominance of negroid peoples throughout the area during the life of all four empires.

By far the most important foundation common to each empire was the economic-geographical situation. Although their areas did not coincide, each empire was situated at a focal point of the trade routes between the forest areas to the south, the commercial centers of the north, and, in certain cases, the Nile valley. The north-south trade was of first importance. In the forest region gold was mined and ivory collected. Both these precious commodities were sought by merchants from the north for resale in northern lands and around the Mediterranean. No doubt some found their way into Europe. The forest people needed a constant supply of salt to meet the demands of their tropical habitat. Salt was not to be found in their own areas, but it was mined at Taghaza in the northern Sahara. Thus the exchange of gold and ivory for salt created a commercial relationship between these two peoples that lasted for perhaps a thousand years. Other commodities were added as the people on both sides learned of each other's needs. Copper was mined at Takedda, just south of the Sahara. Some foodstuffs produced in the forest were welcome to northerners, who, in their turn, brought metal utensils, horses, and various cloths to offer to the southerners. Slaves were a commodity offered by both parties, though most of those exchanged were southerners, for it was in the north that division of labor had advanced to the stage at which manual laborers were in demand.

At the points where these exchanges could most easily take place market towns grew up. Control over these towns and over the sources of the wealth itself—the gold of the forest, the salt mines in the Sahara—became a central issue of struggle between rival groups, and in consequence each group was forced to organize, to seek new weapons, to exact taxes to pay for defense and expeditions. In short, success in these conflicts for the control of wealth necessitated the formation of states; it was this process that led to the creation of the four empires.

It should not be thought that these commercial exchanges were accomplished easily. Travel is hazardous in the Sahara even today; in those days it was dangerous and exhausting in the extreme. Thus in the fourteenth century, when the famous Berber traveler Ibn Battuta crossed the Sahara, he described it as a "desert haunted by demons." He had to purchase four months' provisions for his camels; then, after reaching Taghaza and spending ten fly-bitten days there, "water supplies are laid on [by the caravan captains] for the crossing of the desert that lies beyond it, which is a ten nights' journey with no water on the way except on rare occasions." Beyond Taghaza his party lost one man in the desert; Battuta passed another caravan, which had lost men who had become separated from it, one of whom his caravan later found dead under a desert shrub.

Those who would trade across the desert had to be tough and brave; nor could it have been easy to travel with gold dust and ivory along the forest trails.

Fortunately, by the time Ghana had risen to its full eminence, in the eleventh century, Islam had taken the Arabic language into the furthest corners of the expanding Muslim world, so travelers were able to leave eyewitness accounts of the lands they visited. Thus a Granada Arab from Spain, al Bekri, painted a vivid picture of Ghana of 1067, the year after the Norman invasion of England, offering visual images of both the Ghana court and the basis of the empire's economy:

> The king of Ghana can put two hundred thousand warriors in the field, more than forty thousand of them being armed with bow and arrow. . . . When he gives audience to his people, to listen to their complaints and set them to rights, he sits in a pavilion around which stand ten pages holding shields and gold-mounted swords and on his right hand are the sons of the princes of his empire, splendidly clad and with gold plaited into their hair. The governor of the city is seated on the ground in front of the king, and all around him are his viziers in the same position. . . .
>
> The king exacts the right of one dinar of gold on each donkey-load of salt that enters his country, and two dinars of gold on each load of salt that goes out. A load of copper carries a duty of five mitqals and a load of merchandise ten mitqals. . . . All pieces of native gold found in the mines of the empire belong to the sovereign, although he lets the public have the gold dust that everybody knows about; without this precaution, gold would become so abundant as practically to lose its value.

Mali, successor empire to Ghana, seems to have become even more wealthy. When its famous emperor, Mansa Musa, made a pilgrimage to Mecca in 1324, it was reported that he was accompanied by five hundred slaves, each carrying a staff of gold weighing over sixty pounds. His arrival in Cairo was a glittering event long remembered in that ancient city; apparently, the Mali emperor and his retinue brought so much gold to the Egyptian capital that Egypt's currency was devalued for a dozen years.

The last of the three empires was that of Songhai, based on its capital, Gao. Having freed itself from the domination of Mali by the end of the fourteenth century, in the following century, especially under the leadership of, first, Sunni Ali and, then, Askia Muhammed Toure, the frontiers of Songhai were extended to contain almost all the Sudanese trading towns. The empire lasted until 1591, when it was finally crushed by the Moroccans, who proceeded to occupy its western areas, using Timbuktu as their center.

For nearly a thousand years the empires of the western Sudan had dominated much of the life in this area, one succeeding the other in a continuous line. The Moors of Morocco were unable to maintain this continuity, however; not for another two centuries was another empire of comparable influence to arise in the same region.

These three important empires had arisen from the same basic roots; each declined and eventually disappeared for much the same reasons. While their strength depended on control of the towns that were principally engaged in the trans-Saharan trade, and they developed political systems capable of collecting centralized revenues, raising armies, and regulating commerce, they never developed any form of homogeneity. In each a variety of ethnic communities was brought under one imperial government, but the fiat of the government extended only as far as its military power could stretch at any moment. The empires, therefore, were composed of a congeries of trading towns and certain areas of mineral or crop production. The frontiers were never defined and often changed according to the power of the center. A military leader usually held the central seat of power, and upon his death there was often a struggle for the succession, during which time some of the provinces of the empire would assert their independence. Moreover, the central government commonly represented the dominance of one ethnic group over the rest. Thus Ghana saw the supremacy of the Soninke, Mali of the Mandingo, Songhai of the group of the same name centered on Gao. Although the administration, especially after the arrival of Islam, was usually sufficient to govern the ruling community, it rarely showed enough strength to embrace efficiently the many other groups, each at different levels of development and organization. Consequently, the inborn centrifugal tendencies in the empires were constantly encouraged and took advantage of any weaknesses to undermine the power of the center, especially since the main impact of imperial rule was to levy dues on trade or to recruit men for the imperial armies—both causes of resentment.

External elements also constantly threatened imperial power. Not only did rival ethnic groups contend for control of the center, eventually resulting in a series of successor empires, but in the north bands of nomads frequently took advantage of the lack of imperial military control to raid and sack the northern frontiers. In particular, the Tuaregs, nomadic groups who disliked the idea of settling under a centralized government and who, inflamed by religious revivalism, destroyed Ghana, formed a constant threat to each of the empires. The Tuaregs were never entirely subdued and remained a permanent threat to administration and trade.

Thus, although the period of imperial government under the three empires extended over most of this thousand years, it was only for short periods, when a strong ruler was in power, that administrative order could be said to extend to the whole of the area claimed by a particular empire. Even then, when an empire "worked," the life of most ordinary people was hardly affected, unless their men were conscripted into a military levy. In their round, mud-walled, thatched-roof huts, in the towns, in villages across the grasslands, along riversides, most people were too occupied with growing food or tending cattle to be concerned with imperial politics. The merchants, who were vital to the life of the empire, and who were most seriously affected by the changing fortunes of various imperial administrations, were but a small group. Consequently, so long as the merchants continued to collect what surplus food could be produced or buy a few cattle and provide some implements, utensils, or cloth in exchange, the peasant family was content to leave the worry of taxes and the hazards of travel to them.

At the same time, the effects of the imperial era on the west African peoples should not be underestimated. The trading routes and market towns probably needed protection and some form of administration. In general, the towns prospered within it. As Ibn Battuta wrote of Mali in the fourteenth century: "There is complete security in their country. Neither traveller, nor inhabitant in it, has anything to fear from robbers or men of violence." The same could hardly have been said of Europe at the time. And if the empires of the Sudanese savannah lands, because of their links with the north, the comparative ease of travel within their confines, and the combination of irrigated cultivation with husbandry, tended to dominate, if not exploit, the southern Guinea peoples, they at the same time guaranteed markets for southern products.

Yet perhaps the main contribution of the imperial era was the introduction of Islam to west Africa. Goods were not the only commodities carried across the Sahara along the trading routes protected and fostered by the empires; ideas and techniques often accompanied them, discussed in the towns of the western Sudan and adapted there to local conditions. The most important body of ideas was certainly that contained within the Muslim religion. Until the seventh century Africans had followed the religions of their ancestors, in a wide variety of cults, customs, traditions, and beliefs. In 632 A.D., however, Islam began to make converts in Egypt. From there the Muslim proselytizers and their supporting armies began a series of campaigns to bring the whole of north Africa under their sway. They found little resistance in the towns and cities, only slight enthusiasm in the countryside, and active hostility in the desert. Some of the Berbers, for instance, migrated southward rather than accept the new law. But Islam pursued them. From the towns of southern Algeria and Mauretania the new learning began to penetrate into the Sudan itself. In the eleventh century the western Sudanese towns became centers from which Islam could spread its influence deep into west Africa.

The first impact of the new religion was made by the administrative techniques it introduced. The Islamic conception of a powerful executive coincided with the need of the empires for strong, centralized government. The introduction of the Arabic script and of learned men to write and read it provided, for the first time, a corps of administrators capable of keeping records. The pilgrimages to Mecca that were encouraged among the converts produced more than spiritual satisfaction; they introduced the imperial favored few who were able to make them to new ideas and techniques. Thus it was probably as a result of a sixteenth-century pilgrimage that firearms were first brought to a Sudanese empire. Even the long white robe that has become traditional wear was brought to west Africa by the Muslims.

For the most part these innovations were not imposed from the outside; rather, they were learned and integrated into existing customs. The idea of the strong ruler, for instance, fitted well with Sudanese concepts of monarchy. Yet in some ways Islamic influences weakened the empires. Not only might Islam lead to invasion from rival Muslim sects, as the Almoravids invaded Ghana; by undermining the traditional spiritual role of the monarch and by vesting authority in the class of Islamic scholars, the power of the ruler may well have been weakened. Moreover, Islam tended to be an urban religion, leaving the mass of rural peasants to continue their traditional cults. Indeed, this division between town and countryside, often marked by antagonism and conflict, has persisted to the present day.

Nevertheless, Islam brought to west Africa a wealth of learning and richness of culture never seen before or since, even if it affected only a small minority of the inhabitants. Cities such as Timbuktu and Jenne became famous for their scholarship, with universities and libraries attracting scholars from all over the Muslim world. According to the Moroccan Arab Leo Africanus, who visited Timbuktu in the early sixteenth century, "There are numerous judges, doctors, and clerics in Timbuktu, all receiving good salaries from the king. He pays great respect to men of learning. There is a big demand for books in manuscript, imported from Barbary. More profit is made from the book trade than from any other line of business." And at this same period in the Songhai empire, of which Timbuktu was the brightest star, a system of provinces had been established, each with its own governor, and the central government had been divided into the kind of ministries familiar to the modern world—dealing with finance, justice, internal affairs, agriculture, and the like.

It is proper, however, to conclude this description of life in the three empires with other words from Leo Africanus, this time revealing something of the life of the majority of their inhabitants. Outside the capital of Songhai, Africanus found "nought but villages and hamlets inhabited by husbandmen and shepherds. . . . They are ignorant and rude people and you shall scarce find one learned man in the space of an hundred miles. They are continually burthened with grievous exactions, so that they have scarce any thing remaining to live upon." Neither the riches of the kings and merchants nor the learning of scholars touched the life of these people—but, then, this social situation was no different in the rest of the world.

The three empires were all situated in the western section of Sudan. They all had dealings with areas that are now part of Nigeria, Songhai at one time claiming suzerainty over both Katsina and Kano. But it was the fourth major empire, sited around Lake Chad, that most directly affected the ancestors of modern Nigerians.

Trans-Saharan trade also played a crucial role in the growth, development, and strength of the empire called by the composite name of Kanem-Bornu. Like the others, it was formed through a loose unity between communities living on the southern fringes of the desert. Because of its more easterly location it had communications with Tunis and Tripoli, and it was also well placed to maintain contact with Nubia and Egypt.

The beginnings of Kanem-Bornu are shrouded in myth and mystery. As in other parts of west Africa some traditions link the early ruling peoples with the Middle East, but there is no evidence to support this theory, which probably arose *post hoc* from the influence of Islam. It seems most likely that, as a result of the seventh-century Muslim invasions of north Africa, a southerly movement of groups accustomed to live in the Sahara took place during the next century and a half. This movement would account for the dominance that was established to the east of Lake Chad by a largely caucasoid immigrant group, the Zaghawa, during the seventh and eighth centuries. Following the division of the ruling families of the Zaghawa, one branch established a dynasty that was to last for a thousand years.

The Sefawa dynasty first established a state east of Lake Chad with a capital at Njimi, about the location of which argument still continues. It was from this small state that the first Kanem empire arose. Yet, like the similar states farther west, the empire was formed among a considerable number of groups. The actual delineation of these communities remains obscure; various writers often attribute conflicting names and differing contributions to them.

What seems to be fairly well established is that both the Kanuri and the So peoples were important in the development of the empire. The latter are claimed to have been the earliest inhabitants of the area and to have developed a comparatively advanced society. The name of the So seems to have been derived from a north African source and to indicate a linguistic rather than a social group. The So were probably a varied set of peoples speaking a common language but living in separate communities across central Sudan. However this may be, the So were capable of building their own walled towns, of creating a complicated political system surmounted by a divine king, and of giving women a prominent place in the hierarchy—probably derived from a former matriarchal society. They also modeled clay, being especially clever with animal figures, and made bronze figures of their ancestors. That they could be dominated by nomads indicates that they were more accustomed to the arts of peace than to times of war.

The Kanuri from Bornu, who also were a multiple people, one of a number of groups from which the Zaghawa seem to have come, fought the So for several centuries. The primary task in forging the first Kanem empire was therefore to mold the various groups together into some form of unity. It is interesting to note that in this process the Kanuri adopted many customs learned from the So, including much of their political system and the influential position accorded to women. In the long run, however, the So were unable to resist Kanuri power. By about the sixteenth century their groups were entirely assimilated into Kanuri society.

The Sefawa dynasty, founded at the beginning of the ninth

century, recognized its first and continuous objective as that of uniting as many groups as possible under its rule. It possessed one great advantage over the other three empires in approaching this task: it had solved to a degree hitherto unknown in west Africa the difficulty of the succession. It is usually acknowledged that the Sefawa dynasty lasted in an unbroken line from about 800 to 1846. Yet theirs was no dictatorship. The mais, or kings, always ruled with the advice of a council. The councilors were drawn from two sources, the royal family and dignitaries descended from slaves. The empire was divided into provinces, each governed by a warden, who was also a councilor. The king's mother, elder sister, and first wife also enjoyed great power. Thus the royal family always remained in a position of collective control, and the hereditary character of the monarchy was safeguarded. In order to avoid the danger of revolt from a nobility with a power base in the countryside, often a cause of weakness in other contemporary empires, the most important nobles were kept in the capital, where they could be supervised by the royal family. They were sent to the provinces only to collect taxes or subdue rebellion. Meanwhile, the administration of the fiefs into which the empire was divided was conducted by bureaucrats who owed their positions to the monarch.

At the end of the eleventh century, during the period when the Muslim religion was making its most important strides into the Sudan grasslands and the Almoravid Muslim reformers were invading Ghana, the royal family were converted to Islam. The mai during the last years of the eleventh century, Umme Jilme, certainly became a Muslim, for he died in 1097 in Egypt while on a pilgrimage to Mecca. The acceptance of Islam brought even greater consequences to Kanem than were experienced by its sister empires. Its location made Kanem the obvious center for the diffusion of Islamic thought and custom in the central Sudan and therefore the principal meeting point for the Mediterranean coastal Magreb, the Sudan, and the Middle East. In its turn this focal situation brought economic opportunities. Pilgrimages were important stimulants for trade. The economic links from Kanem could stretch out to Tunisia in the north and Egypt and Arabia to the east. Kanem rulers established an embassy in Tunis and built a rest house in Cairo for its pilgrims and the students it sent to Cairo University. At the height of the empire's powers it even claimed suzerainty over the Fezzan, in modern-day Libya.

Islam also brought writing and scholarship to Kanem, as it did to Mali. The advantages to the administration were considerable, for such skills assisted the royal family to strengthen its control by providing written records and tax receipts. With the addition of Muslim law to traditional customs the judicial system could be tightened without antagonizing the people by sudden change. A corps of judges became established in all the major towns with a high court in the capital, the chief justice ranking second only to the king in the hierarchy.

Economically, the existence of the royal court and a comparatively large class of nobles ensured a ready domestic market for surplus production, and the development of surplus production provided a sound base for foreign trade, though currency seems to have been largely absent, rolls of cloth being the main means of exchange. Grain was exchanged for salt in the desert; potash from the lake was sent to Kano for distribution throughout the grasslands; kola nuts were exported; and the Kanuri seem to have acted as middlemen for copper trade between Darfur and Nupe. Yet, in contrast to its sister empires, Kanem depended more on the trade in slaves than in any other commodity. Indeed, the slave trade, perhaps because of its closer relations with the north and east, underpinned the economic strength of Kanem-Bornu. The slave markets of Tunis, Tripoli, Cairo, Turkey, and the

Levant were always avid for supplies. Slave-trading expeditions were common occurrences for the Kanem military men. During the dry seasons mail-clad horsemen would ride out to the south, where the weaker—agricultural—peoples had only poisoned arrows with which to defend themselves. They were not unresisting—one powerful king was killed by a hoe in one such expedition!—but they were unable to prevent many of their people from being taken for sale in the markets of the Magreb and the Middle East.

Although the Sefawa dynasty showed extraordinary powers of survival and continuity, it was still beset by the kind of dangers that shook the other empires. As it expanded, its lines of communication often became so stretched as to endanger the central power. Nobles and members of the royal family had to be used to conquer and administer outlying provinces; even the precaution of keeping them in the capital could not be employed for the whole time. Consequently, intrigues, revolts, and rebellions occurred, particularly during periods of weak rule. During the first quarter of the thirteenth century members of the royal family itself mounted revolts against the mai, though each was crushed. Later, at the end of the same century, further divisions within the royal family so seriously weakened the empire that it became a prey to outside invaders.

The eastern frontier had always been the most vulnerable. In particular, the Bulala people, usually nomadic and inhabiting an area to the east of the empire, were a constant threat to the authority of the imperial government. During this period, through a combination of internal revolt and the attacks of the Bulala, the Sefawa court was forced to retreat westward to the other side of the lake in Bornu, where some of the Kanuri people had been settling for a long time. A hundred years later the Sefawa family finally abandoned Kanem. Henceforth, the empire was to be known as Bornu; the old frontiers shrank; and it largely confined its direct influence to lands that are now part of Nigeria.

The Bornu state had to face difficulties similar to those encountered by its Kanem predecessor. It still depended on the ability of the central government under the mais to collect tribute from the constituent parts of its empire, with the constant danger of civil war and secession. The communities on its periphery continued to attack it at times of weakness. The empire still depended heavily on the slave trade, inevitably arousing antagonisms, and was by its very nature incapable of stimulating productivity in industry, craft, or cultivation. One additional cause of constant friction was its relationship with the Hausa city states: sometimes the Bornu empire was powerful enough to exact tribute from some of them; at other times the towns not only refused to pay but attacked the empire itself.

It was not until the end of the fifteenth century that the mais of Bornu were able to bring to an end the civil wars that had weakened their power in Kanem. By that time the whole of Bornu had been occupied and they had built a new capital city, Birni N'gazaragamu, on the present borders between Nigeria and Niger. The state was restored to its former equilibrium by a redeployment of its principal officers, whose jealousies and conflicts had been one of the major causes of weakness.

Religion also was used to strengthen the discipline of the empire. Ali Ghaji, who was mainly responsible for the resurrection of Sefawa power at the end of the fifteenth century, recognized the potential influence offered him by Islam. With the assistance of his chief imam he instituted a campaign for stricter observance of Muslim principles, setting an example himself. Ali Ghaji also increased the strength of his army, for his expansionist policies involved war with the Bulala in the east and the Jukun from beside the Benue in the south, the extension of his frontier northward, and demands for contributions to his treasury from the Hausa towns of the west. Meanwhile, since trade flourished, mainly based on an exchange of slaves for horses from the north, the Bornu treasury and the royal coffers began again to see the riches they had enjoyed in Kanem.

In the reign of Ghaji's son the Bornu army returned to Kanem to subdue the Bulala who had troubled them for so long. Kanem now became a province of the Bornu empire, but the Sefawa remained in their new capital in Bornu, which remained the seat of government until the nineteenth century.

The empire was also affected by the troubles of Songhai in the east. In particular, the Kebbi state, which had broken from Songhai, began to encroach on disputed territories between the two empires. The Kebbi, moreover, proved too strong to dislodge from their fortified capital, Surame, and the Bornu army had to retreat, leaving the issue to be determined later.

The apex of Bornu power was reached during the reign of Idris Alooma, who ruled the empire from 1571 to 1603, a period coinciding with the defeat of the Songhai empire by the Moroccans, Elizabethan England, the Iberian destruction of American cultures, the reign of Akbar in India, and the Ming dynasty in China. Alooma possessed one special advantage over his contemporaries in west Africa: he made a kind of defense agreement with the Turks that enabled him to acquire Turkish instructors to train his army and Turkish muskets for use by his soldiers. In so doing he secured the means to accomplish his two main objectives: to unify the empire under his central control and to extend the bounds of imperial power.

It is interesting to note that in seeking the first of these objects Alooma recognized the danger of fratricidal conflicts from within the royal family, which had so often weakened the empire over the past two and a half centuries. He therefore kept the members of his family and the great nobles in the capital, as his early predecessors had attempted to do, and he extended his policy by refusing to give them provincial governorships, appointing instead men who were either slaves or of humble origin on the ground that he could rely on the loyalty of made men to a greater extent than on that of his own kinsmen. It is also significant that the threads of former matrilineal influence still survived; Alooma was certainly strongly influenced by his mother, Aicha, who had acted as regent before he took the throne.

Alooma was fortunate in having an excellent chronicler, his imam, Ahmad ibn Fartuwa, whose accounts of the first twelve years of his reign provide us with a vivid picture of this Bornu period. (Unfortunately, records of the latter part of Alooma's reign seem to have been lost.) The power of the empire and emperor seems to have rested largely on the army, composed of an armored cavalry bearing feathered lances and emblazoned shields in the van, drums and trumpets to inspire their valor after them, a peasant infantry armed with bows and arrows or spears next, and women to carry provisions in the rear. As was the custom in Europe at the time, the spoils were usually the possessions and bodies of defenseless villagers, as booty or slaves.

The numerical superiority of the Bornu army, together with the slight degree of discipline instilled by its Turkish instructors and the muskets provided by them, gave it a superiority over most of its antagonists. By intelligent use of the power the army represented Alooma brought most of the recalcitrant provinces under his suzerainty and ensured that they would pay his taxes, weakened the states on his borders —even Kano was humiliated by his forces, though they could not take the town—and gained control of the most important trading routes. The Kebbi were this time defeated; the Tuareg were forced to sue for peace; and Kanem was attached to the Bornu empire.

Despite this record of successful warfare the Bornu Chronicle records that Alooma "promoted the prosperity of the country and the wealth of the towns." Supplying and provisioning the army no doubt stimulated trade and industry, while the capture of important trans-Saharan trade routes enriched the empire. Mai Alooma was also a devout man, making the pilgrimage to Mecca and building a hostel there for pilgrims from his empire. In his efforts to promote unity in his kingdoms he recognized the value that religion could play and strove to bring all his public men within the Muslim fold. With the same objective he strengthened the Islamic element in the law at the expense of traditional custom, giving greater power to Muslim magistrates and therefore providing a greater degree of conformity.

Idris Alooma was obviously an outstanding ruler of his time; he increased the territories forming the Bornu empire and achieved a greater degree of unity within it. However, one must doubt whether the lot of the ordinary inhabitants was much improved by his rule. His wars must certainly have produced a great deal of rapine, looting, enslavement, and destruction. Still, perhaps some who lived on the empire's perimeter felt greater security; the merchant class probably benefited from supplying his army and from wider opportunities to trade; the law seems to have been codified in clearer terms and more uniformly administered. It is difficult to draw up a balance sheet, but one fact does emerge: society in the empire was becoming more stratified. The distinctions between (1) king, court, and nobility, (2) merchants and traders, (3) farmers, fishermen, and craftsmen, and (4) slaves were becoming clearer.

This social and economic division was accompanied by that other special African stratification, into clans and village, age, and ancestor groups. Yet the division of a society, and particularly of labor, never developed to the extent that was becoming common in Europe and Asia. The production and exchange of goods did not grow to the degree that caused such upheavals in the other two continents and led to the deep divisions between rich and poor. The vertical stratification between communities of various characters and sizes remained more important than the horizontal divisions between social classes. Even slavery was never an entirely static condition: slaves could almost always earn their freedom, and the free might at any time become enslaved through warfare or raiding.

Alooma left a state around which he had built a powerful and wealthy tributary empire. Its influence was felt as far north as the Fezzan and in Kanem, Kano, and the lands of the Jukun for nearly another two hundred years. But Alooma's military strength had contained, but never destroyed, the external dangers. The Tuareg continued to raid the north, the Jukun the south. Whenever a weak ruler, a debilitating civil war, or a natural famine weakened the power of the center, vassal states would take the opportunity to secede and reassert their independence. From the latter years of the seventeenth century the strength of the empire slowly declined; at the start of the nineteenth it was finally destroyed.

Between the empires of Kanem-Bornu and Songhai lay the Hausa city states: Daura, Kano, Zaria, Gobir, Katsina, Rano, and Briam. Often they were the subject of contention between the two empires, both of which were anxious to exact tribute from them; for all were states based on the commercial wealth of trade and therefore usually were economically tempting. Rarely, however, did they fully submit to either empire; more often they maintained their independence, seeking both to increase their wealth and to establish their own sources of tribute in other areas.

The Hausa are a linguistic rather than an ethnic group. They are made up of a complex of peoples who migrated into the northwestern and northern parts of the central area of Nigeria, spreading over the borders to the north and west up to the fringes of the Sahara.

The origins of the Hausa people, like those of their neighbors, remain obscure. Again there is the suggestion in legend that their ancestors came from the Middle East. There is no sure evidence that migrants or invaders from that area ever entered the lands inhabited by the Hausa, but if some did reach Hausaland, there is no doubt that there were inhabitants there before them. Records from both Kano and Katsina dating back to the beginning of the twelfth century make it clear that the Hausa areas were inhabited before any Middle East travelers could have arrived.

A number of charming legends concerning the origins of the Hausa towns have survived, all variations around a central theme that the son of a king of Bagdad, called Bayajidda, fled to Kanem-Bornu, where he married the mai's daughter. Traveling further west, he came to Daura, where he killed a sacred snake that had been preventing the local people from drawing water from their well. In gratitude, the queen of Daura married him and bore him a son named Bawo. The son succeeded his father on the throne and had seven sons: Biram, Daura, Katsina, Zaria, Kano, Rano, and Gobir. These were taken as the names of the Hausa Bakwai—the seven Hausa states. Tradition maintains that each state had a special responsibility: Daura and Katsina in charge of commerce and markets; Kano and Rano as chiefs of the indigo industry; Zaria responsible for labor recruitment, the capture of slaves; and Gobir as the war leader. Biram is not usually included in the list, but actually it became the governmental center.

Each state was governed by a king assisted by ministers. Conversions to Islam probably began in the thirteenth century, but it was not until the fourteenth that the Muslim influence was seriously felt. As elsewhere, Islam became much more popular among the court and merchant classes than among the common people, most of whom held to their local pagan cults until much later. One of the strongest Islamic influences came from the incursion of the Fulani, a people from Mali who brought with them books on divinity from the university of Timbuktu. We know that they had appeared in Kano by the mid-fifteenth century. From Islam the towns were able to draw new resources in government, law, and administration and to develop a sound system of taxation.

Each town was strongly fortified, for their commercial wealth made them objects of frequent attack. Baked mud walls and deep ditches were built around them. Often towns would help each other to repel attacks, though at times they would attack each other in an effort to secure ascendancy. Not only had these city states to defend themselves against the empires on the borders of Hausaland, they also had to repel attacks from the predatory enemies of the empires themselves; the Tuareg and the Jukun, for example, were accustomed to raid them.

Moreover, the Hausa had expansionist ambitions of their own. In addition to the Hausa Bakwai, tradition related that there was a Banza Bakwai, or bastard seven. These consisted of other areas not actually part of Hausaland proper: Zamfara, Kebbi, Gwari, Yauri, Nupe, Ilorin, and Kwarafafa. In each of these areas the Hausa languages and culture took root, and each was at some time or another claimed to be under the influence of Hausaland. During the eighteenth century warfare was frequent between these various Hausa towns. In 1700 Zamfara conquered Kano, already weakened by wars with Katsina and the Jukun. Later it was Gobir's turn to become aggressive, and by the end of the eighteenth century most of Hausaland was debilitated by fratricidal conflict.

Across the whole of the Sudanese grasslands empires and states contended with each other for power, trade, and wealth for over a thousand years. They brought some degree of unity to hundreds of small communities, but their wars and slave raids also brought misery, destruction, and enslavement to many of the common people. The empires provided a fertile base for the spread of Islam, which was accompanied by the arts of writing and the techniques of law and administration, yet the arrival of Islam itself was not an unmixed blessing: it often set Muslim societies against pagan, while the divisions within the religious order itself at times provoked invasion and warfare. During this period, though, despite the rise and fall of empires, the contention between ruling groups, the destruction and slavery, communities in west Africa were learning better methods of production, exchanging their goods on an ever widening basis, and learning more of the ideas of the world beyond them.

These developments were slow and rarely broke down society so completely as was common during the same period in Europe and Asia. Many of the old traditions and customary ways of life persisted, perhaps preserving a closer harmony, a greater degree of international relations, than was possible in the budding industrialism of the other two continents. In any case, it is this combination of internation strife with local social cohesion that laid the foundations for the modern society of northern Nigeria.

4

THE MIDDLE BELT, OYO, AND BENIN

JUST AS the savannah grasslands of the north offered the greatest opportunities for societies to settle and grow into states and empires, it took longer to master the natural hazards of the rain forest that covers much of southern west Africa. So, as a general rule, the farther south one looks in west Africa, the later was the development of strong societies. Nevertheless, states and empires just as strong as those in the north were built in the south, playing just as important a role in the historical drama of west Africa. One has only to mention the names of Benin, Oyo, Dahomey, and Asante to realize that the forest belt was no permanent barrier to the growth of powerful states.

Between the extremes of north and south in west Africa there lies a middle belt of land the peoples of which also can claim to have played a part on this stage. In Nigeria this belt is marked by the Jos plateau, over four thousand feet high, and by the Benue and Niger plains. In that region many of the soils are poor, water scarce, rainfall variable, and tsetse widespread. Since the middle belt also was an area of frequent slave raiding, much of the territory was thinly populated. Nevertheless, certain communities managed not only to settle but to develop sufficiently cohesive societies as to challenge the greatest states of their time.

The Jukun have already been encountered. Also known as the Kororofa, Kororofawa, and Kwararafa, the Jukun eventually settled beside the Benue, where their capital, Kororofa, was situated. That much is sure, but their origins and original homelands are as obscure as those of most west Africans. One meets again the legend that the Jukun first came from the Middle East, but this time the legend is elaborated: they left Mecca because of a quarrel with the Prophet Muhammed. Another tradition suggests that the Jukun traveled with the Kanuri from the Yemen but left Bornu after disputes with their fellow migrants. The first definite evidence of the Jukun's existence seems to be a record in the Kano Chronicle: during the second half of the fourteenth century the king of Kano approached the borders of their lands, whereupon the Jukun fled. Later in the century, it is reported, the Jukun had to pay tribute to Kano to the tune of two hundred slaves.

It was in the seventeenth century that the Jukun became significantly powerful among contemporary states and empires, at times presenting a threat to both Bornu and the Hausa towns. As early as the late sixteenth century, however, Jukun attacks on Kano had forced its inhabitants to flee the town for neighboring Daura. Further attacks destroyed much of Kano, and at the end of the century the Jukun were sufficiently powerful to force Zaria to pay tribute to them.

The Jukun state structure fitted into the general west African patterns of the period. It was a monarchical state, the king, or aku, being "divine" and possibly theocratic, too. It has been suggested that he was held to represent the gods and the link between them and his people. A superficial view of his position would be that he was an absolute monarch, but to make this assessment would be to miss the set of checks and balances crucially woven into African custom. The king had a number of councilors, with a leader, the abo, who acted as a kind of prime minister. There were also priests, whose main responsibility was to guard the sacred relics left by former kings. In cases of unpopular rule or tyranny, councilors and priests had access to varied and effective sanctions. An aku who wished to remain on the throne and preserve his life would not dare to rule against the wishes of his people.

The second important community of the central region was that of the Tiv, who also lived beside the Benue, west of the Jukun. It is believed that the Tiv came from farther south, migrating northward to escape their enemies and finding a new home on better-protected hills. Later, pressure of their own population probably induced some of the more adventurous Tiv spirits to spread out into the open country.

It was from this latter expansion that the Tiv came into contact with other communities of the area, notably the Jukun, who were to make a deep impression on Tiv society, and the Fulani. As is common in most African societies, interrelationships have been of paramount significance to the Tiv. According to their central philosophy, all members of their community are descended from Adam, one of whose sons was called Tiv, their original ancestor, another being the ancestor of all other people. Before the influence of the Jukun was felt, the government of the Tiv community was dominated by a secret society that appointed the rulers. Authority was divided between two leaders: one who was supposed to use his powers of magic to ensure prosperity for the community and made responsible for both spiritual affairs and the laws; another who seems to have had more of an executive function. Both were elected by a council, which also played an advisory role in both civil and legal administration.

The influence of the Jukun radically altered the elements

of Tiv society. The two initial Tiv rulers were replaced by a system of chiefs, thus tending to a localization of social organization. New rulers, the "drum chiefs," as they were called, were appointed by and subject to the king of the Jukun; consequently, as the system gradually spread from those clans first in contact with the Jukun, Tiv society as a whole came under the authority of their neighboring state.

Farther west still, beside the Niger, as it bends southeast, and its tributary, the Kaduna, which flows south, lived the people known as Nupe. Their society consisted of a number of separate communities that cooperated at times of danger or sometimes for the purpose of military adventure. Usually the Nupe, or certain of their communities, were under the influence of some more powerful group, but in the sixteenth century they seem to have established their independence as a kingdom and begun to use it to expand their own power over others. This new unity and strength is usually attributed to Tsoede, their warrior-king of the period, who is said to have lived to the age of 120!

The dates of Nupe achievements during the sixteenth century are doubtful, for it is clear that Tsoede's feats have become legendary, making historical accuracy nearly impossible. What does seem certain is that the Nupe under Tsoede invaded Yorubaland and destroyed Old Oyo. Warfare seems to have continued between the Nupe and the Yoruba for many years, though the Nupe were eventually repulsed. According to Nupe legend, Tsoede introduced various arts and techniques from Idah—including canoe-building, smithing, human sacrifice, and bronze-casting—where his father was a prince. The truth of at least part of the legend is in doubt, for although it is claimed that the art of bronze-casting had been learned in Idah from Benin, the most famous bronzes found in Nupe, including a magnificent seated figure, seem to have been derived stylistically from Ife.

Toward the end of the eighteenth century Nupe began to

suffer the debilitating effects of the centrifugal factors that were weakening states throughout west Africa. Quarrels about the succession resulted in the state's being divided. Fulani groups participated in the conflict and eventually emerged as the paramount element in the state, placing their puppet on the throne early in the nineteenth century and maintaining him until they were ready to take complete control themselves.

There were many other communities in the middle region —the Idoma, the Igara, the Igbira, and others—who were either too small or more concerned with other affairs to develop powerful state systems. Many others lived in village communities without interest in building state systems, content to live more peaceful, localized lives. Yet most of the communities that developed beside the Niger and the Benue seem to have forged links with each other from very early times. The payment of tribute to a succession of overlords was a frequent feature in the area, the overlords often changing according to the political circumstances of different periods. Sometimes, too, one community would be subject to another yet still have groups subservient to itself. In this way it is clear that communications between the various societies of the region were constantly maintained.

It is equally clear that trading activities sustained relations between the different peoples. Markets were widespread, attended not only by locals but by Arabs, by Hausa, and, in certain cases, by traders from the coast. In some ways, therefore, the region began to develop as the crossroads of commerce in what is now Nigeria and parts of the Cameroons. Many foodstuffs were exchanged; cloth, robes, harnesses, implements, utensils, ivory, and slaves formed the main wares. The markets also served as centers for discussion, where ideas as well as goods were exchanged. Hausa became the common language of traders, while all the main local languages were descended from a common family. In short, this area of the

Niger bend and the Benue became one of the formative cultural cradles for an important section of modern Nigerian society.

Finally, one comes to the peoples of the southern areas, in particular the Yoruba, Bini, and Ibo societies. For many centuries channels of communication have linked all the southern societies that cover the main rain forest area, from Oyo on the northern borders of the forest to the coast and the Niger delta. Though their development into settled, progressive societies came a little later than in the northern grasslands because of the additional problems posed by their forest environment, when it came, it was as virile and creative as that in the north. States were built and, as they began to experience their power, expanded into various types of empire. Trade was conducted between the forest states—southward to the coast—and with some of the Hausa and Kanuri towns to the north. Wars, tribute, and enslavement were all features of these societies; at the same time, some of the societies produced artistic creations that have been universally acknowledged to be among the finest of their kind in the history of mankind.

All these activities involved frequent intercourse between the peoples of the forest area. Thus it is not surprising to find that many of them have retained legends of common origin, and that neighboring influences on forms of government are common. For example, the Yoruba had a strong influence on the Bini, whose main dynasty originated in Yorubaland; the Bini had considerable impact on the western Ibo; and the Ibo had frequent commercial contact with the peoples of the delta. Consequently, the cultures of each of these communities, and of many smaller ones in the region, have grown out of a melting pot of ethnic interchange.

The Yoruba can claim some pride of place in this multihistory, if only because their main rivals, the Bini, believe that their rulers originally sprang from the Yoruba. Like many others, Yoruba legends assert that their people originally came from the east. Sometimes these legends seem to be affirmed by the similarities between religion, art, and burial customs of the Yoruba and the peoples of the Nile. The legends vary—the ancestors came from Egypt, Kush, or Arabia —but no certain historical facts relating to this early history have yet been established. One may only guess that the "east" the Yoruba legends speak about was some part of the western or central Sudanese savannah, that the similarity in certain cultural habits was acquired by the exchange of ideas that took place between that area and the Nile valley, and that Yoruba ancestors moved southward into the verges of the forest around 1000 A.D.

Wherever the Yoruba came from, they certainly found many people already inhabiting the lands they reached, for the forest lands were populated long before the birth of Christ. Indeed, the earlier inhabitants used metals, created fine sculptures in terra cotta, and probably had some connections with the peoples who were responsible for the Nok culture.

Almost certainly the immigrants brought new ideas of government and administration with them. They seem to have dominated and then assimilated existing communities, producing an amalgam of techniques that introduced profound social changes around the turn of the first millennium, a time of movement and change in many parts of west Africa. Kanem was expanding rapidly, inevitably causing displacement and migration among many peoples. The Hausa towns were just establishing themselves. Ghana was in its prime. It is therefore not surprising to find that it was during this broad period that the Yoruba seem to have arrived in their new home and begun to build towns or clear settlements in the forest.

Ile-Ife has always been regarded as the traditional lodeplace of the Yoruba. Although their society seems to have been more varied than those of the others we have examined, all sections of their people appear to have regarded Ife as their traditional home. So, although each town, village, and settlement had its own web of clan or family allegiance, with its hierarchy of elders and chiefs, the bond that bound them together was their common regard for Ife.

This unifying factor in Yoruba life even survived the transfer of political power from Ife to Old Oyo. Ife remained the spiritual focus of Yoruba life, with its oni as religious leader, though it was Oyo that developed the most powerful empire, traditionally founded by Oranmiyan in the late fourteenth or early fifteenth century.

For three centuries the Yoruba empire expanded, until it reached the Niger in the north, Benin in the east, modern Togoland in the west, and the coastal mangrove swamps in the south. Those vast territories were divided into provinces, each administered by a king who owed allegiance to the imperial supreme ruler, the alafin of Oyo. As in the case of the other west African empires, however, the farther the province was situated from its power center—in this case Oyo—the weaker its allegiance and the more independent it tended to be. So the Oyo empire was as loosely knit as its predecessors and contemporaries.

The political system of Oyo was complex. The alafin was selected from among the royal family by a kind of cabinet formed from the principal councilors of state and known as the mesi. It also controlled state policy under the leadership of the basorun, a type of prime minister. The eldest son of the alafin not only never succeeded to the throne but was expected to commit suicide on his father's death. Experience of conflicts between factions within royal families and of the danger of an ambitious son's assassinating his father seem to have taught the Oyo important lessons. Nominally, the king was absolute, but the system was clearly designed to ensure that he ruled in accordance with the wishes of his people: if his subjects considered that he was misusing his power, he was both deposed and had to commit suicide.

As the people's will had to be expressed in some organized form, it was inevitably the mesi who assumed the role of popular voice. Thus the mesi always held considerable power over the king's actions, for he knew that to defy them would mean deposition and death. Yet the mesi itself could not claim autocratic powers, for a secret society, known as the Ogboni and composed of religious and political leaders, was sufficiently influential to inhibit its actions. The threat of death also hung over the military commander, for if his army was defeated, he, too, had to commit suicide.

In the provinces government took a slightly different form. Each of the kingdoms and towns, some of which had twenty thousand inhabitants by the eighteenth century, was ruled by an oba, who was supposed to be descended from the town's founder and was selected from one of the ruling lineages by the chiefs of other lineage groups. It was common for a council to be formed from the chiefs, together with heads of various political and religious associations, a system that ensured that a large proportion of the townspeople were represented in decision-making on their town's affairs and that popular control was exercised over the actions of the oba.

In the early years of the sixteenth century Oyo faced its first serious crisis. As we have seen, this period saw the Nupe invade Yorubaland and destroy Old Oyo. The inhabitants fled to Borgu. In the succeeding reign, however, the alafin repulsed the Nupe and set out to lead his people home; though he died on the way, his son took the refugees back into Yorubaland, where he had to establish a new capital at Oyo Igboho. (Oyo Igboho remained the capital while the continued attacks of the Nupe and Bussa were repelled.)

Eventually, the crisis was overcome, and Old Oyo was reoccupied as the capital, but in the eighteenth century Oyo was again challenged on a serious scale. This time it was the new state of Dahomey, founded only in the seventeenth century, to the southwest, that contested its supremacy. By this time the central objective of the southern states in west Africa was to gain footholds on the coast, both to increase their influence over the slave trade and to gain a share of European imports, particularly of firearms. Oyo had already seized Great Ardra on the coast at the end of the seventeenth century and made it into a tributary state. In 1724 Dahomey retaliated by invading the same state in its efforts to gain access to the coast. After initial repulses the Dahomey army defeated the Oyo forces, but they were so fearful of the consequences of their own success that they tried to placate Oyo by offering gifts, for the Oyo army was at this time considered to be an all-avenging monster. According to an eighteenth century writer:

> The Dahomans, to give an idea of the strength of an Eyoe [Oyo] army, assert that when they go to war, the general spreads the hide of a buffalo before the door of his tent, and pitches a spear in the ground, on each side of it; between which the soldiers march, until the multitude, which pass over the hide, have worn a hole through it; as soon as this happens, he presumes that his forces are numerous enough to take the field.

And a Dutch merchant declared that "This nation [Oyo] strikes such a terror into all the circumjacent Negroes, that they can scarce hear from them mention'd without trembling: And they tell a thousand strange things of them."

Three years after its defeat by Dahomey, Oyo took advantage of a war between its conquerors and Ouidah to intervene effectively on the latter's side. There had long been an understanding, amounting almost to an alliance, between Oyo and Ouidah. In the war of 1698 Ouidah had helped Oyo to attack Great Ardra, and thus when Ouidah was invaded by Dahomey, again as part of Dahomey's effort to establish itself on the coast, it was the turn of Oyo to come to its ally's assistance, especially since it was still smarting from the defeat of 1724.

In the new war the armies of Oyo surged through Dahomey, laying waste much of the countryside, and in 1729 the king of Dahomey had to sue for peace. Part of the peace settlement was that Dahomey agreed to pay tribute to Oyo—sweet revenge for the disgrace of five years earlier—but the tribute was not paid, so in 1738 Oyo armies again invaded Dahomey, on this occasion laying siege to the capital, Abomey, to ensure that the settlement was honored. The treaty terms were stiff. Oyo demanded a tribute of forty men, forty women, forty guns, and four thousand loads of cowries and corals (used as currency) per annum, backdated to 1728. At first Dahomey refused the terms, but by 1747 the persistent Oyo threats persuaded it to submit, continuing to pay the substantial tribute into the nineteenth century. The supremacy of the Oyo empire was convincingly reestablished.

Before long, however, internal troubles began to weaken the power of the Oyo empire. In the mid-eighteenth century a power-hungry basorun maneuvered himself into a position of dominance over a succession of alafins. For twenty years he retained his supremacy, until he was outwitted by Alafin Abiodun, who killed him and his whole family. A period of peace ensued, but the damage had been done. The central governing institution had been undermined. Tributary states began to seek excuses to refuse to pay their dues. Dahomey defied the empire in 1781 and 1784. The Egba seceded and repulsed a punitive force sent from Oyo. The Bariba revolted and defeated an imperial army sent to discipline them. The coastal provinces began to quarrel during the 1780s; the empire found itself incapable of imposing its authority on them. The very army that had been responsible for imperial expansion and internal order itself showed increasing signs of weakness—sure evidence that central authority was disintegrating.

Perhaps the most important indications of the disintegration of Oyo were the signs of economic decline. Tribute from subject states and provinces had brought in considerable revenues, although so much of the tribute was spent in warfare that there was little benefit to either industrial productivity or the economic strength of the empire. The location of Oyo gave it an advantageous position as a center of trade between north and south, but the resistance of the constituent states to imperial authority and to demands for tribute affected the revenues, revealing the decline in central authority. Oyo, in short, fell victim to the trend in west African history whereby during the slave era trading attractions moved steadily southward. The profits to be gained from trading with the Europeans on the coast and receiving the goods they brought from overseas, especially firearms, gradually outweighed the benefits of northern-directed commerce. The Yoruba were looking ever more directly south in seeking commercial opportunities; Oyo found that it was increasingly regarded as being situated too far north to provide the commercial base Yoruba merchants were seeking. By the end of the eighteenth century it had become clear that Oyo's days of preeminence were over.

The Oyo empire had played a long and important part in the development of the Yoruba peoples. It had always possessed a central core that provided the Yoruba with a sense of cohesion, based on a common language pattern, a common religion, and a widespread feeling of kinship. The empire was well organized through most of its history and had involved a large proportion of its inhabitants, freemen and slaves, in its administration. Many of its rulers had been wise, shrewd, and good strategists. The empire had brought to the Yoruba peoples fine institutions, a cohesive spirit, and creative artistic inspiration. Its influence survived long after its structure disintegrated.

The second great forest empire, contemporary with Oyo, was that of Benin. The origins of the Bini, who formed the core community, are as indefinite as those of other west Africans. According to Egharevba, the historian of Benin:

> Many, many years ago, the Binis came all the way from Egypt to found a more secure shelter in this part of the world after a short stay in the Sudan and at Ile-Ife. . . . Before coming here, a band of hunters was sent from Ife to inspect this land and the report furnished was very favorable. Tradition says that they met some people who were in the land before their arrival. These people are said to have come from the Sudan originally.

Thus, according to tradition, legend, and what few facts we possess, the Benin area was inhabited before the arrival of the Bini, the newcomers came from the east, and they had close connections with the Yoruba of Ife.

From this combination of sources we can build a picture of a first Benin state, founded probably around 900 A.D. with a dynasty of kings known as the Ogiso. Sometime in the twelfth century the migrants from Ife seem to have arrived. Tradition now has it that the Bini became dissatisfied with the rule of the Ogiso and sent to Ife to ask the oni for a prince to act as their ruler. Egharevba has a charming legend to tell of how the oni reacted to this request:

> In order to test the ability of the Binis to look after his son, Odudua first of all sent seven lice to the Benin chiefs to be cared for and returned after three years. This condition was fulfilled and Odudua was greatly surprised to see the lice in increased sizes when they were sent back to him by the chiefs. He exclaimed that "the people who can take care of such minute pests as lice can undoubtedly take care of my son."

Thus began the dynasty that was to create the second Benin state and expand it into another powerful west African empire. According to the legend, Odudua's son, Oranmiyan, went to Usama in Benin, fathered a son by a local woman, and left his son to become the first oba, considering that only a man born and bred in the country could make a good ruler. Traditionally, too, it was another son of Oranmiyan who became the first alafin of Oyo, so the dynasties of the two most powerful forest empires had a common ancestry.

It was the first oba, Eweka, son of Oranmiyan, who founded Benin's administrative system: a hereditary state council of six members, one of whose tasks was to act as king-makers. But as Benin had a hereditary concept of monarchy, combined with primogeniture, the council's responsibility was not to select a new monarch but rather to ensure that the king's eldest son was duly and securely installed. Moreover, the chiefs who administered the provinces were directly responsible to the king, and Eweka improved the king's central position by appointing his children to be chiefs in many of the villages. When the state council began to interfere too often, as it did in the reign of Eweka's grandson, the oba ensured that his authority was seen to be supreme: he moved the capital to Benin City, though he had to fight his way in, and quickly reduced the pretensions of his council.

Clearly, the obas of Benin were considerably more powerful than the rulers of most contemporary empires. They could not be removed from office, like the alafins of Oyo, and they could grant chieftaincies to their own nominees instead of having to observe lineage claims. But perhaps the most important source of Benin monarchical power was the commercial monopolies imposed by the obas. The monarch had absolute power over trade, and industries and crafts also were under his control. He appointed special officials to conduct commercial activities, and the guild system for craftsmen, such as goldsmiths and brass-smiths, was organized under regulations made by the king. Only after the royal agents had finished their commercial transactions were the common merchants allowed to participate, and even then they had to secure permission from the king; the special crafts could only be practiced through ward guilds in Benin City under royal direction.

It may be, too, that the composition of Benin, compared with that of Oyo, strengthened central authority. The Yoruba were and still are essentially an urban people. Each town tended to become the nucleus of a faction, rendering centralized government difficult and encouraging divisive tendencies. Benin, on the other hand, was almost entirely a village society. The smaller units of political government and economic activity did not allow local leaders to acquire such power as might challenge the control of the oba, and, as we have seen, the oba often adopted policies designed to use his advantage to the full.

Benin reached the zenith of its power in the fifteenth and sixteenth centuries. It had a large and comparatively efficient army that was able to extend the influence of the empire to the north, to the Niger, to Bonny in the delta, and as far as Lagos and Badagri along the coast. The oba of the mid-fifteenth century, Ewuare, was not only a successful military leader, increasing the imperial revenues by forcing many towns and villages to pay tribute, but, according to tradition:

> He made good roads in Benin City. It was he who had the innermost and greatest of the walls and ditches made around the city, and he also made powerful charms and had them buried at each of the nine gateways of the city, so as to ward against any evil charms which might be brought by people of other countries in order to injure his subjects.

It was in the reign of Ewuare that Benin received its greatest stimulus: the appearance of the first Europeans. In this respect the empire had a great advantage over its rivals, for it had a position on the coast and could be reached by river. When the Portuguese arrived, first, during an exploratory voyage in the Bight of Benin in 1472 and, then, from 1485 in search of trade, Benin was a strong, well-organized empire, an obvious magnet to attract the Portuguese merchants. The Portuguese found Benin willing to supply pepper, skins, palm kernels, and ivory in exchange for manufactured goods brought from Europe. Soon slaves were requested, particularly for the settlement made by Portugal on the island of São Thomé. Since slavery was common throughout west Africa, slaves were supplied to the Portuguese in the way that had been customary in inter-African commercial or military transactions, except that the Portuguese traders quickly found that firearms were even more acceptable to west Africans than other manufactured goods. Of course, it was not long before the new firearms were providing still greater strength to the armies of Benin.

Missionaries followed the merchants and began to make converts, including members of the Benin royal family. Then ambassadors were exchanged between Lisbon and Benin. In the middle of the sixteenth century the first English arrivals at the Benin court found that Portuguese was spoken there. The friendliness that existed in these early days between the oba and the Portuguese is well expressed in a letter written by a Portuguese representative, Duarte Pires, to his king in 1516:

> The favour which the king of Benin accords us is due to his love of your highness; and thus he pays us high honour and sets us at table to dine with his son, and no part of his court is hidden from us but all the doors are open. Sir, when these priests arrived in Benin, the delight of the king of Benin was so great that I do not know how to describe it, and likewise that of all his people; and he sent for them at once; and they remained with him for one whole year in war.

Soon after the beginning of the sixteenth century, however, the trade in slaves became dangerously dominant. At the main port used for this trade and, to a much lesser extent, for the export of pepper, Gwato, on the Benin coast, a factory was built so that slaves could be housed for later sale to merchants from Europe. The oba imposed the same regulations on the slave trade as on all other forms of commerce, exercising a royal monopoly, and appointed his own agents to negotiate with the European merchants. In addition, Benin was uniquely situated, with access to the sea and rivers and dominance over the slave-supplying forests.

In the mid-sixteenth century the English made their first appearance in Benin. According to one chronicler, who related the events of the first voyage in 1553, they sailed up the river and then walked ten leagues from the river to the king's court. Here they were well received and asked what they sought. On telling the king that they wanted to exchange the goods they had brought with them for commodities of his country:

> The king then having of old lying in a certain store-house 30 or 40 kintails of pepper (every kintail being a hundred weight) willed them to look upon the same, and again to bring him a sight of such merchandises as they had brought with them. . . . And in case their merchandises would not extend to the value of so much pepper, he [the king] promised to credite them to their next return, and thereupon sent the country round about to gather pepper, causing the same to be brought to the court: so that within the space of 30 days they gathered fourscore ton of pepper.

Although the English tried to follow up this initial voyage with further expeditions to the west coast and continued to trade occasionally with west Africans for fifteen years, they were not at first strong enough to challenge the Portuguese, who controlled all the positions on the coast itself. The fact that in 1562 John Hawkins led an English slaving expedition to west Africa, the first, also seems to have been a factor in the failure of England. By that time some Africans had become hostile to slaving, and others had discovered how to play one set of European merchants off against another. In any case, after Hawkins's disaster at the hands of the Spaniards in 1568 at the end of a slaving voyage from west Africa to south America, English merchants withdrew from the slave trade until the following century. They also seem to have abandoned other forms of trade to west Africa at the same time.

Benin continued to prosper during the slaving era. At the beginning of the seventeenth century one Dutchman described the city thus:

> When you go into it you enter a great broad street, which is not payed, and seems to be seven or eight times broader than the Warmoes street in Amsterdam. This street is straight, and does not bend at any point. It is thought to be four miles long.
>
> At the gate where I went in on horseback, I saw a very big wall, very thick and made of earth, with a very deep and broad ditch outside it. . . . And outside this gate there is also a big suburb. Inside the gate, and along the great street just mentioned, you see many other great streets on either side, and these are also straight and do not bend. . . .
>
> The houses in this town stand a good order, one close and evenly spaced with its neighbours, just as the houses of Holland stand. . . .
>
> The king's court is very great. It is built around many square shaped yards. These yards have surrounding galleries where sentries are always placed. I myself went into the court far enough to pass through four great yards like this, and yet whereever I looked I could still see gate after gate which opened into other yards.

A comparison of this picture of Benin with most European towns of the seventeenth century would show that economic and social conditions were roughly similar, given the differences between tropical and temperate environments. It was to be largely the contrasting impacts of the slave trade on west Africa and Europe that was to separate their respective paths into the future.

The city of Benin remained a place of comfort, good manners, and prosperity until toward the end of the eighteenth century, yet it did so in the midst of an empire rapidly contracting and declining in power. The tremendous increase in the slave trade, and the accompanying desire on the part of west Africans to obtain firearms, made it impossible for the oba to retain his trading monopoly for long. Communities that had previously accepted Benin's rule sought greater independence in order to secure their share of the fruits offered by trade with the Europeans. Warfare and competition proliferated; various African communities quickly learned of the benefits to be attained from making alliances with different European groups; the firearms they obtained as the price for their help were used not only to capture slaves and repel invaders but also to resist the imperial power of the obas. Government, public life, and the social customs of the wealthy could be sustained in Benin City, but society there became increasingly isolated from the generally rapacious life of the rest of the empire.

As the provinces revolted or collapsed into chaos through the effects of slaving raids and intercommunal wars, the empire crumbled. Eventually even the city itself began to be affected. During the eighteenth century reports of increasingly dictatorial obas, chiefs, and priests provide evidence of declining standards under the pressures of growing insecurity. Benin, like its contemporaries, had provided order, security, unity, and progressive prosperity; it had given the world the splendors of its incomparable brass sculptures; but the very commercial life on which much of its later prosperity and power had been built became its Achilles's heel. Order, unity, law, and prosperity could not survive under the destructive forces of the slave trade and the growth of the social values consequent on its pursuit.

5

THE IBO

THE OTHER large community in the south of present-day Nigeria was the Ibo, and with the Ibo one encounters something quite different from the experience of the other peoples considered. One can compare the states and empires of the north with each other and with those of Oyo and Benin; there are similarities between them all, and, although they show variation, they were based on related foundations. The Ibo lived quite differently. They had neither states nor empires, never developed centralized government, and therefore used totally different institutions.

Very little is known about how the Ibo originally came to inhabit their lands. The absence of state systems led to lack of interest in dynastic records, even in oral tradition. The lack of contact with European traders resulted in an absence of the Benin-type written records stretching back to the fifteenth century, and, of course, like both Oyo and Benin society, Ibo society was nonliterate, never having been penetrated by Islam. It is possible that there was once an Ibo "core," probably around Awka and Orlu, from where groups of Ibo spread across surrounding areas. Yet the picture is so obscure, with many groups claiming to have originated from different regions—such as Benin and Idah—that little purpose is served at present in trying to bring the core theory into what may turn out to be an artificial focus.

It is more important to explain why it can be claimed that the Ibo are a single people when they have always been so fragmented and scattered. First, they inhabited a recognized geographic area: it stretched from Benin to Igala, from the Cross River to the Niger delta. Second, they spoke a common language, which certainly developed various dialects but nevertheless was broadly understood among all groups. Third, their cultural patterns were, if not identical, closely related, based on similar cults and social institutions. And fourth, the whole Ibo people believed in a common supreme god, known as Chuku or Chineke, who was responsible for everything in this world and the next. It is, therefore, because of these common denominators, and despite their fragmentation and lack of centralized institutions, that the Ibo can reasonably be considered as one ethnic community.

Within these common characteristics the Ibo may be divided into five main cultural groups: a western community, on the west bank of the Niger and around Onitsha; the northern group, around Awka, northward to Nsukka and southward to Okigwi; the Owerri, around the town of that name; the Cross River Ibo, near Bende and Arochuku; and the Ogoja, who lived between Afikpo and Abakalika. Throughout the area east of the Niger and south of the Benue, plus an enclave on the west bank of the Niger around Asaba, the Ibo lived in thousands of small villages. They never built recognizable towns or cities, but their village life was coherent, often cohesive, linked together by a variety of interlocking allegiances.

The basis of social life was the extended family, a concept common to many parts of the African continent. All relatives, however remote, were members of the family structure. Their place in the family guaranteed them social and economic security; their contributions in economic activity and personal relations were made within the family's framework. Indeed, among the Ibo the extended family was the foundation on which villages and the system of communal land holding were based.

At times, this structure burst its confines, for the family would become so large that quarrels developed among its members. Then the village would splinter into separate units, and new villages might be formed. On the other hand, small related groups might decide to amalgamate in order to form a larger village to ensure greater protection.

Despite this fragmentation and the small size of the political units a number of factors were continually operating within Ibo society to strengthen cohesion and the sense of community. First, villages were bound together into clans, all the inhabitants of which claimed to be descended from a common ancestor. Thus each cultural group would be composed of perhaps a hundred clans, which would speak a similar dialect and share certain common customs and traditions. Each village was itself divided into a number of wards consisting of extended families. Thus, every Ibo had an immediate, a median, and a more remote allegiance binding him to a wide variety of his fellows: family, village, and clan loyalties all played roles in developing and preserving Ibo cohesion.

Second, the system of government, which was based on the village, added to the sense of community. In the general pattern there were two political institutions: the council of elders and the village assembly. Respect for age was universal, so the council of elders usually consisted of the heads of extended families, though the Ibo belief in equality is illustrated by the right of any adult male to sit on the council, especially when a decision was being taken affecting the individual. The recognition of this right also acted as a curb on any elders who might be tempted to make an arbitrary decision or form an unrepresentative hierarchy.

The village assembly strengthened popular participation in important decision-making. All controversial issues had to be placed before it, and on such matters all adult men had the right to speak. The decisions then taken had to be unanimous, thus ensuring government by consent.

The judicial system also encouraged popular involvement. When quarrels occurred between members of different families, other members of the families, including their elders, could arbitrate. More serious disputes and crimes were usually heard by the elders' council and the village assembly.

The broad uniformity of these patterns of government and law provided one strong element of unity, and the unifying trend was reinforced by the third cohesive factor: the age groups common to most Ibo communities. Age group members shared initiation rites, and from that time on worked together in communal services and competed together against other similar groups in sports or other activities. In some communities the leaders of the age groups were given positions on the council of elders, thus giving the young men a role in government, and in all cases the experience of a common life provided for each age set bound together young men and women, beyond the family, to the village. Indeed, since the institution existed in most communities, this common experience also tended to bind together young people of neighboring villages.

In certain Ibo communities title societies also contributed a strand to the web of communal life. Title societies were a kind of insurance societies, open to any freeborn male who could pay the initiation fee. Payment of the fee authorized the purchaser to take a title, and as he made further payments, he moved up the grades. In the top grades members received a pension or dividend as their share of the lower-grade fees. Again, in some villages the leaders of these societies were allocated places on the council.

Another similar kind of organization, particularly prevalent among the Cross River and Ibibio clans, was the secret society. As well as incorporating the initiation and grade fees, the titles and pensions, these societies practiced a secret ritual that was supposed to confer on the participants special powers from the gods. Such societies often played an important role in the government of the village. The higher-grade members would make major political decisions, while the lower ones were entrusted with administration. This degree of hierarchical government provided an exception to the general Ibo pattern; among the clans in which such societies took a leading role the power of the village assembly was inevitably reduced, with an elite gaining greater influence than usual. Yet so long as the hierarchy was acceptable, this concentration of power may have brought greater cohesion, though it also invited more resentment and political intrigue.

A few communities went even further in their centralization of government than those with secret societies. Beside the Niger and at Nri, near Awka, a few instances occurred of actual states, with kings, assisted by the leaders of title societies, the lineage elders, and leaders of age groups, holding governmental powers. One example of this structure was that in Onitsha, where the obi was chosen from and by a royal family and ruled with senior members of a title society as his council. These states, however, were exceptions.

A fourth feature of Ibo life that assisted the cohesive trend was the wide prevalence of markets. Among the Ibo the village market was, and still is, the focal point of social as well as of economic activity. People gathered there not just to buy and sell, important though these functions were; it was in the market that most arrangements for the social life of the village and surrounding areas were made. Moreover, on a wider scale, the main market of a clan, or group of villages, played a role similar to that the local market played: the affairs of the clan were settled there and considerable economic exchange was conducted for the whole area. Indeed, one communal task decided upon at the market—the hewing out, keeping clear, and maintaining the radial paths that led to the center of the villages—itself involved communal labor and cooperative organization, which in turn deepened the roots of cohesion between the group of villagers.

Fifth, marriage custom widened the sense of community. The Ibo were generally an exogamous people; they encouraged their men to seek wives from outside their own lineage or village. Thus the personal relationships established had a very wide connotation. Links were forged within a family stretching across several villages, as wives, mothers, and the husbands of sisters usually all came from different villages. Not only did this custom encourage multiple personal contacts, these contacts themselves, and the many family visits they entailed, encouraged inter-village trading. Then, too, these marriage relationships also provided a basis for the organization of mutual defense and, when quarrels arose, modified the severity of warfare between villages.

Sixth, the cult of oracles and the commercial web that largely depended on it perhaps was the strongest organizational network drawing the various Ibo communities together. The Ibo relied on a large number of oracles, which could be consulted to provide verdicts for the mass of disputes that inevitably arose in such a fragmented but related society. The dominant oracle was Chuku, the high god, recognized by most Ibo to be supreme but there were also many others in localized use, some with considerable powers.

The belief in oracles provided not simply spiritual satisfaction or supernatural sanction; it was a crucial factor in political power and economic activity. The oracular organization was made up of agents and mercenary forces. The agents would travel the countryside persuading villagers to consult their particular oracle. When the oracle had spoken, those found guilty would be ordered to pay a number of slaves, supposedly to be sacrificed to the oracle but actually to be sold to slave merchants. Fees paid by the successful litigants might also be in the same currency and be disposed of in the same manner. Those consulting the oracle would be warned that the gods would punish them if they ignored the verdict; to ensure that their oracle maintained its reputation the agents often employed mercenaries to burn down the villages of those who refused to accept the verdict and to capture the offenders to add to the toll of slaves.

While these practices were widespread in Iboland, two particular clans dominated their conduct. The Awka were famous for their traveling blacksmiths, and their blacksmith guilds took it in turns to tour the country. However, once they had proved their skill in a village by forging farm implements, swords, or spears, the smiths used their reputation to persuade the villagers to refer their disputes to the Awka oracle, Agbala.

The Aro made even more extensive use of the system. They had the advantage of possessing the supreme oracle, the Arochuku, the voice of Chuku, which was considered to be the most objective because of its remoteness from the location of most disputes, and, therefore, because of its lack of direct interest in the outcome. Yet this was a naive supposition. The Aro traders had a widespread network of trading routes and found the oracle invaluable to their activities. They would first persuade the disputants to accept their oracle, then conduct them to Arochuku, where they would collect a fee for accommodating them in their family compound. Finally, the agent would provide the oracle priests with such background information concerning the dispute, details of the locality concerned, and histories of the litigants as to enable the priests to impress the contestants with their supernatural knowledge!

Armed with this great advantage the Aro became the most powerful trading community in the country. They opened long-distance trade routes right across the lands of the Ibo and could always deploy Chuku's mercenaries when resistance was met. Their main commercial strength developed out of the slave trade with the Europeans, beginning in the sixteenth century. For some years the Aro held a monopoly for supplying slaves to the delta states. They would buy slaves in the north and march them to the main market in Bende. From there these human cargoes would be marched to Bonny and Calabar to be sold for transport across the Atlantic. Along the routes trodden by the slave traders and their captives the Aro established settlements where the slaves could be fed, and these new villages grew as halting places for caravans carrying ordinary merchandise and for mercenaries.

Because of the fame of their oracle the Aro were believed to be divinely protected, and since their mercenaries were accustomed to revive this belief by their actions against anyone daring to doubt it, the Aro were able to trade and settle where they wished without fear of molestation. Inevitably, the Aro thus came to have some influence on the clans among whom they moved. However, they seem to have had sufficient sensitivity to the spirit of Ibo independence to limit their influence to issues important to their commercial activities. Characteristically, when the slave trade was prohibited by Britain and replaced by trade in palm oil, the Aro readily turned to the new customs.

The virile commerce practiced by the Aro and the powerful organization built by them to conduct it certainly brought an economic unifying factor to the Ibo. Yet, at the same time, the commerce also led many Ibo to the slave ships and a life of slavery on the other side of the Atlantic, for the lucrative slave trade was a crucial part of the Aro commercial mastery, while the small-scale nature of Ibo government left clans, villages, and families constantly exposed to the raiders, traders, and extortioners of the oracles.

The fact that the Ibo people survived such depredations is itself witness to the strength of their culture and the stamina of their institutions. It is estimated that toward the end of the eighteenth century sixteen thousand Ibo were sold every year in Bonny alone; others were certainly being sold in the Calabar markets. Despite these continually heavy losses Iboland remained closely populated, its inhabitants apparently having the spirit and determination to rebuild their depopulated villages and to maintain, against the enormous odds, the social order on which their survival depended.

Fortunately, there exists a first-hand account of life in Iboland, written by a remarkable man, Olaudah Equiano, who was kidnapped from his home in the mid-eighteenth century, taken in a slave ship across the Atlantic, and sold as a slave in Virginia. Later, Equiano was taken to England and again sold there. Some years afterward he purchased his liberty and traveled to many lands as a seaman. He then took an active part in the anti-slavery agitation in England, particularly in the preparations for the foundation of the colony for released slaves in Sierra Leone. In 1792 he married a Cambridge girl. His autobiography, published in 1789, gives a fascinating account of his travels and also describes his Iboland home around the middle of the century. Extracts from it can provide us with a picture of daily life in Ibo society at that time.

> This kingdom is divided into many provinces or districts. . . . I had never heard of white men or Europeans, nor of the sea . . . every transaction of the government . . . was conducted by the chiefs or elders. . . . Those Embrenche, or chief men, decided disputes, and punished crimes . . . Adultery, however, was sometimes punished with slavery or death . . . so sacred among them is the honor of the marriage-bed, and so jealous are they of the fidelity of their wives. . . . The men, however, do not preserve the same constancy to their wives which they expect from them; for they indulge in a plurality, though seldom in more than two. . . .
>
> We are almost a nation of dancers, musicians, and poets. Thus every great event, such as a triumphant return from

battle, or other cause of public rejoicing, is celebrated in public dances, which are accompanied with songs and music suited to the occasion. . . . As our manners are simple, our luxuries are few. The dress of both sexes are nearly the same. It generally consists of a long calico, or muslin, wrapped loosely round the body. . . . Besides this, our women of distinction wear golden ornaments, which they dispose with some profusion on their arms and legs. When our women are not employed with the men in tillage, their usual occupation is spinning and weaving cotton, which they afterwards dye, and make into garments. They also manufacture earthen vessels, of which we have many kinds. . . .

Bullocks, goats, and poultry, supply the greatest part of their food. These constitute likewise the principal wealth of the country, and the chief article of its commerce. The flesh is usually stewed in a pan. To make it savory we sometimes use also pepper and other spices; and we have salt made of wood ashes. Our vegetables are mostly plantains, eadas, yams, beans and Indian corn. . . . their principal beverage is palm wine. . . .

Each master of a family has a large square piece of ground, surrounded by a moat or fence, or enclosed with a wall made of red earth tempered, which, when dry, is as hard as brick. Within this are his houses to accommodate his family and slaves; which, if numerous, frequently present the appearance of a village. . . . These houses never exceed one storey in height; they are always built of wood, of stakes driven into the ground, crossed with wattles, and neatly plastered within and without. The roof is thatched with reeds. . . . The whole neighborhood afford their unanimous assistance in building them [the houses], and in return expect no other recompense than a feast. . . .

. . . We have few manufactures. They consist for the most part of calicoes, earthen ware, ornaments, and instruments of war and husbandry. . . . In such a state money is of little use; however, we have some small pieces of coin, if I may call them such. They are made something like an anchor. . . . We have also markets, at which I have been frequently with my mother.

They are sometimes visited by stout mahogany-coloured men from the southwest of us: we call them Oye-Eboe, which term signifies red men living at a distance. They generally bring us fire-arms, gunpowder, hats, beads, and dried fish. . . . These articles they barter with us for odoriferous woods and earth, and our salt of wood-ashes. They always carry slaves through our lands, but the strictest account is exacted of their manner of procuring them before they are suffered to pass. Sometimes indeed we sold slaves to them, but they were only prisoners of war, or such among us as had been convicted of kidnapping, or adultery, and some other crimes, which we esteemed heinous. . . .

Our tillage is exercised in a large plain or common, some hours walk from our dwellings, and all the neighbours resort thither in a body. They use no beasts of husbandry; and their only instruments are hoes, axes, shovels, and beaks, or pointed iron to dig with. . . . This common is often the theatre of war; and therefore when our people go out to till their land, they not only go in a body, but generally take their arms with them, for fear of a surprise; and, when they apprehend an invasion, they guard the avenues to their dwellings, by driving sticks into the ground, which are so sharp at one end as to pierce the foot, and are generally dipt in poison. From what I can recollect of these battles, they appear to have been irruptions of one little state or district on the other, to obtain prisoners or booty. Perhaps they were incited to this by those traders who brought the European goods I mentioned amongst us. . . . When a trader wants slaves, he applies to a chief for them, and tempts him with his wares. It is not extraordinary, if on those occasions he yields to the temptation with as little firmness, and accepts the price of his fellow creature's liberty with as little reluctance, as the enlightened merchant. Accordingly, he falls on his neighbours, and a desperate battle ensues. If he prevails, and takes prisoners, he gratifies his avarice by selling them; but, if his party be vanquished, and he falls into the hands of the enemy, he is put to death. . . . We have fire-arms, bows and arrows, broad two-edged swords and javelins;

> we have shields also, which cover a man from head to foot. All are taught the use of these weapons. Even our women are warriors, and march boldly out to fight along with the men. . . . The spoils were divided according to the merit of the warriors. Those prisoners which were not sold or redeemed we kept as slaves; but how different was their condition from that of the slaves in the West Indies! With us they do no more work than other members of the community, even their master; their food, clothing, and lodging, were nearly the same as theirs (except that they were not permitted to eat with those who were freeborn) and there was scarce any other difference between them than a superior degree of importance which the head of a family possesses in our state, and that authority which, as such, he exercises over every part of his household. Some of these slaves have even slaves under them, as their own property and for their own use.
>
> As to religion, the natives believe that there is one Creator of all things, and that he lives in the sun, and is girded round with a belt, that he may never eat or drink; but according to some, he smokes a pipe, which is our own favourite luxury. They believe he governs events, especially our deaths or captivity. . . .
>
> Though we had no places of public worship, we had priests and magicians or wise men. . . . They calculated our time, and foretold events. . . . These magicians were also our doctors or physicians. They practised bleeding by cupping; and were very successful in healing wounds, and expelling poisons. . . .

The Ibo and the people of Benin had long contacts with the inhabitants of the mangrove swamps of the Niger delta. Especially after the Europeans began to visit the coast the delta became one of the most important trading areas in west Africa. But the areas around the delta were inhabited before the arrival of Europeans. The main population consisted of the Ijo people, most of whom lived in scattered fishing villages. It is suggested that the Ijo came originally from the Benin area and that they may be one of the oldest-established communities in Nigeria.

After the arrival of the Portuguese the Ijo settlements found themselves excellently situated to attain a foremost position in the slave trade. They quickly developed trading stations, with New Calabar, Bonny, and Brass in the van. By the early seventeenth century these towns had all grown into ports of crucial importance to both European merchants and African slavers. Further along the coast, at the mouth of the Cross River, Old Calabar, an ancient Efik trading state, also rose in importance to meet the needs of the slave trade. In the western delta Warri, which we have already mentioned, developed into what was virtually an independent state from the same source of commercial wealth.

The sudden growth of these fishing villages into substantial towns as the impact of the new trade was felt forced the villages to make administrative changes. Up to this time the usual method of government in the villages had been through an assembly, which all adult male inhabitants had the right to attend, under the presidency of a senior chief known as the amanyanabo. As trade expanded rapidly, however, power moved into the hands of the most successful merchants and the "house" rule system developed.

The house system became the dominant socioeconomic institution in the delta—the basis of the commercial relationship between African and European merchants—until the latter years of the nineteenth century. The system began as a structure built on the extended family of the principal trader of a district, but it was soon widened to include subordinate traders as well as members of the family. Simply put, in the system the head of the house exacted taxes from each member of his extended house to meet the expenses of the organization and to equip a war canoe of thirty men to serve it. It was usual for the head to be succeeded by one of his children, but since the succession was decided by a house meeting that could be attended by all members, slave as well as freeborn, the choice was sometimes varied. On occasion, an outstanding slave was chosen as the new head;

for commercial prowess tended to take precedence over personal considerations.

The head of the house became an increasingly powerful person, particularly in the most successful houses and as trade increased. He had considerable authority over every member of his house and could settle internal disputes or punish crimes. Since he was responsible for conducting negotiations with foreign merchants, African and European, his power extended to economic, political, administrative, and legal affairs.

When disputes arose between rival houses, they were settled by the town assembly, still under the presidency of the amanyanabo, who was also head of his own house, was responsible for the conduct of warfare, led the battle fleet, and initiated general policy.

Inevitably, as trade grew to dominate the life of the delta towns, and town administration grew more complex than had been customary in the former fishing villages, the heads of houses, on whose activities prosperity depended, were increasingly accepted as being responsible for government. Under the chairmanship of the amanyanabo they formed a kind of council, superseding the authority of the general assembly. Although the organization of each town showed considerable variation, domination by groups of powerful merchants became characteristic in Bonny, Old and New Calabar, Brass, and Warri. And one might note that the supremacy of commercial influence in political institutions displayed in the delta reflected similar trends witnessed in European towns during the eighteenth and nineteenth centuries.

Finally, in tracing the origins of modern Nigerian society, we turn to Lagos, now the Nigerian capital, but only of any considerable influence since the nineteenth century. Lagos was founded by a group of Yoruba who, under the leadership of a junior member of the royal family, settled at Isheri, about a dozen miles from the site of the modern city. The settlers spread southward to an area of the mainland opposite Iddo Island. As civil wars among the main body of Yoruba began to threaten this settlement, the inhabitants moved across the water to Iddo Island itself.

The whole area is a mass of mangrove swamps, creeks, and islands. Consequently, as the population increased and the mainland proved to be vulnerable to attack, expansion had to take place on other islands, including Lagos Island itself, and it says much for the ingenuity and adaptability of the Yoruba that they were able to make homes and sustain themselves in such an inhospitable environment.

It was not only the mainland Yoruba who threatened the early settlements. Benin also tried to invade Iddo, but under the leadership of the Iddo king, or olafin, the Bini were repulsed, and their subsequent attacks were equally unsuccessful.

Foiled in their attempts at invasion, the Bini began to migrate peacefully and settle in Lagos, and as their influence grew from within, they gradually became the dominant community in the settlement. But the Benin empire was not satisfied with such pacific influence: marauders from Benin began to attack the islanders' possessions on the mainland. Matters never became too serious, however, because, it will be recalled, the royal rulers of both Lagos and Benin were related to the royal family of Oyo and therefore were of common ancestry. The quarrels of their peoples were not allowed to rupture entirely the sense of relationship, and the problems were solved when the oba of Benin, anxious not to jeopardize Bini influence in Lagos, appointed the Isheri chief, Ashipa, king of the island kingdom of Lagos, which thus became a colony of Benin, paying tribute until well into the nineteenth century.

At the time Benin became supreme in Lagos, the relative importance of Iddo and Lagos was being reversed. Although

Iddo never acknowledged the formal suzerainty of Benin, as the settlement lost its supremacy before the rapid rise of Lagos, it became in practice another colony of Benin.

Lagos, meanwhile, was seeing great increases in its trading wealth and consequently in its political power. Portuguese traders had long visited the island; in the late eighteenth century, recognizing Lagos' advantageous situation for the slave trade, they began to settle on the island. Their presence increased the number of shrewd, skilled merchants living in Lagos, while its strategic position for controlling the slave trade from Yorubaland gave it advantages that rivaled those of the delta towns. These advantages were still further augmented by the effects of the destructive Yoruba civil wars: by weakening its rivals and greatly increasing the supply of slaves, the wars provided Lagos with an accretion of wealth and power that prepared the island city for its paramount role in the nineteenth and twentieth centuries.

One may aptly conclude this account of the coastal towns that played such a vital part in fostering the commercial life of Nigeria with extracts from a book written by a ship's captain who visited the west coast frequently during the last fifteen years of the eighteenth century:

> The town of Lagos is built on a bank or island, which appears to have been raised from Cradoo lake, by the eddies, after the sea and periodical rains had broken down the boundary which separated it from the ocean. The island is of inconsiderable size, about four miles from the sea, and a foot only above the level of the lake at high water, which is so shallow that boats of only ten or fifteen tons burden can approach the town. . . .
>
> It has always been the policy of the Lagos people, like those of Bonny, to be themselves the traders and not brokers. . . .
>
> The necessaries of life are here extremely abundant and cheap, and are brought chiefly from the country or northern margin of Cradoo lake, which communicates with Jaboo, a very fertile kingdom, and inhabited by an agricultural and manufacturing people.

It is these people who send so much cloth to Lagos and Ardrah, which the Portuguese traders from the Brazils purchase for that market, and which is held there in much estimation by the black population. . . .

The population of the town of Lagos may amount to 5,000; but there are two or three populous villages on the north side of Cradoo lake, over which the caboceer of Lagos has jurisdiction. The chief's power is absolute and his disposition tyrannical to excess. . . .

When I first paid him [the king] a visit he was holding a levée. . . . The entrance to the audience-chamber presented a very curious spectacle. It was an oblong room of considerable length, having an opening along the centre of the roof to admit the light and air. . . . On each side of the apartment, there were tumbled together, promiscuously, articles of trade, and costly presents, in a state of dilapidation; namely, rolls of tobacco, boxes of pipes, cases of gin, ankers of brandy, pieces of cloth, of Indian and European manufacture, iron bars, earthenware, a beautiful hand-organ, the bellows of which were burst, two elegant chairs of state, having rich crimson damask covers, all in tatters; a handsome sedan chair, without a bottom, and two expensive sofas, without legs. These, I presume, were placed thus conspicuously with a view to impress the minds of those persons who were permitted to approach the royal presence, with the ideas of the wealth and grandeur of his sable Majesty; and politically, might perhaps be considered as something similar to the pageantry with which it is thought necessary to surround royalty in civilized countries, and which have so captivating and imposing an effect on the unthinking and vulgar. . . .

6

THE IMPACT OF EUROPEANS

> Twelve or thirteen leagues upstream from here [Lagos] there is a large town called "Geebuu" [Ijebu-Ode], surrounded by a very large ditch. The river of this country is called in our days Agusale [Ogun], and the trade which one can conduct here is the trade in slaves, who are sold for brass bracelets, at a rate of 12 to 15 bracelets for a slave. . . .

THUS WROTE a Portuguese participant in west African exploration at the end of the fifteenth century. A Dutch factor with the Dutch West India Company wrote thus:

> When these Slaves come to Fida, they are put in Prison all together, and when we treat concerning buying them, they are all brought out together in a large Plain; where, by our Chirugeons, whose Province it is, they are thoroughly examined, even to the smallest Member, and that naked too both Men and Women, without the least Distinction or Modesty. Those which are approved as good are set on one side; and the lame or faulty are set by as Invalides. . . .

The Invalides and the Maimed being thrown out . . . the remainder are numbered, and it is entered who delivered them. In the mean while a burning Iron, with the Arms or Name of the Companies, lyes in the fire; with which ours are marked on the Breast. . . .

When we have agreed with the Owners of the Slaves, they are returned to their Prison; where from that time forwards they are kept at our charge, cost us two pence a day a Slave; which serves to subsist them, like our Criminals, on Bread and Water: So that to save Charges we send them on Board our Ships with the very first Opportunity; before which their Masters strip them of all they have on their Backs; so that they come Aboard stark-naked as well Women as Men. . . .

An eyewitness on a voyage to New Calabar described negotiations on shore thus:

The thirtieth of June, 1699, being ashore, had a new conference which produced nothing; and then Pepprell [Pepple] the King's brother, made us a discourse, as from the King, importing, "He was sorry we would not accept of his proposals; that it was not his fault, he having a great esteem and regard for the Whites, who had much inriched him by trade; That what he so earnestly insisted on, thirteen bars for male, and ten for female slaves, came from the country people holding up the price of slaves at their inland markets, seeing so many large ships resort to Bandy [Bonny] for them; but to moderate matters, and incourage trading with us, he would be contented with thirteen bars for males and nine bars and two brass rings for females, etc." Upon which we offered thirteen bars for men, and nine for women, and proportionably for boys and girls, according to their ages; after this we parted, without concluding any thing farther. . . .

We gave the usual presents to the King, etc. To Captain Forty, the King's general, Captain Pepprell, Captain Boileau, alderman Boughsby, my lord Willyby, duke of Monmouth, drunken Henry and some others two firelocks, eight hats, nine narrow Guinea stuffs: We adjusted with them the reduction of

> our merchandise into bars of iron, as the standard coin, viz.: One bunch of beads, one bar. Four strings of rings, ten rings in each, one ditto. Four copper bars, one ditto. . . .
>
> The price of provisions and wood was also regulated. Sixty King's yams, one bar; one hundred and sixty slave's yams, one bar; for fifty thousand yams to be delivered to us. A butt of water, two rings. For the length of wood, seven bars, which is dear; but they were to deliver it ready cut into our boat. For a goat, one bar. A cow, ten or eight bars, according to its bigness. A hog, two bars. A calf, eight bars. A jar of palm oil, one bar and a quarter.
>
> We paid also the King's duties in goods; five hundred slaves, to be purchased at two copper rings a head.
>
> We also advanced to the King, by way of loan, the value of a hundred and fifty bars of iron, in sundry goods; and to his principal men, and others, as much again, each in proportion to his quality and ability.

A factor who worked in the slave trade during the eighteenth century reported that the space between decks in slave ships was a bare five feet, with rows of ledges on which the chained slaves were laid

> in two rows above the other, on each side of the ship, close to each other, like books upon a shelf. I have known them so close that the shelf would not easily contain one more—And every morning perhaps more instances than one are found of the living and dead, like the captives of Mezentius, fastened together.

An American slaver of the nineteenth century added:

> I took my round of the half-deck, holding a camphor bag in my teeth; for the stench was hideous. The sick and the dying were chained together. I saw pregnant women give birth to babies whilst still chained to corpses, which our drunken overseers had not removed. The blacks were literally jammed between decks as if in a coffin; and a coffin that dreadful hold became to nearly one half of our cargo before we reached Bahia.

According to a captain who visited the west coast frequently during the last fifteen years of the eighteenth century:

> This place is the wholesale market for slaves, as not fewer than 20,000 are annually sold here; 16,000 of whom are natives of one nation, called Heebo [Ibo], so that this single nation has not exported a less number of its people, during the last twenty years, than 320,000; and those of the same nation sold at New and Old Calabar, probably amounted in the same period of time to 50,000 more, making an aggregate amount of 370,000 Heebos. The remaining part of the above 20,000 is composed of the natives of the brass country, called Allakoos, and also of Ibbibbys [Ibibios] or Quaws [Ibibio Kwa].
>
> Fairs, where the slaves of the Heebo nation are obtained, are held every five or six weeks at several villages, which are situated on the banks of the rivers and creeks in the interior, and to which the traders of Bonny resort to purchase them.
>
> Their [the slaves'] dispositions are naturally timid and desponding, and their despair on being sent on board of a ship is often such, that they use every stratagem to effect the commission of suicide. . . .
>
> Some of the traders have become extremely opulent in consequence of the great extent to which the trade in slaves has been carried on by them, and are in possession of European articles to a considerable amount, especially unwrought iron and copper. . . .
>
> A trader here, named John Africa, and who has been several voyages to England, is endowed with an extraordinary memory. I have known him to have open running accounts with fourteen or fifteen vessels at the same time, wherein the debit sides exhibited long lists of various articles received by him at different periods on credit; yet, he could tell to a bunch of beads the exact state of each account when he came to settle it, although he could neither read nor write. . . .
>
> Many of the natives write English; an art first acquired by some of the traders' sons, who had visited England, and which they have had the sagacity to retain up to the present period. They have established schools and schoolmasters, for the pur-

pose of instructing in this art the youths belonging to families of consequence.

A Liverpool man, who had made eleven voyages to west Africa, told the British Privy Council in 1789:

> At Bonny Slaves are purchased of the King, who is the principal Trader, and of other Traders. These Traders go up into the Country to purchase Slaves. They go up the Rivers to the Distance of about Eighty Miles from Bonny, and the same from New Calabar, in large Canoes with Two or Three principal Persons, and about Forty Men in each. . . . At the Head of these Two Rivers there is a Mart for Trade, where the Black Traders purchase these Slaves of other Black Traders, who bring them from the interior Country.

Fifty years later Commander Robert Craigie was trying to convince King Pepple of Bonny and Anna Pepple, head of the Anna Pepple trading house, that the English had changed their policies and now were determined to abolish the slave trade. He was told by Anna Pepple, "If we cease to sell slaves to foreign ships, our principal source of wealth will be gone; the English were our first customers, and the trade has since been our chief means of support." When Craigie asked how much they would lose by giving up the slave trade, she said, "Too much—very much—we gain more by one slave ship than by five palm-oil ships." Craigie then tried a different tack, suggesting that the English government might be prepared to compensate Bonny for the loss of income for as long as five years. "The King will take 4,000 dollars yearly," said Anna Pepple. And it was only after further argument that Craigie got the sum down to two thousand dollars, an indication of the extraordinary value for both parties of the slave trade.

The major impact of Europeans on west Africa was due to the slave trade. The trade dwarfed all the other effects put together. For the greater part of four centuries the trade dominated relations between the two peoples, and it continued to affect them profoundly even when it was officially ended. No one can understand the psychological attitude of Africans toward Europeans—nor, indeed, of black to white Americans—without comprehending the trauma of the slave trade and the heritage it bequeathed to modern Africans or slave descendants in the United States. Nor can the issue be minimized by the knowledge that generations of Africans also took a vital part in this commerce in human commodities. Feelings of guilt always aggravate emotional anger, often resulting in excuses, self-justification, or sheer denial, all of which add fantasy to other barriers against acceptance of guilt.

I have analyzed elsewhere the consequences of the slave trade on west Africa and Britain.[1] Here it will suffice to summarize the major effects on African society.

In the first place, African participation in the trade, amply documented above, should not divert attention from the fact that the overseas slave trade began with the arrival of Europeans, continued so long as the Europeans required slave labor, and ended at European convenience. At the beginning of the period of European contact with west Africa, marked by the Portuguese voyages of the fifteenth century, Africans were seen as a source of labor, whether on Portuguese farms or in the new settlement on São Thomé. Only a few slaves were taken during the first years, but from early in the sixteenth century they became the major commercial interest for the succession of European traders who accompanied and followed the Portuguese.

The crucial factor in this massive demand for labor was, of course, the colonization of the Caribbean and the Americas. As the indigenous inhabitants of those lands proved unable, unwilling, or insufficiently numerous to perform the arduous tasks required in a plantation society, the peoples of Africa appeared to offer the only alternative, large-scale source of

[1] *See* the author's *The History of Britain in Africa* (Praeger: New York, 1969), Chs. II and III.

labor. Indentured labor or the methods of the press gang—both forms of slavery—were common practices applied by Europeans to their fellow countrymen at this time. The sale of Africans as slaves by other Africans had been habitual for many centuries. In both instances, the form of slavery had usually been much milder than that which developed in the Americas and the Caribbean. Yet the existence of modified slave practices and their acceptance in each society paved the way for the growth of that transatlantic commerce in human cargoes that was to have such profound effects on Africa, America, and Europe.

There was an insistent demand for labor in the new American and Caribbean colonies. Merchants in western Europe therefore saw the opportunity for large profit making. They had no power to capture Africans themselves; nor did they see any necessity to do so: they simply altered the main item in the order books from "pepper" to "slaves." African merchants—mainly kings and their agents—accepted slaving as part of normal commercial practice. They had been accustomed to regard the sale of slaves—mainly into domestic slavery—as part of their usual commercial pattern, so, if the Europeans asked for slaves instead of pepper, this was no more than a change in commodity.

Three major factors altered the character of the slave trade from that of a normal commercial transaction. First came the problem of transport. In Africa itself slaves had usually been transported in caravans when they had to be moved long distances, though many of them were either enslaved in their own villages or moved to towns or villages in the same region. No doubt, some had to undertake long marches, but usually they traveled no farther than their masters, and they were accustomed to halt for sleep and refreshment. It was quite a different matter to transport large numbers of slaves across the Atlantic. Ship travel in those days was both hazardous and unhealthy for ordinary sailors, as the necessity for press gangs testifies. For a cargo of human beings in circumstances where the larger the number and the fewer the rations the greater the profits conditions were indescribably brutal.

The second factor lay in the form of slavery that developed in the plantation society of the Americas. No longer were African slaves treated as individual members of the community, with rights as well as duties. They were considered to be the absolute possessions of their master, with as little claim to personal rights as farm animals. Yet they played a vital role in building the new American—north, central, and south—and Caribbean societies. Often their skill in mining or tropical agriculture was the crucial element in the survival and growth of a colonial society, and Africans certainly contributed an essential share to the creation of America's civilizations, African culture becoming an important element in their varied amalgams. But the contribution was made at the cost of a massive loss of human dignity and identity.

The third factor that altered the character of the trade was its size. There is no record of a large number of slaves ever being transferred from one society to another within Africa. Estimates of the number of human beings transported across the Atlantic during the four slave centuries vary widely, but the lowest is counted in many millions, the highest in several tens of millions. No such colossal transfers of population had ever been known to human history. Nor can the consequences of such losses to African societies be measured in terms merely of a commercial transaction. The slave trade was a crime against vast numbers of men, women, and children, a profound loss to innumerable communities, and an affront to the dignity of human life.

It might have been supposed that once the destructive effects of the new trade had become apparent, it would have provoked resentment and protests. Yet there is no evidence that protests often occurred. Certainly there were slave revolts, both in the ships crossing the Atlantic and on the plantations, but these were the desperate efforts of the actual sufferers to avoid the fate that awaited them or to break out of intolerable conditions (some even committed suicide by leaping into the sea rather than face the prospect of the slave life). Among those in direct contact with the enslavement that preceded the journeys, little evidence is shown of any rejection of the system. King Affonso of the Bakongo made one early plea to the king of Portugal, asking that Portuguese traders be recalled because of their participation in the slave trade; two hundred years later, in the early eighteenth century, a Dahomey king seems to have tried to stop the export of his people; and later in the same century a ruler in Senegal actually passed a law prohibiting the transport of slaves through his territory. But these were isolated instances; the trade brought too many riches, the goods of the Europeans were too tempting, and the slaving process developed too powerful a momentum for any serious resistance to arise against it. Slave raiding became inextricably entwined with dynastic or communal conflict: wars, which might not originate as the result of actual slaving, were easier to start than end, particularly when they provided so much of the human commodity demanded on the coast. Society inevitably became insecure, more authoritarian and violent, thus weakening the popular influence that might have tried to halt the trade to protect its own members, while the ruling groups who made the major profits were encouraged to promote the trade with still greater vigor.

In Europe critical voices were few and muted. Beginning in the seventeenth century a few, mainly Quaker, protests were heard, and by the middle of the eighteenth century hints that the tide was turning could be gleaned from the speeches and writings of a small minority. Horace Walpole, for instance, could write in 1750:

> We have been sitting this fortnight on the African Company: we, the British Senate, that temple of liberty, and bulwark of Protestant Christianity, have this fortnight been pondering methods to make more effectual that horrid traffic of selling

> negroes. It has appeared to us that six-and-forty thousand of these wretches are sold every year to our plantations alone! It chills one's blood.

Yet, whatever the blood temperature of British members of Parliament, the slave trade on which much of Britain's commercial profit depended was to continue for over another half-century and slavery itself for more than eighty years.

In any case, during most of the three main slaving centuries —the sixteenth through the eighteenth—protest would have been irrelevant, even if it had been heard; for as the Dutch governor of Elmina Castle explained in 1700, his fellow countrymen continued to supply Africans with firearms because ". . . we are are forced to do this. For if we did not do it, they would easily get enough muskets from the English, or from the Danes, or from the Prussians. And even if we governors could all agree to stop selling firearms, the private traders of the English or the Dutch would still go on selling them."

The system of commercial competition relied so heavily on the lucrative trade in slaves, paid for in arms, and the demand for capital accumulation had become so obsessive, that no counter-influence could prevail against the trade.

Moreover, the main slave period coincided with the period in which Europe began to break out of its continental environment. The hope of discovering the sources of the gold that had been entering Europe via north Africa for several centuries had long attracted the more adventurous Europeans; they soon realized they must also seek the sources of the spices, silks, and jewels distributed by the Arabs to the West as it became likely, with the Turks approaching Constantinople, which fell in 1451, that Europe might be barred from the Middle East.

This search took the Europeans around Africa to India and southeast Asia, across the Atlantic to the Caribbean and the Americas, and to the northern seas of Russia and Canada. It engendered its own momentum, fueled by the new commodities it encountered; the mercantile forces that had initiated it were reinforced by its activities and urged the explorers on to still more remote areas in the search for still greater opportunities for commercial dividend.

Then, too, the mercantilist assumptions that dominated European economic thought in the sixteenth and seventeenth centuries inevitably provoked colonial and commercial warfare. Starting from the belief that the volume of world trade was static, each commercial state aimed to secure a larger share of that trade for itself at the expense of its rivals. Inevitably, therefore, the lands newly discovered by the Europeans, and especially those of major commercial value, were fought over by countries that were able to take advantage of their Atlantic seaboards to participate in the new trading opportunities. During the sixteenth and seventeenth centuries the slave trade from the west African coast, designed to supply the plantation colonies on the other side of the Atlantic with a labor force, together with the rich rewards of the return trade from the colonies, came to be the most lucrative of all these international attractions. In the first half of the eighteenth century it dominated all others. It has been estimated that in 1790 Britain had $170 million invested in the West Indies compared with $43 million in Asia, and that British trade with the Caribbean was almost double that of the East India Company.

Just as the first colonies were made monopolies of royal families or their chartered companies, so, at first, the same system applied to the slave trade. Thus the competition that developed between the companies of different nations, sometimes resulting in warfare, often took on a national character. At one time or another the Portuguese, Spaniards, Dutch, Swedes, Danes, Brandenburgers, French, and British were all engaged in this bitter conflict to secure a major share of the slave trade. Alliances were made with different African communities, bribes were offered, ships were attacked, kidnappings were arranged, threats of diplomatic action or of war itself were hurled around.

Portuguese domination of the slave trade was succeeded by that of the Dutch, who in turn were superseded by the French and British. During the eighteenth century these latter two nations were almost constantly at war with each other, and the slave trade, especially the "asiento"—the contract for supplying slaves to the Spanish colonies—was one of the factors in their international rivalry. Britain emerged the victor, and its victory was marked by the fact that by the middle of the century half the slaves crossing the Atlantic were carried in British ships. London, Bristol, Liverpool, Glasgow thrived on the proceeds. In Birmingham one hundred thousand muskets a year were manufactured solely for barter in the trade; the textile mills of Lancashire turned out cloth to be used both to clothe the slaves of the plantations and to buy slaves in west Africa; some merchants even bought cheap cloth in India to export to the African slave markets.

The mid-eighteenth century, however, saw the rise to prominence of an independent merchant class. Royal monopolies were broken; merchant companies were opened to all who could afford to join; and competition, more fragmented, became even fiercer. As the old form of international commercial organization fractured, British merchants became the new pacesetters, garnering huge profits and laying the groundwork for future international ascendancy. In particular, the immense profits made in the slave trade contributed substantially to the foundations, then being laid, on which was to be built that industrial superstructure that was to give Britain the predominant international position in the nineteenth-century world.

Throughout these centuries European culture, clearly the strongest in the world, was penetrating America, Asia, and Africa. The focus of global power moved to Europe, exhibiting there tendencies never before witnessed. At various times societies in the Middle East, around the Mediterranean, and in Asia had known periods of international paramountcy, but they had never been able to dominate the life of the six continents, as became possible for Europeans. In the nineteenth century European values, techniques, literature, languages, and customs were assumed to have universal application. Many ordered civilizations in the Americas and Asia broke down under this impact, to be replaced by those of the various Europeans who wielded power over them. New societies were built in the Americas based on European cultures, with scant regard for those that had existed before the European conquest. In particular, India became the victim of European ambitions: much of its wealth taken as booty to European capitals, its industrial structure destroyed under the impact of European techniques, its cultures undermined by European pressures.

Significantly, however, even under the severe weight of four centuries of slave trading, African society did not suffer the same fate as the societies of the Americas. Whether or not it was owing to the greater strength of African culture, with its more dispersed communities, the natural barriers that prevented easy travel into the interior, or sheer lack of attraction, European domination of Africa was not imposed until the last quarter of the nineteenth century, long after the process had been completed in America and Asia.

Then, European participation was confined almost entirely to the coast, to the castles and forts, the creeks and deltas of west Africa. In the coastal area there was some little European influence evident. For instance, a number of Portuguese settled along the coast or on the islands off the coast and a portion of the factors and traders who engaged in the slave trade came to be mulattoes. But the European influence was slight, and largely confined to commercial techniques and customs. And since virtually all the operations in the interior were conducted by Africans, the inland communities were scarcely touched by European cultural influences.

The basic effect of the slave trade on west African society was its destructive impact on social and economic life. Although the European and African merchant classes understood each other and recognized their mutual interests, the uses to which each put its profits were in sharp contrast. Whereas the Europeans, and particularly the British, invested their gains in constructive channels—financing further expeditions or, later, supporting mechanical experiments and industrial growth—most of the African profit was either destroyed through being employed in warfare, often for the purpose of capturing more slaves, or in building greater royal power. The very goods exported demonstrated the contrary influences of the trade on its two bases. The European merchants exported firearms, cottons, utensils, iron bars, alcohol, ornaments; the Africans exported human labor, some well skilled, thus weakening their social economy. Similarly with imports: Europe was not importing the slaves its merchants bought in Africa but rather the products of their labor; it was exchanging slaves for coffee, tea, sugar, cotton, and bullion, all of which assisted its home economies. Africa, in contrast, was importing either weapons of war, which helped to dislocate its economies, or goods, such as textiles and metalware, that undermined its own industrial production. The consequence was, therefore, that European economic and social life benefited enormously from the slave trade, whereas African life was positively harmed by its operations. The textile industry, in particular, which had been such a strong economic bulwark of west African economies, shrank disastrously under the pressure of European imports.

On the other hand, contact with European traders brought some advantages to certain west Africans. One particular craft certainly benefited. The bronze imported from Europe allowed the craftsmen of Benin to produce many of their famous sculptures. The increase in the number of commodities available through European imports, despite their nature, also stimulated trade. Many more people were encouraged to travel around the country; markets displayed a wider variety of goods; communities previously remote were brought into social contact with others. One factor especially encouraged the extension of the trading patterns already in existence: the introduction of credit, particularly in the Niger delta, where the head of the trading house would be given goods by European traders on credit against future delivery of slaves. The credit system also spread to lesser traders, for the Europeans knew that if anyone defaulted, the king or chief would honor the debt, often selling the family of the guilty trader to pay for it. The introduction of the credit system not only encouraged the expansion of the slave trade but also supplied a foundation for commerce that facilitated trading activities long after slavery had been abolished.

Also encouraged by the slave trade was the use of currency in place of barter. As we have seen from the records, the value of many goods came to be measured in terms of iron bars and copper rings. The copper or brass rings, sometimes called "manillas," were widely used in the delta. They were shaped into the form of bracelets, often with beautifully intricate patterns worked on them. Cowrie shells, long used in the northern belt of west Africa and on the east African coast, also were employed as currency. Such currencies often did not have to change hands; they become staples of exchange, a constant measure against which the respective value of different commodities could be judged. In this respect the European usually had the advantage, for the African had no means of knowing what the European traders had to pay for the goods they brought with them. Nevertheless, African traders, too, had tactics at their disposal: they could bargain with rival European traders, and often they would insist on selling a complete group of slaves when the supply was short, with the buyer having to accept the old, sick, or maimed as part of the bargain.

Finally, the presence of European merchants constantly seeking slaves also assisted the treasuries of the west African rulers. The Europeans had to pay several dues—rents, commissions, customs, and "dashes" (tips)—all of which added to the wealth and power of the rulers, enabling them to strengthen their administrations. Whether the trade brought any benefit to the common people is more doubtful.

On balance, there is no doubt that west Africa suffered more than it gained from the era of the slave trade. Social life was seriously dislocated under the burden of frequent wars and slave raids; industry, crafts, and skilled labor declined under the competition of European imports and the export of productive young men and women; most of the benefits accruing from the trade were gained by a small class of kings, chiefs, and merchants, thus encouraging authoritarianism, militarism, and parasitical commercialism; and the economies of west Africa were increasingly tied to those of the European powers as ever greater dependence was placed on European imports. These were all crucial factors in widening the power chasm opening between the societies of Europe and west Africa.

7

NINETEENTH-CENTURY TURMOILS

THREE major factors combined to effect a radical transformation of the west African scene during the first three-quarters of the nineteenth century: the Muslim jihads and Yoruba civil wars, exploration and Christian missionary efforts, and a revolution in trade. The combination of these factors effectively prepared west Africa for the imposition of European colonial rule, which came during the final quarter of the century.

It has already been observed that toward the end of the eighteenth century the large states of the region that now is Nigeria were under severe pressure from a number of centrifugal forces. Many of their constituent provinces were either claiming independence or revolting against imperial rule, particularly against imperial taxation. Slave raiding, warfare and an increasing use of firearms, and the diffusion of wealth from European traders, after first strengthening the central governments, gradually began to undermine the power of centralized administration and to give greater opportunities for independent existence to the peripheral communities. At the same time the mounting attractions of trade with Europeans on the coast were shifting the center of economic power southward, toward the sea, where the trading bases were centered. By the beginning of the nineteenth century, therefore, it could be said that most of these states and empires were ripe for destruction.

The first agent of disintegration was a Muslim reformist movement mainly conducted by the Fulani. Just as the Almoravids of the eleventh century, caught up in a similar puritanical movement within Islam, had taken advantage of the weakness of Ghana to destroy its empire, so at the beginning of the nineteenth century a series of Fulani jihads undermined the Hausa states. Bornu was attacked, and Oyo defeated. The movement set in motion a series of chain reactions that kept a large belt of west Africa in a state of insecurity and frequent civil war for much of the nineteenth century.

Within the Islamic faith two types of duty are laid down by the Koran. Each Muslim has an individual duty to say five daily prayers, fast through Ramadan, and make a pilgrimage to Mecca. The second kind of duty is owed by the whole Muslim community, though it can be undertaken by a section acting on behalf of the whole. The principal part of this communal duty is to bring unbelievers into the Muslim fold. The process is to invite those outside Muslim rule to join Islam. If they refuse, war is to be declared on them. In the event of a Muslim victory all prisoners may be made slaves and their possessions sequestered by the treasury of the victorious Muslim state. The conquered inhabitants are not necessarily forced to join Islam—they may be allowed to practice their own religion—but they are placed under the military protection of the Muslim state and must pay taxes to it.

The jihad, or holy war, however, has often taken on a more complicated character. There have been frequent disputes within the Muslim world and various reformist movements. In many cases, the reformers have accused their opponents of not being Muslims, of being, in fact, "unbelievers," because they have not accepted the strict, often austere doctrines asserted by the priests to be the true faith. In such cases, which were a frequent occurrence during the late eighteenth and early nineteenth centuries, the jihad was fought at least in part against states and communities themselves professing the Muslim faith.

The Fulani, who came originally from Senegal, became a largely nomadic people in about the thirteenth century. From the middle of the fifteenth century they are reported as appearing in Hausaland, bringing with them many books on Islamic law and theology. Most Fulani were traditional cattle herders, and they spread through a wide area of the western Sudan, as far as Adamawa on the northern slopes of the Cameroon Mountains. As a result of their travels, many Fulani settled down in various towns and villages in Hausaland, intermarried with the Hausa, and became part of urbanized communities; others adopted a semi-nomadic life. Most of the settled and semi-nomadic Fulani were attached to the Muslim faith; those who were entirely nomadic and pastoral were not usually Muslim.

The chief inspirer of the main Fulani jihad was a scholar born in Maratta, Gobir, in 1754. Usuman dan Fodio was a member of a community related to the Fulani, the Toronkawa, who claimed to have some Arab ancestors. Many of the community were teachers or preachers, and there was a strong missionary spirit in it. Dan Fodio, who became known as the shehu, the Hausa form of shaikh, or chief, became a profound student of Islamic law and theology. He began to preach while still young and went on tours, making visits to both Kebbi and Zamfara. Fodio preached what he believed to be the pure, orthodox doctrines of Islam, and thus challenged the concepts and practices that had grown up among those who, resident in the towns, had become more concerned with retaining the favors of urban rulers. Others followed Fodio's lead, and his followers began to take on the appearance of a separate community.

The fact that Fodio did not accept the patronage of the courts, although he preached to rulers, gave his campaign a certain spirit of antagonism to the ruling class. This was particularly evident in Gobir, then the most powerful of the Hausa towns. The sultan of Gobir tried to have Fodio killed, and, when the attempt failed, the sultan hoped to bribe him. But Fodio carried on with his teaching and preaching, writing pamphlets in Arabic and poems in Hausa and Fulani, all of which sold widely throughout Hausaland.

At the mystic age of forty, the same age as Mohammed when he received his first revelation, Fodio asserted that he had seen a vision calling on him to "unsheath the sword of truth." He therefore began to add to his teaching the notion that the Prophet had advised that arms be prepared. The challenge to authority was clearly approaching. The new sultan of Gobir tried to restrict Fodio's activities and the rights of his followers. The sultan's son, Yunfa, who succeeded him in 1802 and had been taught by Fodio, attempted even harsher methods. Both sultans went to the extreme of prohibiting further conversions to Islam and ordered that those who had not been born in the faith but had been converted should recant.

The rulers of Gobir were well aware that Fodio's reformation directly challenged their traditional methods of government, and thus a political element was added to the movement of religious reform and intellectual renaissance. Conversely, when Fodio fled from Gobir in 1804 and proclaimed his jihad, the war was not only against religious laxity but also against the decadence of Hausa rulers.

The declaration of war soon revealed that there were many grievances in the Hausa states quite outside the religious sphere. Hausa farmers were ready to take advantage of the opportunity to rid themselves of what they considered unfair taxes; pagan Fulani cattle-herders resented the obligation to pay taxes and obey laws when they were accorded few rights by the Hausa rulers. Thus the war took on the character of a popular movement—a kind of "peasants' revolt"—beneath its religious sanctions. Already weakened by divisive elements, and traditionally refusing to cooperate with each other, the Hausa rulers were incapable of resisting this populist tide for long: by 1809 the Fulani rebels had conquered them all, including the great cities of Kano and Katsina, and emirs owing allegiance to Fodio were appointed in the defeated states.

The Fulani then attacked Bornu. In Bornu, however, they met stiffer resistance. At first it seemed that Bornu, like the Hausa states, would fall, for its monarchy was as unpopular. But the ancient state found a new leader, al-Kanemi, a Muslim scholar from Kanem, who rallied the physical and moral forces of Bornu. Not only did al-Kanemi lead the army, he engaged in virile disputation with the Fulani, rejecting their assumption of superior Islamic morality. The armies of the Fodio jihad were repulsed, and al-Kanemi, though keeping the Sefawa mais on the throne for ceremonial purposes, became the de facto ruler of Bornu and Kanem.

However, farther east the Fulani were successful. Many of the community settled in the northern Cameroons and helped in establishing the powerful emirate of Adamawa, which represented the easternmost extent of Fulani dominance.

During this vast jihad Fodio's brother, Abdullahi, and son, Bello, were in charge of military operations. These two also were left in charge of the administration of the newly conquered territories, Bello over the eastern lands, based in the new capital at Sokoto, and Abdullahi in the west. Fodio lived in Sokoto, studying and preaching until he died there in 1817. On his brother's death Abdullahi recognized the son as successor shehu, and Bello's descendants ruled from Sokoto until recent times.

Having established their power in the north, the Fulani

began to interfere in the affairs of southern states. In Nupe civil war divided the ruling family, and a Fulani mallam, Dendo, opened another jihad. By intriguing between the rival factions of the royal family, Dendo eventually gained control over most of the state. In Oyo, also, civil strife assisted the imposition of Fulani rule. The empire had always been loosely controlled, on the assumption that Yoruba kings would accept the ultimate authority of the alafin. But as the southern Yoruba became wealthier through their contact with coastal trade, their allegiance became progressively weaker. Revolt in the army about 1817 revealed the feebleness of central authority, but the army rebels made the mistake of believing that they could call on Fulani assistance without paying a price. They were mistaken: the Fulani took control of the northern town of Ilorin, thus opening the way to Muslim conversions and Fulani pressure on the alafins in Oyo. By 1835, when the ruling alafin was defeated and killed, the capital had to be abandoned, its people fleeing south and building a new capital, which they called New Oyo.

The capture of Ilorin by the Fulani cut off Oyo's main source of slaves from the Niger areas. Oyo's merchants hoped to make good this loss by securing slaves from other Yoruba states, an intention that only encouraged further civil wars among Yoruba communities. Owu and Ife fought each other, the latter supported by the Ijebu and refugees from Fulani attacks on Oyo. Owu was destroyed, its inhabitants driven into the lands of the Egba.

The general strife in the towns encouraged armies of bandits to start raiding throughout northern Yorubaland, mainly for the purpose of capturing slaves who could be sold in the coastal ports. About 1829, indeed, parties of the bandits who had settled in a war camp founded the great city of Ibadan. And many Egba, together with refugees from Owu, settled in Abeokuta and prepared to defend the town. The stabilizing influence of settlement was reinforced by an alliance that Ibadan and the new Oyo capital made by which Ibadan was to undertake responsibility for common defense against further Fulani incursions, but the settlements and alliance did not end the civil wars of the Yoruba. There was jealousy of Ibadan as the new town displayed ambitions to lead the Yoruba; rivalries about the trade routes to the coast added further fire; and the teachings of Islam were undermining traditional Yoruba customs. To the west, however, the power of Dahomey constantly hung over the safety of all Yoruba, and in the south in the middle of the century Britain took possession of Lagos.

It would be an exaggeration to attribute all this civil strife, terror, and disintegration to the Fulani jihads. Certainly, the continuing slave trade played as important a role as the Fulani, yet the Fulani took advantage of the dislocation and added to it by their political intrigues and military attacks. By the 1830s they controlled all the north of modern Nigeria except Bornu, parts of Kebbi, Gobir, and the hill areas of the middle belt. They provided a broadly uniform system of administration over a vast area with a central administrative unit at Sokoto.

In Sokoto, Bello received tribute from the provinces and was accepted as the final authority on the most important issues of administration. On the whole government was just, taxation reasonably fair, the civil service efficient, the law improved by reforms. The emirates were constantly supervised, officials visiting them to check on the administration of the provinces. The sultan himself often appointed officials in his empire and supervised the higher matters of the administration. During the first years of the new regime, under Bello and his immediate successors, the empire and its constituent towns enjoyed a period of prosperity. The Hausa states were no longer weakened by rivalries and continual warfare, or by weak, oppressive government. They therefore gained the opportunity of conducting their trade in comparative peace and safety, their main concern.

Meanwhile, the effects of Fodio's intellectual criticisms

had some result. Discussion within Islamic society became much more vigorous and profound, scholarship was revived, and a literary revolution followed his radical inspiration. One of the most important social reforms resulting from Fodio's teachings was the beginning of some emancipation for women, many of whom gained an opportunity to become highly educated. Fodio wrote—early in the nineteenth century!—

> . . . to instruct one's wives, daughters, and captives is a positive duty, while to impart knowledge to students is only a work of supererogation, and there is no doubt but that the one takes precedence over the other. Muslim women, do not listen to the speech of those who are misguided and who sow the seed of error in the heart of another. . . . They seek only their own satisfaction and that is why they impose upon you tasks which the Law of God and that of his Prophet have never especially assigned to you. Such are—the preparation of foodstuffs, the washing of clothes, and other duties which they like to impose upon you, while they neglect to teach you what God and the Prophet had prescribed for you.

Such injunctions certainly led to much greater freedom for some women in Muslim society, though to what extent it penetrated the common Muslim homes is a matter of doubt. Certainly, such precepts for the treatment of women are by no means universal in the Muslim areas in modern times.

Late in the nineteenth century, as the idealism of the revolution began to wane, graft and corruption crept back. The taxation system was adulterated by a series of illegal levies and inequitable taxes. Many emirates became corrupt as the opportunities for personal wealth increased. Above all, local slave trading increased again, bringing with it devastated areas, depopulation, and the corroding effects on economic development we have seen take place elsewhere. Nevertheless, the administrative system never collapsed, remaining into the twentieth century a framework built under the inspiration of Fodio.

The second factor involving major change was the effect of explorer and missionary activity. Why this period—the late eighteenth and most of the nineteenth centuries—should have seen a sudden rise in the desire of Europeans to know more about Africa is a matter of considerable argument. Perhaps it was the result of the additional leisure that western Europeans were enjoying as a result of their infant industrialism. Perhaps it was the consequence of the age of reason and scientific inquiry then beginning to burgeon. It could hardly be attributed to the activities of the traders, for they had been visiting Africa since the sixteenth century. But whatever the reason, contact between Britain and west Africa became considerably closer during the eighteenth century: a sprinkling of Africans came to Britain for their education or training, though they cannot have influenced more than a handful of people; the issue of slavery had an impact on many minds, at least among the middle class, while at the time of the Mansfield Judgment of 1772, which declared slavery illegal in England, there were about fifteen thousand West Indian slaves in the country (it will be recalled that Dr. Johnson's servant, Francis Barber, was a freed slave and inherited money and goods in the learned doctor's will).

There is as much difficulty in determining the cause of the outburst of proselytizing that took European missionaries to Africa during the same period. The Reformation was long in the past, the Victorian era of self-righteousness and duty some way in the future, when the evangelical wave began. The movement also had connections with the anti-slavery campaign, perhaps being the product of a mixture of guilt and reformist fervor. It is clear from contemporary records, too, especially in letters written from mission stations, that escape from the new, unaccustomed, and unacceptable pressures of industrial society played a part in persuading Europeans to seek the simpler, "natural" life of primitive Africa. On the other hand, there was also a sense that Christian missionaries were taking to the "poor, benighted natives" what was assumed to be the better and more advanced life of Europe and the values on which it was based—often for very laudable motives.

In this study effects are more important to us than causes. It is the part played by the explorers and missionaries in linking Africa to Europe, rather than the reasons for their travels, that concerns us. The fact is that while at the beginning of the nineteenth century Europeans knew virtually nothing of the interior, despite three and a half centuries' acquaintance with west Africa, by the end of the century the general geography of the continent was known to Europe, some Europeans had traveled to most regions, and European governments had divided virtually the whole continent between themselves. Much of this new knowledge came from explorers and missionaries.

It is intriguing to note how little of Africa was known to Europeans at the start of what was to be regarded as the imperialist century. Soon after contact between Africans and Europeans was made, the Portuguese learned something of the large Bakongo society around the mouth of the Congo River. The Portuguese also traded with Benin, which could be reached up the Niger. To both places Portuguese missionaries followed merchants and sailors. As we have seen, the English, guided by a Portuguese pilot, also visited Benin in the sixteenth century. The French sailed up the Senegal and the English up the Gambia, but they rarely ventured away from the river banks. North Africa was, of course, part of Mediterranean society from very early times, but the hinterland was closed to Europe by the Sahara and Muslim domination throughout the Middle Ages. The Portuguese visited the east coast in the late fifteenth century and subsequently sacked, captured, and occupied most of the port states during long conflicts with the Arabs. In the west, apart from the few minor exceptions mentioned above, for centuries the slave trade was conducted between European traders and African kings, agents, and merchants on the sea coast, with Africans being solely responsible for the task of capturing or buying the slaves in the interior. Indeed, Europeans, after over three hundreds years' trading, did not even know the course of the two mighty rivers, the Niger and Congo.

The one exception to this almost universal lack of contact between Europeans and African societies away from the coast was in the south, where, in the mid-seventeenth century, the Dutch had established a settlement at the Cape. The "garden and refreshment station" for Dutch ships sailing to the East Indies began to expand into the interior. Farmers sought new lands; fresh settlers arrived from a Europe torn by sectarian strife; and the frontiers were pushed farther east and north. By the second half of the eighteenth century they had reached as far as the outposts of African societies that had been expanding southward and westward. Africans had lived in the eastern regions of South Africa before the Europeans had appeared at the Cape, as is made clear by the stories of shipwrecked Portuguese sailors who made their way across these lands to the east-coast cities controlled by their countrymen. But it was not until the two societies had been living within the same region for some hundred years or so that they encountered each other in any serious numbers.

The south was the only major exception—though it was to be a very important exception to future relations between Africa and Europe—and when the Europeans began to be interested in the geography of the continent or concerned with converting the souls of its inhabitants, they had to find the means of penetrating into the interior. The late eighteenth and most of the nineteenth centuries thus became a new "age of discovery" for Europeans with regard to Africa, as the fifteenth and sixteenth centuries had been with regard to transatlantic and Asian exploration.

In many ways the exploration of Africa proved to be a

more arduous task than those of the Atlantic, the Indian Ocean, or the lands that they lapped. The conventional method of penetrating a new land—by sailing up its rivers from the sea—offered only occasional possibilities; for almost all Africa's major rivers develop waterfalls or cataracts within a short distance of the coast where the high land falls steeply to the coastal plains. Then again, many of the rivers—among them the Niger—form wide, swampy deltas at their mouths. Not only were the deltas extremely unhealthy, but they were virtually unnavigable. And even when these immediate hazards were overcome, the thick tangles of rain forest in the west and the arid, tsetse-infested plains of the east, in places accompanied by high, precipitous mountains, presented barriers to travel never before encountered on such a massive scale by Europeans. And Africa, finally, is a huge continent—second only to Asia in size—five thousand miles from north to south and never less than two thousand miles wide.

A further, and equally dangerous, hazard confronting explorers in the African continent was its diseases. Not for nothing was much of west Africa termed the "white man's grave." It literally became so. Early attempts to live on the coast or to penetrate the interior brought death to large numbers of Europeans. Malaria was the special scourge, though there were many other dangerous diseases, and the blazing heat and sticky humidity proved severely debilitating to Europeans. Moreover, it was not until the middle of the nineteenth century that a method of combating malaria, by quinine, was discovered.

Despite these hazards, a number of Britishers were determined to discover what lay beyond the African coasts. In 1788 an African Association was formed in London to support the exploration of Africa and, in particular, to sponsor expeditions to discover the source of the Niger. The association collected funds to pay the expenses of such expeditions and found that there were many adventurers eager to meet the challenge of what was termed the "Dark Continent."

The first few attempts met with disaster. It was known that for many centuries caravans had been crossing the Sahara from north Africa to such places as Bornu and Hausaland, which were rumored in Europe to be very wealthy and powerful. So expeditions were prepared, first from Cairo and then from Tripoli. Both were failures. At the beginning of the 1790s two more attempts, one from Gambia and the other from Sierra Leone, met with a similar fate. In fact, the first expedition to meet with any important success was that of a young Scots doctor, Mungo Park, in 1795. Park followed the route of the abortive Gambian expedition and was involved in many adventures and much suffering. He was robbed by African chiefs, insulted by Moorish merchants, and held prisoner by a Moorish chieftain. Despite these hazards he carried on and reached the Niger in July, 1796. Following its course, he confirmed that the great river actually flowed eastward—though he failed to discover its source—before he started his arduous journey back to the coast. Again he was robbed, and this time, bereft of followers, he had to struggle on alone until he reached a friendly village, where he lay, wracked with fever, for five weeks. It was almost a year after reaching the Niger that he managed to return to Gambia as a member of a slave caravan.

Following the relative success of Mungo Park's courageous expedition, the association financed another set of journeys, which again proved abortive. One expedition, this time led by two Germans, one of whom died in Cairo while the other actually reached Bornu but died in Nupe, tried to cross to the west from Cairo. Yet another German was murdered by his African servant. A Swiss, sent to north Africa, discovered nothing of note. An unproductive attempt to ascend the Old Calabar River in the hope of proving it to be part of the Niger delta was equally unsuccessful.

Nevertheless, the persistence and heroism of these pioneers had some effect: the British government began to show interest in the Niger. It decided to finance another expedition by Mungo Park; this time he would lead a party of forty-three other Europeans consisting of officers and various journeymen capable of devising methods of overcoming the difficulties by then all too well known. The company was guided by a Mandingo and set off from Gorée on the west coast in April, 1805.

Few of the earlier lessons seem to have been taken to heart. For some reason, Africans were not included in the expedition, despite their acclimatization and ability to work hard in extreme heat. The Europeans soon began to feel the strain, to fall sick, and die. Others of the expedition were murdered by robbers. When Park reached the Niger four months after his departure, only nine of his men survived with him. All were almost totally exhausted. Eventually, Park had only four Europeans left to accompany him on what he now believed would be a journey downstream, to the mouth of the Congo (he believed the Niger and Congo to be the same river). He had recruited a new guide and three slaves and had built a boat out of two canoes. The new guide was sent back overland with a journal and letters; nothing further was heard of Mungo Park. They probably reached Bussa, where Africans think that his boat struck a rock and that he and his crew perished in the waters, but it is unlikely that their fate will ever be effectively established.

It was not until the Napoleonic wars were over that attempts to gain more knowledge from the harsh environment of west Africa were resumed, but the attempts were no more successful than previously and again cost many lives. Further progress was then delayed until 1822, and then it was not so much a matter of unraveling the mysteries of the Niger as of gaining knowledge of Hausaland. Again the British government provided the money for an expedition, to start from Tripoli and to include Major Denham, Lieutenant Clapperton, and Dr. Oudney. The party followed the trail of one of the main caravan routes, which was well marked by skeletons of slaves who had perished on the journey to the coast. They reached Lake Chad, the first Europeans to see the lake, and soon afterward arrived in the capital of Bornu, where they were greeted by al-Kanemi, the leader who had led Bornu in its successful resistance to the Fulani.

The members of the party then divided. Denham joined a slave raid and was lucky to escape when the raiders were routed by their intended victims; he then went off to explore Lake Chad. Clapperton and Oudney set off for the Hausa states. The doctor died, but Clapperton arrived in Kano in January, 1824. His descriptions of the city provided the first British eyewitness account of a place that had been the subject of much rumor in Europe. As the most important mercantile center of the area, Kano was the market that most impressed Clapperton. His description could almost have been written today, so little has Kano market changed.

> The soug, or market, is well supplied with every necessary and luxury in request among the people of the interior. . . . The sheikh of the soug lets the stalls at so much a month, and the rent forms part of the revenues of the governor. The sheikh of the soug also fixes the prices of all wares, for which he is entitled to a small commission. . . . Particular quarters are appropriated to distinct articles; the smaller wares being set out in booths in the middle, and cattle and bulky commodities being exposed to sale in the outskirts of the market-place; wood, dried grass, bean straw for provender, beans, Guinea corn, Indian corn, wheat, &c. are in one quarter; goats, sheep, asses, bullocks, horses, and camels, in another; earthenware and indigo in a third; vegetables and fruit of all descriptions, such as yams, sweet potatoes, water and musk melons, pawpaw fruit, limes, cashew nuts, plums, mangoes, shaddocks, dates, &c., in a fourth, and so on. . . .
>
> The interior of the market is filled with stalls of bamboo, laid out in regular streets, where the more costly wares are sold, and articles of dress, and other little matters of use or ornament made and repaired. Bands of musicians parade up and down

> to attract purchasers to particular booths. Here are displayed coarse writing paper, of French manufacture, brought from Barbary; scissors and knives, of native workmanship; crude antimony and tin, both the produce of the country; unwrought silk of a red colour, which they make into belts and slings, or weave in stripes into the finest cotton tobes; armlets and bracelets of brass; beads of glass, coral, and amber; finger rings of pewter, and a few silver trinkets, but none of gold; tobes, turkadees, and turban shawls; coarse woollen cloths of all colours; coarse calico; Moorish dresses; the cast off gaudy garbs of the Mamelukes of Barbary; pieces of Egyptian linen, checked or striped with gold; sword blades from Malta, &c. &c. . . .
>
> The slave market is held in two long sheds, one for males, the other for females, where they are seated in rows, and carefully decked out for the exhibition. . . . The male slaves are employed in the various trades of building, working in iron, weaving, making shoes or clothes, and in traffic; the female slaves in spinning, baking, and selling water in the street. . . .

Leaving Kano, Clapperton proceeded to Sokoto, where he was welcomed by Bello, the son of Fodio. Bello was hesitant about helping the Englishman to journey further toward the Niger because of the dangers it might entail, but he did provide Clapperton with some useful information, including a map of Sokoto and the surrounding territory. The sultan also showed himself much impressed by the interest Britain was showing in his land; he suggested that a British consul and physician be sent to Sokoto. In fact, one of the party was left behind, not in Sokoto, but in Bornu, where he was to act as consul, though he did not survive long. Denham and Clapperton then rejoined forces and returned to Tripoli with the survivors of their expedition.

By the 1820s other Europeans were interested in the Sudan and the Niger. An Italian tried, but failed, to reach Timbuktu. A Frenchman, Caillie, succeeded in 1827–1828 where the Italian had failed; he journeyed from Tangiers to Timbuktu and returned safely. However, further British attempts to reach the Niger brought only death and disaster.

Within a year of returning to Britain, Clapperton was off again, this time making his base at Badagri on the Guinea coast. Accompanied by his servant, Richard Lander, he returned to Kano and Sokoto. This time, however, he found himself welcomed much less cordially than on his previous visit. Africans were becoming suspicious of the European travelers, and their suspicions were being fed by Arabs anxious to preserve their influence and markets. Bello, preoccupied by civil wars within his empire and conflict in Bornu, bitterly resented the knowledge that Clapperton had brought arms as presents for his enemies as well as for himself. The lack of cooperation was clearly fatal to his plans, and Clapperton died near Sokoto in 1827.

Lander, however, continued to explore north of the Benue until he had to retrace his steps to Badagri, where he had a most alarming experience. The Portuguese slave merchants, who were suspicious of all Britishers because the British government was using its navy to put an end to the slave trade, persuaded the inhabitants of Badagri that Lander was a spy, and he was put on trial. Forced to submit to ordeal by poison, Lander saved himself by immediately taking a powerful emetic, and he returned safely to England in 1828.

This fortunate and ingenious escape saved the life of the man who was to succeed in solving the age-old problem of the Niger. In 1830 Richard Lander took his brother John on yet another attempt to chart the course of the river. Supported this time by the British government, they again made Badagri their base, despite the previous alarming experience. The two brothers then made their way to Bussa and started downstream in two canoes. Finding little difficulty for many miles, they successfully passed the confluence with the Benue. Finally, as they approached Asaba in Iboland, they encountered trouble: they were attacked by fifty Ibo canoes and taken as prisoners to the chief at Abo. On hearing of their plight, the king of Brass, in the Niger delta itself, ransomed the two Englishmen, after receiving a promise from the captain of a British ship anchored in his territory that he would recover the ransom. On the brothers' release, however, the captain refused to honor his debt, the king was duped, and the two men escaped on the ship to Fernando Po, from where they returned to England.

At least, their journey and adventures had solved the riddle: it was established not only that the great river flowed eastward, as had been shown a quarter of a century earlier, but that it then turned south and reached the sea through the maze of delta rivers amid which Brass stood. It would not be long before missionaries and merchants would seek means to exploit this significant discovery.

The persistent efforts to explore the Niger were only one part of the awakening European, and particularly British, interest in the African continent. They formed the earliest cohesive group of expeditions, probably because of the long-standing connections between Britain and the west African coast and the rumors that British visitors had heard of the wealthy, powerful empires in the north.

In any case, in the early stages of exploration it was rivers that were sought as channels leading to the interior. Thus in 1816, according to the *Quarterly Review,* a Captain Tuckey led an expedition to explore "the River Zaire, usually called the Congo." It was hoped that Tuckey, working on Mungo Park's assumption that the two rivers were one, would meet up with another expedition traveling from the Atlantic coast to the Niger. Both ventures failed, each leader losing his life. But Tuckey's expedition throws significant light on the attitude taken toward these explorations. One of its purposes was to gather "information respecting an important part of that ill-fated country, whose unhappy natives, without laws to restrain or government to protect them, have too long been the prey of a senseless domestic superstition, and the victims of a foreign infamous and rapacious commerce." Yet the purveyors of the "superior culture" seem to have been imprudent: "spiritous liquors were not to be obtained; but excesses of another kind were freely indulged, to which they were prompted by the native blacks, who were always ready to give up their sisters, daughters, or even their wives, for the hope only of getting in return a small quantity of spirits." The editor of the *Review* assumed that "they were trained to this offensive custom by the European slave-dealers."

In South Africa traders had begun to move among the large African communities of the Transkei and elsewhere; the Afrikaner Voortrekkers, escaping from what they considered suffocating British government in the Cape, played a role in taking a particular form of European culture into the interior. At the same time itinerant traders were also moving into the northern lands beyond the Cape. Livingstone, Speke, Burton, Grant, Baker, and, later, Joseph Thompson explored the center and east of the continent. Frenchmen, among them Faidherbe and Brazza, and Germans, including Nachtigal and Barth, followed similar paths, sometimes financed from Britain, which had the strongest motives for opening the African interior. Stanley combined journalism, exploration, and commercial enterprise. Throughout the African continent, the whole of the central period of the century became an era of Rider Haggard adventures, eagerly devoured by the British public.

Efforts at exploration were most concentrated and pursued most vigorously in the west. The invention of the steamship greatly assisted these endeavors, especially since it was soon adapted for sailing up rivers. Hardly had the Landers' news been heard than a Liverpool merchant, Macgregor Laird—a name that was to scale the heights of fame in west African shipping—formed a company to trade on the Niger. In 1832 he sent two small steamers to explore the river. Yet, though the secrets of the river might have been prised open, the hazards of disease and African hostility remained undiminished. Some navigation within the delta and up the Benue was achieved, but only nine of the forty-eight Europeans survived. Richard Lander, the old hand at west African exploration, was killed by armed canoeists in the delta itself.

Still the expeditions continued. In 1835 John Beecroft used one of Laird's original steamers to ascend the Niger as far as Lokoja, near the Benue confluence; five years later he nearly reached Bussa and explored the Benin river, this time in a boat owned by a west African merchant. In 1842 he explored the Old Calabar River and three years later reached Rabba, capital of Nupe.

The most impressive expedition of the era was that mounted by the British government in 1841. It consisted of three steamers and a schooner under the command of naval officers who were empowered to make treaties for the abolition of the slave trade with the chiefs they encountered. They also took with them a number of missionaries, including an African, Samuel Crowther, and equipment to establish a model farm. However, the environment again defeated the expedition. It got as far as Lokoja, where the leaders bought land from local chiefs and started the farm—only to have sickness strike them once more. A third of the Europeans died; the rest were evacuated; and the project was abandoned as one more disaster.

Still the British government persisted in its efforts to learn the facts of west Africa. In 1850 it financed another expedition to the northern territories. The party included two Germans, and one of them, Heinrich Barth, made considerable progress. Barth was away for five years and returned with much valuable information about the city states of the north.

One result of Barth's journeys was that the government renewed its efforts to utilize the river system, and it was the next expedition that achieved the first significant breakthrough in the struggle to preserve European life in the hostile climate. The party, under the leadership of Dr. Baikie, was to try to discover whether the Benue, which had been crossed by Barth, was the same river that had been explored by Lander twenty years earlier. Another ship was supplied by Laird, and careful surveys were made by the naval officers aboard as it sailed among the rivers. There was also a little successful trading along the river banks, but the greatest achievement was the prevention of death, a direct result of the use of quinine, the discovery of the correct use of which was to play as important a role in European contact with west Africa as had the charting of the Niger twenty-four years earlier. By 1861 most of the geography of the area was established; quinine allowed Europeans to survive the ravages of malaria, although health hazards persisted for many years. The way was therefore open to develop those commercial activities that were the central objective of nineteenth-century British life, in the pursuit of which the remaining gaps in geographical knowledge would be filled.

Another agent that was to play an important part in both widening knowledge of the interior and promoting British trade was, as we have indicated, the missionary effort. As the 1841 expedition made clear, exploration, Christianity, and labor were considered to be three paths to a single uplifting goal. Missionaries were taken by the explorers so that they could not only convert the heathen but also demonstrate to them the virtues of hard work. This dictum of "Bible and plow," which was later to be adopted and adapted by David Livingstone, was strongly propounded by Sir Thomas Fowell Buxton in his book, *The African Slave Trade and Its Remedy*. The way to save Africans from the ravages of the slave trade, Buxton asserted, was to teach them how to make money by other means, so that they could buy goods from Europe, and at the same time save their souls. This doctrine was, of course, popular not only in the churches of Britain, where collecting boxes for saving the "poor black natives" were becoming popular, but also among British merchants. It was opposed, however, both by the deeply rooted Islam in the north and by many established coastal merchants, who found their activities hindered by the distracting effects of missionary work on their customers and suppliers.

For many years the hostile climate of west Africa prevented all but a few hardy European missionaries from staying more than a short time in the area, so the early Christian efforts had to be undertaken largely by Africans. The Church Missionary Society (CMS) actually aimed to establish a self-sufficient Sierra Leone church. Samuel Ajayi Crowther, who, as we have already seen, was a member of the 1841 Niger expedition, had been a slave. Released by a British anti-slaver naval patrol stationed off west Africa, Crowther was landed at Freetown. He was educated by the CMS in Sierra Leone before being sent to England and then to Fourah Bay College in Freetown. Later he revisited England to be ordained and eventually become the first African bishop in the Church of England.

Crowther was also a close friend of Henry Venn, Honorary Secretary of the CMS, and since Venn agreed with Buxton on the beneficent combination of Christianity and economic development, he taught his African disciple the doctrine. Crowther thus became a fervent proponent of British culture and of an Anglicizing policy. In one of his journals he wrote, "When trade and agriculture engage the attention of the people, and with the gentle and peaceful teaching of Christianity, the minds of the people will gradually be won from war and marauding expeditions to peaceful trade and commerce." These sentiments could be taken as the central text of missionary endeavor in west Africa during the middle years of the century.

Another feature in Crowther's history illustrates an important factor in both missionary activity and the dispersion of British culture that accompanied it. Crowther was a member of the distinctive Yoruba community of released slaves in Sierra Leone, a community that preserved a cultural cohesion. Some of the ex-slaves were dissatisfied with conditions in their adopted country, though they were aware that to return to their homes was to risk reenslavement during the wars that were being fought there. Nevertheless, from 1839, parties of emigrants sailed back to Lagos and Badagri, many then proceeding to Abeokuta in Yorubaland. A mission was opened there; several hundred immigrants from Sierra Leone settled; and Crowther became one of its members. On the way, hindered by political upheavals and the threat of the slavers, the returning exiles stayed in Badagri and opened a mission, schools, an experimental farm, and a corn mill. A mission was also established in Calabar by the Church of Scotland, and the Methodists and the Baptists were active in Yorubaland, too.

The advent of the migrants from Sierra Leone had a profound effect on the Yoruba. They introduced a more intimate knowledge of European culture than anything previously experienced in the area, for Sierra Leone had been under British tutelage since its inception in the eighteenth century whereas no more than a few individual Europeans had penetrated from the coast to Yoruba towns and villages. The new perspectives stimulated fresh ambitions, ideas, and techniques. The old customs of slave trading and human sacrifice were attacked; European values were posed against African traditions. Conflict ensued, and often the members of the missions found themselves in great danger. Yet they gained new respect when, in 1851, they rallied to the defense of Abeokuta when it was attacked from Dahomey. Both the Anglican CMS and the Baptists took part in the defense of the town, the Baptists being led by Bowen, who, along with Davy Crockett, had fought Indians in Texas and Alabama. The Abeokuta and Badagri missions also gained strength from the establishment of factories in their neighborhoods; both towns developed into commercial centers that attracted legitimate trade as well as remaining slave centers. Before long each of the missions was expanding its influence by establishing new stations in "feeder" areas.

The Muslim jihads had changed the character of the interior states; exploration had provided knowledge of west African geography, the hazards it presented, and some means of overcoming them; Christian missionary activity had brought European cultural influence into the region, a part of which concentrated in the beneficent effects of labor, consumer ambitions, and an exchange of goods. And it was through the organization of these latter activities that the peoples of west Africa were to be most profoundly affected by their contact with Europe.

The principal agent in this process of organization was Britain. By taking the lead in abolishing the slave trade, the British were mainly responsible for what was bound to be a major change in economic conditions. For three hundred years the only serious relationship between west Africans and Europeans had been their contact through the slave trade, either as victims and shippers or as black and white merchants. By the end of the eighteenth century British merchants conducted over half this business. The economic life of the Gold Coast, the Slave Coast, and the Niger delta, together with the hinterlands of each of these areas, was dominated by the trade. To abolish it by a stroke of the pen in London was to destroy the economic life of large communities—even though it might save many of their members from a life of slavery. It is true that it was not until the 1820s that Britain began to interfere seriously with the slave trade; it is also true that, despite the abolition by Britain in 1807 and the outlawing of the trade by several other nations, its volume actually increased during the following years (the demands of the American plantations and of Brazil ensured that means would be found to circumvent the law). Nevertheless, once Britain took its responsibility seriously enough to station a naval squadron consisting of twenty warships and over one thousand men off the west coast to intercept slavers, west African trade with the outside world was bound to diminish.

The effects of this British policy were serious. Much of west Africa's indigenous industry and crafts had been undermined by contact with Europe. Textiles, metal-working, pottery, and the organization of agriculture to feed local populations all suffered from the competition of cheap, mass-produced commodities. The warfare and dislocation of society resulting from slave raiding and the consequent shifts in political power aggravated the trends. The moves to abolish the slave trade added to the confusion of peoples, many of whom had lost the ability to sustain themselves without it.

It was not only Africans who suffered economic loss from Britain's new policies, many British merchants also were dependent on the trade. The merchants found that the burgeoning strength of British industry was too powerful for them to preserve their commercial stake in the slave trade; for the first notable effect of the industrial revolution was the precedence industry took over trade. The landed aristocracy that still controlled British government in the eighteenth century took a supercilious attitude to commerce, even though many of them participated in its profits, but the prospect of industrial growth on their estates was regarded with favor and equal avarice. Indeed, the supremacy established by industrial interests proved to be one factor in the campaign to abolish the slave trade, which was held to be reducing investment in industry. The growth of mechanized textile manufacture, under a policy of strong protection, established the value of industry over commerce. Exports multiplied, much of the cotton cloth being sent to Africa, and Britain began to look to the outside world for raw materials rather than for slaves.

The end of the slave period left Africa as no more than

marginal to Britain's new economic power. Slaving had played a dominant role in the capital accumulation of the eighteenth century, but the continent possessed few of the raw materials sought for British factories, though Egypt and Uganda came to supply a proportion of their cotton. Nor was Africa an attractive area for investment, most of which went to the rapidly industrializing lands in America, Europe, Australia, and Canada, where capital goods could be sold and new markets were arising. It was not until diamonds and gold were discovered in South Africa toward the end of the nineteenth century that the City of London showed any serious interest in the African continent.

Yet, though not of first- or second-rate importance in the new economic climate of Britain, Africa was still of concern to a few sections of British economic society. In particular, those who had been involved in the slave trade sought alternative commodities to fill the gap left by abolition. They were fortunate in discovering one substance in much the same area that had previously supplied many of their slave cargoes: palm oil, found mainly in the forests of Yorubaland and Iboland. Palm oil could easily be prepared by boiling the husks in water, skimming off the oil, and selling it to the traders who traveled to the markets. But these were not European traders; as in the slave trade, African merchants bought the oil, took it to Lagos or the ports of the delta (the "oil rivers"), and there sold it to the British, almost entirely representing firms in Liverpool.

Liverpool was not only the main port for Lancashire's new textile industry, it was also the center of the infant chemical industry. The mills needed ever greater supplies of lubricating oil; the chemical industry was manufacturing increasing quantities of soap, no longer the luxury it had previously been but instead an essential because of the urban filth that was an integral part of the industrial revolution. Palm oil was found to produce the best lather and to be suitable for lubrication.

Thus the perfect alternative to the slave trade was found ready to hand. Gradually, those who had been dependent on the slave trade on and behind the coast turned to the collection and sale of the new product, though slaving was maintained for many years, especially in Lagos. Meanwhile, Liverpool merchants moved into Bonny, Calabar, Brass, and Lagos. They took with them cloth, firearms, liquor, beads, lead, copper, and a varied selection of second-rate goods scavenged from the back streets of Lancashire's grim industrial towns. Liverpool merchants acquired huge profits from their monopoly of the oil trade, but the African middlemen who bought the oil from the producers and sold it to the British traders also made handsome profits and often gained great power.

In fact, the growth of the oil trade extended and exaggerated the form of relationship between African and European merchant classes that had been established by the slave trade. The delta trade houses that had been created to organize the trade in slaves were now adapted to the sale of the new commodity. Their hierarchy was usually strengthened by the more sophisticated commercial techniques adopted, and certain merchant kings became extremely powerful over both their own traders and the Europeans with whom they dealt. The shift of political power southward toward the coast was accentuated, as were the corroding effects on native industries and crafts. And strengthening the whole process was the importation of European culture and values; for such trade was considered "legitimate" by the missionaries, who contrasted it with the commerce in human beings. Indeed, those who returned home from Sierra Leone, where they had been inculcated in British qualities after being torn from their homes and family communities, were encouraged to develop those attributes of competitive individualism that the Victorian British assumed would be the salvation of Africa, just as they were the sinews of their own industrial power. The interiors of some Itsekiri houses became virtual replicas of Victorian middle-class homes—down to the armchairs, antimacassars, pianos, and tea-sets!

During the first half of the nineteenth century the Fulani had destroyed most of the former power of the northern empires and, based on Sokoto, had established themselves as suzerains of the north. They had also plunged deeply into Yorubaland, extending their power southward and exacerbating the civil strife that seemed to have become an endemic feature of that society. As a result of conflicts between different Yoruba groups, the power of their states was also in decline. They were under threats not only from the Fulani but from their ancient foe, Dahomey. In the delta and Lagos a state of near anarchy prevailed, with African and European traders engaged in every kind of bribery, deceit, and violence in their efforts to appropriate the maximum commercial advantage to themselves, whether it be from the continuing slave trade or from new palm-oil wealth.

Meanwhile, by charting the interior and discovering the prophylactic qualities of quinine against malaria, the explorers made it possible for Europeans, missionaries, and traders to seek the paths leading to those communities living behind the coastal states. Christian culture had begun to pose a challenge to Islam and indigenous traditions, European values to those of Africa and the Muslim world. The interests of missionaries and merchants alike brought the most powerful of European governments, that of Britain, into an uneasy contact with west Africa. The French had also begun to play an active role in the area. The future fate of the peoples of west Africa was to be profoundly influenced by this impact of European industrial powers on the social, economic, and political affairs of their societies.

8

THE RACE TO IMPERIALISM

THE POPULAR idea that Europeans—particularly the British—seized Africa as part of an atavistic imperialist policy, induced by their rise to international dominance in the nineteenth century, has increasingly come under the fire of historical analysts. Nor can the conventional Marxist theory—that imperialism inevitably arose out of the export of surplus capital and the need for its protection—any longer be given serious credence. In any case, this latter theory, which neither Marx nor Lenin supported by the profound study of data that characterized much of their other work, was largely based on the work of J. A. Hobson, who confined his examination largely to South Africa.

The fact is that for most of the nineteenth century the British, supreme in world economic power, were deeply influenced by anti-colonial doctrines. Conventional economists, under the sway of Adam Smith, had discarded their earlier mercantilist theories and come to a virtually unanimous conclusion that the possession of colonies undermined the nation's economic health. Their argument was that the cost of administration and defense of colonies would be a waste of public money and therefore a drain on the country's economy. For this reason British governments from 1839—when the Durham report on Canada was published—introduced progressively representative and then responsible government into white-settled colonies—Canada, Australasia, and South Africa—while trying to rely on informal relations based on industrial and manufacturing power in nonwhite colonies. The major exception to this trend was, of course, India, but India was an exception to almost every rule.

During the nineteenth century, too, the changing pattern of British international policy strengthened the anti-colonial mood. Britain's early manufactures had been fostered by a policy of protection. Before the middle of the century, however, protection was more and more thought to be an artificial restraint on international trade. This change in attitude reflected the growing dominance of British trade throughout the world. Once British industry lost all fear of competition—even from goods produced by cheap labor—any form of interference with free trade, whether by Britain or through reaction by others, was held to reduce the commercial opportunities of its merchants. Moreover, British trade had, by mid-century, expanded so widely that Britain could afford to encourage the Indians to export to the United States, Japan, and Europe, because thereby India would earn revenues both to buy British capital exports and to pay the expenses of British administration.

In this situation the paramount objective of British policy was to avoid all restraints on international trade, one of which was still considered to be the possession and administration of colonies. Indeed, the main purpose of maintaining the comparatively small British empire during the first three-quarters of the nineteenth century was to retain coaling stations and bases for the British navy, the chief task of which was to keep the sea lanes open against any obstruction to trade, and particularly to safeguard the routes to India.

At the same time a double dichotomy was apparent in British policy, especially in west Africa. Given that British opinion was generally opposed to colonial activity, it yet became increasingly apparent that certain of the traders and missionaries needed government intervention in order to pursue their tasks to their satisfaction. Traders wanted intervention to prevent African middlemen, kings, and agents from blackmailing them into accepting their terms and submitting to their jurisdiction; missionaries believed that only the British government could halt the slave trade and abolish such brutal practices as human sacrifice.

At the same time, the British government was always sensitive to attempts by rival nations to preempt territories that might have commercial or strategic value. Thus, even at the height of the anti-colonial, free-trade era, voices were frequently heard urging government intervention, and government ministers themselves constantly were wary about the activities of fellow Europeans. Morever, as we have seen, the British government also took a leading role in supporting the most important exploratory expeditions that opened up the interior of the African continent to trade and Christianity.

The fact was that west Africa, and particularly the southern areas of present-day Nigeria, had become a vast market of consumer and wholesale exchange, vital to the economic life of the indigenous inhabitants and, although peripheral to the total British economic scene, nevertheless important to profit-making for an influential section of the British and French merchant classes. The area was covered by a multiplicity of markets—large, medium, and small—linking through their activities the Hausa cities, Benin, Bornu, Yorubaland, the Benue area, and Iboland with Lagos and the delta ports. Thus the trans-Saharan trade was directly connected, by a stream of traders, across the savannah to the middle belt, the forest region, and the coast. In some cases, there were even mobile markets, composed of the caravans trekking across west Africa selling their wares en route. In the delta, in Lagos, and in Badagri "legitimate" trade vied with the continuing slave trade, producing conditions of violence and ruffianism.

Thus it was that despite a general aversion to colonial matters in Britain, the central Nigerian issue of the mid-nineteenth century was who was to establish authority over this great market area. Particularly, it was a matter of control over the important centers of exchange on the coast, for it was clear that the northern area, under the domination of its ancient Islamic culture, would retain the authority of its indigenous rulers. For the first part of the period, too, African rulers were in complete control of the coastal towns; European traders had to obey their rules and suffered sanctions such as boycotts if they challenged them. But when European missionaries followed the Sierra Leonean emigrants to the Niger mission, and when British merchants began to chafe under the regulations of coastal chiefs, attempts were made to persuade the British government to introduce at least some minor supervisory role.

The first specific occasion to assert British control arose out of the anti-slavery campaign. In 1836 British warships entered Bonny harbor to seize a Spanish slave ship. The Bonny ruler was enraged by this violation of his town's right to trade with whomever it wished and imprisoned the British merchants trading in Bonny. In retaliation the British threatened to destroy the town unless the merchants were released and, with the assistance of some African rivals of the ruler, deposed him. Immediately, the new ruler of Bonny found himself dependent on British support. Thus the new ruler was forced to promise to abolish the slave trade—in exchange for compensation, which was never paid. Then, some years later, he seized a British ship in lieu of the compensation and was himself deposed in favor of the previous incumbent. Clearly, the winner in this game of musical chairs was the British.

A more serious British move was made in 1849. A British

consul, John Beecroft, himself a trader, was appointed as consul to the Bights of Benin and Biafra with headquarters in Fernando Po, with the task of continuing the campaign against the slave trade and of protecting the interests of British merchants. One of Beecroft's first missions was to try and persuade the king of Dahomey to stop his slave trading, but, as the king reasonably pointed out, for him to cease trading would only bring advantage to Lagos, where the trade was flourishing. In Lagos the king, Kosoko, who had seized the crown from his uncle in 1845, was both encouraging the slave trade and interfering with British merchants. At the end of 1851, therefore, Beecroft took a naval expedition to Lagos and, after his men had suffered many casualties, took the island, with the help of the deposed uncle's followers. Kosoko was deposed, uncle Akitoye reinstated, and an antislavery treaty signed. The British had taken another step toward control.

Gradually, other coastal towns signed similar treaties, though it was not until the U.S. Civil War and the subsequent proclamation of emancipation and U.S. agreement that the British navy should be allowed to stop American slavers that the slave trade began to decline. In any case, one result of Britain's campaign against the trade was that British power over the states and kingdoms of the coastal area, debilitated by the effects of slaving and civil war, grew appreciably.

The British government did not have it all its own way, however. It learned that it could not intervene in the affairs of west Africa without repercussions. On the one hand, the installation of a puppet king in Lagos did not end the intrigues and conflicts that had persisted there for the previous twenty years. On the other, the 1851 intervention whetted the appetite of those who hoped to see British authority established along the unruly coast.

The progress of British expansion was thereafter continuous, if sporadic. The success of Baikie's voyage up the Niger in 1854 and the trading profit it made helped to stimulate the appetite for expansion. Traders from London, Glasgow, and Manchester, who had hitherto been excluded by the Liverpool-African middlemen monopoly, began to be accompanied by naval ships on their trading expeditions. Missionaries, merchants, the Sierra Leone émigrés, including Samuel Crowther, pressed for more resolute British action.

Then, too, local British officials entertained ambitions of higher status and greater glory. Thus by 1861 the British consul at Fernando Po had persuaded the British foreign secretary so far to breach British anti-colonial policy as to enable him to occupy Lagos. The island became a British colony, and a governor was appointed, but in view of its dependence on the mainland and vulnerability to mainland incursions, intervention in the hinterland inevitably followed. Two years later Palma, Lekki, Badagri, Ado, and Oke-Odan were added to the colony, and military action was being taken in other areas.

Strong anti-British action gradually built up. The Egba, for example, traditional friends of the British, were antagonized by the occupation of Lagos, which they saw as a direct threat to their own independence. However, their own wars with other Yoruba clans disrupted Lagos trade and began to threaten the safety of the colony, so the British authorities, having failed to persuade the Egba to withdraw from the environs of Lagos, sent a military force against them. In reprisal the Egba expelled all European missionaries from Abeokuta for a decade.

This first deliberate move by Britain to impose its political authority on a section of the west African coast seemed for a time as though it might set off a European competition in African colonization. The French were already well established in Senegal, where the governor, Faidherbe, who built up a formidable African army (a significant pointer to the future French policy), had begun to take an aggressive attitude in the 1850s. It seemed, too, that French expansion up the Senegal River might take French merchants into the Muslim states and across to the Niger. The British and the French each began to fear that the other would restrain the trade of their respective merchants by imposing discriminatory customs duties, and when France declared protectorates over Porto Novo and Cotonou, on the coast of Dahomey, it appeared that open conflict might ensue between the rival claimants to the west African coast. That there was no conflict was largely owing to the restraining hands of the governments in Paris and London, which were not prepared to allow their local officials, or their missionaries and merchants, to involve them in the risk of war.

Why was it possible for this breach to be made in Britain's conventional assumption that colonization handicapped trade? The fact is that there were always at least two voices in British government circles. The economists constantly warned against intervention abroad, while certain politicians, no less concerned for the health of British trade, believed that the government must protect commercial interests, when necessary by the exercise of its power. At different times, one or the other opinion prevailed, but Palmerston, who once expressed his belief "that commerce may go freely forth, leading civilization with one hand and peace with the other, to render mankind happier, wiser, better," represented the latter attitude. And it was Palmerston who appointed Beecroft as consul: to protect the interests of British merchants in the area and to suppress the slave trade that damaged those interests. Equally, when Lagos was made a colony of the British empire, it was to be Lagos's responsibility to defend the mission in Abeokuta and to control the main trading channels of the oil trade.

At the same time there was still strong feeling in Britain that the local officials, traders, and missionaries had pushed the government into dangerous paths. This opinion was most clearly expressed when a select committee of Parliament reported in 1865

> That all further extension of territory or assumption of government, or new treaties offering any protection to native tribes, would be inexpedient, and that the object of our policy should be to encourage in the natives the exercise of those qualities which may render it possible for us more and more to transfer to them the administration of all the governments, with a view of our ultimate withdrawal from all, except, probably, Sierra Leone.

Sierra Leone, of course, always had a special niche in British policies, for not only had it been created as a haven for released slaves, but it had become an important base for the anti-slavery naval squadron. Indeed, the only practical effect of the select committee report seems to have been that in the year following its publication the seat of government for all west African settlements was transferred to Sierra Leone. (Authority over Lagos remained in Sierra Leone until 1874, when it was moved to the Gold Coast; it finally returned to Lagos itself in 1886.)

The parliamentary report bore witness to the strength of opposition in high British circles to incurring expense in foreign territories. Opposition sentiments were probably provoked by the renewal of Ashanti attacks on the trade routes into the interior of the Gold Coast and by the fear that the British government would be urged by traders in the locality to take expensive measures to reopen them. The report was far from representing a sincere desire to promote colonial self-government, as might be supposed from its terms. In 1871, for example, the Fante, traditional allies of Britain in the Gold Coast, tried to create a confederation, partly to unite their forces against the Ashanti and partly to provide a representative system based on elections, with a government responsible for social and economic development. The project was immediately condemned by the British in the territory, and when the British government was asked by the Fante for advice and support, the proposal was treated as an attack on British authority. Many of those who had shown the audacity to devise a scheme for self-government were arrested for their pains.

Britain clearly was not prepared to spend its money on administering its colonies, but neither was it willing to allow their own people to govern themselves. In short, Britain's objective seems to have been to treat such countries as open markets in which its merchants could buy and sell without danger of restrictions being imposed by local inhabitants or of costly supervision by itself.

The British government was always reluctant to participate in the search for bases of authority, though its officials and British merchants on African soil were able on occasion to place the government in positions from which it seemed craven to withdraw. This tactic became more feasible when the consulate was moved from Fernando Po to Calabar; henceforth the consuls were able to call in the navy whenever recalcitrant chiefs obstructed the trade of British merchants. In 1877, for instance, a punitive expedition was sent against Brass, and in 1879 Onitsha was shelled for three days by a British warship, an action that the consul considered would have a "most salutary effect up and down the Niger."

Indeed, by the 1870s the struggle for authority was appreciably intensifying. The central reason can be appreciated from trade-return figures. During the decade 1853–1862 the total trade of British west Africa amounted to $21.36 million, of which Britain's share was 64 percent. During the following decade trade more than doubled, but Britain's proportion fell to 50 percent, remaining at that level until 1882.

What was happening was that Americans, Frenchmen, and Germans were exploiting the advantages of Britain's free-trade policy to move into the market. The trade in palm oil and groundnuts, despite frequent fluctuations in prices, was beginning to attract competitors. Competition accelerated trade, aggravated conflicts, and led to further immigration from countryside to towns (Lagos, for example, nearly doubled its population during the 1860s and 1870s, reaching fifty thousand by 1881). Such commercial pressures inevitably intensified the search for authority.

During the early 1870s the main struggle was between British and African merchants, with the power of Britain increasingly employed in support of the former. The rout of the French army by Bismarck's Prussians in 1870, the collapse of the French state, and the Parisian civil war virtually eliminated France from colonial competition for a decade. There was even a possibility that the French colonies might be seized by Germany; so complete was the French defeat that Prussia would not have found such an action particularly difficult. France even offered Prussia the colonies as an alternative to Alsace and Lorraine, and it is an illustration of Bismarck's lack of interest in colonies that he resisted the pressures—by 1870, indeed, quite strong influences in Germany were engaged in west African trade—put on him to take the place of France in west Africa. Like his British counterparts, Bismarck accepted the conventional economic analysis: colonies would be expensive, a burden on his economy. In any case, he had no navy to guard colonial routes.

But if Germany itself presented no threat to Britain in west Africa in the 1870s, German merchants remained active. German merchants, especially from Bremen and Hamburg, were trading in Sierra Leone and Liberia; in 1852 the German firm of O'Swald, which had been carrying cowrie shells from east Africa, settled in Lagos. When O'Swald sold out, its successor created the largest palm oil business in Germany. Germans established a position in the Cameroons, and some of them used their profits to support missionary endeavors in the Gold Coast and Togoland.

During most of the 1870s, in fact, while Britain had little

to fear from its European rivals in the power game, commercial competition was mounting. And even while the calm lasted, Britain merchants were occupied by constantly shifting understandings with the Africans: monarchs, chiefs, and traders. The *modi vivendi* varied according to local circumstances. Where a shrewd, astute ruler, such as Ja Ja of the Bonny house, was in power, British merchants had to accept his terms and consuls dare not interfere. Yet there were few African rulers who could approach the skill of Ja Ja; more commonly they found their authority eroded because British merchants were able to call in consular and naval support. Coercion was becoming increasingly common and effective. In 1873, for instance, an Order in Council established new authority for the Courts of Equity under the consul; he was given the power to fine or imprison those who broke regulations.

This increase in British authority did not go unchallenged by the local Africans. The Lagos consul was unable to prevent Ja Ja from building a substantial kingdom out of the major houses in Bonny. Lokoja, where a consulate had been established in 1865 to protect the activities of British merchants along the Niger, was blockaded for six months by riverside communities determined to prevent the Europeans from taking away their trade. In 1871 a British steamer was sunk in the Niger for much the same reasons. Further attacks on steamers resulted in a situation in which no British vessel dared sail up the river. The African middlemen struggled hard to preserve their trading role against the attempts of Europeans to cut them out and deal directly with the producers.

It was at this stage that a decisive factor entered into both the commercial and the political situations. The British trading posts along the rivers were bringing in large profits, but they were being placed in jeopardy by attacks by Africans. The posts could sometimes be protected by the navy, yet punitive expeditions were only possible during the wet season, when the river was sufficiently high. The chief weakness of the British merchants was division of control and direction, for the main companies came from separate cities: Liverpool, Manchester, Glasgow, and London. The appearance of George Goldie on the Niger in 1877 changed the scene.

Recognizing the British weakness in the face of African attacks and in competition with the French and Germans, Goldie welded the four British companies into one monopolistic group, known first as the United Africa Company and later as the National African Company. When the French refused to amalgamate with him, Goldie began a bitter price-cutting war that so enfeebled them that he was able to buy them out. The Germans, who actually purchased a beach near Lagos for a brief period, were forestalled on the coast by the presence of the British navy and in the interior by Goldie's shrewdness in making treaties with local chiefs. Goldie then built up a fleet of gunboats that proved effective in warding off his competitors, in bombarding those riverine communities that dared to attack his trading posts, and in helping his friends, such as the emir of Nupe, to suppress rebellions. By 1886, when the Conservatives replaced the Liberal free traders at Westminster, Goldie had secured a charter for his company that enabled it to administer justice and maintain security, establishing a virtual "protectorate" (in practice, he had been acting as though he had possessed the charter for several years before his company received it).

The activities of Goldie and his commercial colleagues broke through the defenses of traditional British anti-colonialism. Yet Goldie represented not the initiation of a totally new policy but, as we have seen, the climax of a process that had begun years before he saw the Niger.

As consuls were appointed, as Lagos and coastal areas of the Gold Coast were added to Sierra Leone as part of the British empire in west Africa, and as the navy was used in support of British commercial interests, the issue of revenues arose. Yet though the theory of governmental nonparticipation had to be waived on increasingly numerous occasions, it was still thought to be outrageous to suggest that the government should pay its officials and the expenses incurred by their actions solely or even mainly from British taxpayers' money. Moreover, actual colonization implied government (Lagos was given a governor, an executive, and a legislative council). Roads had to be built, ports supervised, customs collected, order maintained. The Colonial Office was able to bully the Treasury with sufficient success to maintain a subsidy for ships carrying mail—Lagos even secured a loan amounting to $48,000—but governmental activities had to be financed, principally if not solely, from duties raised to provide a local revenue.

From the 1830s British colonial ports were open to foreign goods without discrimination, but duties were levied on trade in order to raise money for administrative expenses. Duties, however, provided another issue of international dispute. French traders, for example, harbored a continual grievance against the duties levied by the British on wines and spirits, which they felt handicapped their particular trade.

Moreover, although Goldie was able to put a virtual end to French commercial activities along the Niger, it was not before the British had been given a considerable fright that their rivals might succeed in gaining the adherence of important African rulers. The French were advancing into the Sudan from Senegal, fighting campaigns to establish themselves from the Senegal to the Niger, building a railway from Dakar to St. Louis. They were influential in Gabon, and their explorer, Brazza, succeeded in establishing French power on the north bank of the Congo. It was not idle rumor that caused the British consul in the delta, Hewett, to express fears that the French might move into the Cameroons and Iboland, thus gaining direct access to the oil producers and isolating the British traders and their African partners from the producing areas.

The consul's remedy was to make further treaties with the chiefs and to create a new colony to include the Cameroons. In this, however, the consul came up against a curious situation within British government circles. The Colonial Office was entirely opposed to any extension of its responsibilities, so the Foreign Office had to deal with the affair. There was more than departmental rivalry in this transfer of authority; for the use of consular officials and the decisions on establishing protectorates were directed more to meeting the challenges of rival European nations than to colonial issues. The most important factor governing the British government's attitude toward African rulers was their relations with other European powers. This interest was perfectly illustrated in the definition the consul gave in 1884 to Ja Ja, who had demanded to know what the word "protection" meant before he agreed to sign a proffered treaty. The consul replied:

> I write as you request with reference to the word "protection" as used in the proposed treaty that the Queen does not want to take your country or your markets, but at the same time is anxious that no other nation should take them. She undertakes to extend her gracious favour and protection, which will leave your country still under your government.

The Colonial Office rejected the consul's advice on creating a new colony, and only belatedly was he provided with the money to bribe chiefs into signing new treaties and told to establish a protectorate that would be under the authority of the Foreign Office. He succeeded in the former task, but when he arrived in the Cameroons, he found that the Germans had forestalled him. They had just declared both Togoland and the Cameroons to be their protectorates. It seemed that Bismarck, like governments in London, could change his mind under the pressure of events.

Bismarck was certainly influenced by the changing political, industrial and commercial scene of Europe, but to what extent one can isolate any of these elements from each other is doubtful. Commercial diplomacy, based on the foundations of industrial strength, was the dominant feature of European international life during the later nineteenth century. From 1870 British industrial supremacy was increasingly challenged, particularly by Germany and the United States, and one of the commonest delusions was that the paramountcy of Britain in the commercial and industrial world had resulted from the possession of an empire. The truth was the reverse: the British empire had been acquired as a consequence of British industrial and commercial activities. Nevertheless, many bankers and merchants in Europe believed that to compete with Britain they must persuade their governments to seek colonial empires, which would provide them with markets for their industrial products, opportunities for investment, supplies of raw materials for their factories, and bases for the armies and navies that would protect their commercial lifelines.

By the turn of the 1880s German merchants were acting in much the same way as those of Britain and France; they were involving themselves in commercial ventures, in both west and east Africa, that led to conflicts with other Europeans and with Africans. They expected their government to protect them in the same way as their British and French rivals were protected.

Moreover, colonial maneuvers could play an important role in Bismarck's political policies. He had defeated France in 1870, but he had no desire to make France a permanent enemy, intent on revenge. He would like to divert the French revanchists into fields in which their aggression could find a less dangerous outlet. Now that Germany was allied to Russia, Austria, and Italy, only France and Britain remained outside Bismarck's circle of amity. If he could encourage hostility between France and Britain, one or both might be induced to join him. Thus when he supported the British occupation of Egypt in 1882, he knew that the French would be furious with the British action. Conversely, when he allowed his merchant and banker friends to have their way in west Africa, he made it clear that his protectorates were aimed against British influence in the Gold Coast and Niger.

Meanwhile, the French, under the premiership of an unashamed imperialist, Jules Ferry, had resumed their position in Dahomey, annexing a series of towns, including, as we have seen, Cotonou and Porto Novo. The French were thus cutting off the British settlements in Lagos and the Gold Coast from each other. With the Belgian king, Leopold, busy carving out an empire for himself on the Congo, with rivalry growing between Britain, Germany, and Portugal in south, central, and east Africa, and with an increasing trend toward protectionism in those African areas under European influence, tension in the imperial field was rapidly mounting.

It was at this moment that Bismarck succeeded in convening a conference on Africa in Berlin. His object, shared by the French and Belgians, was to raise barriers to British expansion. International control and free river navigation would prevent Britain from exerting a monopolistic influence on the Niger. Diplomatic support for Leopold would obstruct Britain's ambitions along the Congo. In practice, the conference did not provide Bismarck with the successes he envisaged. Leopold secured his opportunity to develop his Association on the Congo, which blocked British pretensions in the area, but the French soon abandoned their uneasy cooperative role with Germany, and the intention of undermining Britain's position on the Niger accordingly had to be forsaken.

Bismarck once more displayed his flexibility, quickly switching his ground and coming to terms with the British. He persuaded Britain to recognize the German protectorate in Southwest Africa, despite its proximity to the Cape; to abandon the treaty it had made with the Portuguese aimed at obstructing French and Belgian ambitions on the Congo; and to allow Germany a substantial degree of freedom in east Africa. In return, Bismarck guided the conference into accepting Britain's special position on the lower reaches of the Niger and gave up the attempt to create an international commission in the area. Navigation was supposed to be free to all on both the Niger and the Congo, but in practice this clause of the agreement was never implemented.

During the Berlin conference the significance of Goldie's activities first became apparent. The Germans had insisted that the test of any country's right to declare a paramount influence in a colony should be its effective occupation of that territory. (In fact, strict application of this rule would have excluded the Europeans from virtually all their African colonies and protectorates, but the conference accepted the convention.) In conjunction with the projected establishment of an international commission, the Germans expected that the test for occupation would effectively destroy Britain's claims on the Niger. It did nothing of the sort. Just two weeks before the conference assembled, Goldie had bought out the French companies and was therefore able to display an impressive collection of treaties, which clearly established that no one could challenge Britain's claim to paramount influence along the Niger. Immediately after the conference ended the British government seemed to have abandoned its anti-colonial philosophy; it declared a protectorate over the Niger districts—including the immediate hinterland of Lagos—the territories on both banks of the Niger from Lokoja to the sea, and both banks of the Benue up to Ibi.

The age of European imperialism had officially opened. In Berlin the African continent was vaguely partitioned into separate European spheres of influence; it was now incumbent on each power to establish authority in its allocated territories before rivals could challenge its claims.

9

THE IMPOSITION OF BRITISH AUTHORITY

THE FIRST task of each European power after the Berlin conference was to make good its claim to the territories in which rivals had agreed that its fiat should run. This was by no means an easy task, for there had been a great deal of bluffing in Berlin: claims were made to territories in which no European authority had ever been exercised and in which there had never been any form of European occupation. Moreover, although it appeared on the surface that the British and German governments had abandoned their traditional reluctance to build empires in Africa, this was too simplistic a view. The French were certainly committed to an expansionist policy in the continent, but France was always conscious of its comparatively small population, low birth rate, and vulnerable military position in Europe. France hoped to rectify these disadvantages by bolstering its strength through the addition of African colonies that could provide soldiers as well as economic resources.

The British and German governments, however, though coerced by circumstances into accepting more specific responsibilities than they had desired, never conceived of these extending to the actual use of national revenues for colonial administration. Both governments were quick to realize that unless they found alternative means of financing their new colonies or protectorates, they would be unable to escape from such painful necessity. Both sought an identical sanctuary. If the merchants who had been so insistent on their governments' taking political responsibility for the regions in which they wished to trade were to be given chartered companies, they could be saddled with the burdens of administration, justice, and security—and with the necessity to raise the money to pay for their services.

The British were more successful in this ploy than the Germans. Goldie had been pressing for a royal charter since 1881. He had at first been denied the charter, for there was always the danger that a chartered company might get into political difficulties and then expect the government to rescue it—a likely occurrence during expansive operations. However, once vast territories were allocated to Britain at the Berlin conference, and as it became apparent that if Britain refused responsibility for them, they would gladly be taken by Britain's rivals, the issue had become more urgent. It seemed that either the government must risk indiscretion by the company in exchange for its financing the administration or that government revenues must inevitably become liable for that purpose. In the nineteenth century the former alternative automatically appeared the lesser evil.

Thus Goldie received his charter, in 1886—only a year after the Berlin conference had ended—thus enabling his company, as we have seen, to add an administrative superstructure to its existing commercial organization. A supreme court was established at Asaba with a chief justice; a military constabulary was created under a commandant; and the company agent-general headed an administrative bureaucracy consisting of executive officers who controlled the large regions into which the company's territory was divided. Under the executive officers agents had charge of subdivisions or districts.

Theoretically, the British government passed over to Goldie's company, now the Royal Niger Company, most of its own responsibilities as outlined at the Berlin conference. Bismarck hoped to do the same in Togoland and the Cameroons. He expected the German merchants who had been pressing him to support their ventures to follow the same road as Goldie: to set up chartered companies that would create administrative machines. In this hope Bismarck was disappointed. German officials were forced to demarcate the boundaries of the two protectorates, sometimes to the alarm of the British and French, but little more was done in the territories. Indeed, Germany never placed much importance on these possessions. After the flurry caused by its original intervention Germany left the field almost entirely to its former rivals: Britain and France.

The administrative structure created by Goldie's company may have satisfied the British government, in its anxiety to be free of expense, but it brought little satisfaction to anyone else. The company, for example, was bitterly attacked by the African middlemen in the delta and their Liverpool associates, both of whom were now excluded from their chief markets by the company's monopoly. The government had hoped that the company and the delta merchants would form one large company capable of administering the delta and river areas, thus relieving itself of responsibility within its 1885 protectorate, which was bisected by company lands and under the jurisdiction of Foreign Office consuls. But Goldie aimed at his own monopoly. He claimed territories in which his company had virtually no influence, such as the northern emirates where, in 1885, Joseph Thompson, the explorer, had made treaties for him with Sokoto and Gwandu. Goldie's treaties, in contrast to the definition of royal protection, claimed cession of land in perpetuity—thus giving his company sovereignty in the areas it administered—though the chiefs had little conception of the actual meaning of the agreements they signed. The company constabulary was used to punish towns or villages that challenged Goldie's authority.

It is significant, too, that when Goldie originally formed his amalgamated company in 1879, he dismissed all the senior African managers and agents of the firms he absorbed. The mid-century idealism of Livingstone, Buxton, and Venn had no place in the Niger Company's philosophy. Its objective was to crush the competition of African producers and merchants alike, together with that of those European traders who had formed an alliance with them. The Royal Niger Company's monopoly enabled it to reduce prices to producers, and its power was used to exclude African and European merchants from its territories. It thus halted the movement of African traders across west Africa that had been an historical feature of life in the region and, particularly since the migration of the Yoruba from Sierra Leone in the 1830s, had introduced new ideas and techniques from the outside world.

Because of the Royal Niger Company's limited capital and lack of interest in economic development, little positive progress was made in the territories under its rule. Its monopoly excluded those Africans and Europeans who might have contributed to economic growth, especially in the commercial sector of the economy, and of the two specific projects initiated by the company—an attempt to introduce cultivated rubber and some tin prospecting around Bauchi—the former made little impression, and the latter, though more successful, only became of practical importance after the turn of the century, when colonial government took over.

In the late nineteenth century two main factors influenced British policy toward the coast and its hinterland. The first factor was continued fear of French and German interference, whether from the west into Yorubaland, in the northwest, or along the coast west and east of Lagos. By the early 1880s the Germans had seized the coasts of Togoland and the Cameroons, despite traditional British missionary and commercial activities in the latter territory. The French had established themselves in Dahomey and were soon to use military force to bend that kingdom under their will. Dahomey could provide the French with an opportunity to intervene in Yorubaland, while their interest in the upper Niger and the Lake Chad area might enable them to gain some control in the north. The British Foreign Office was therefore constantly under pressure to authorize British intervention to prevent these regions from falling into foreign hands.

The second factor was the commercial conflict around the oil rivers and up the Niger. Resentment over the Niger Company's monopoly led African traders and clergy to demand that its charter be rescinded and that the British government take over direct rule. Some of the Liverpool merchants were inclined to sympathize with this attitude as they saw their established trade with the interior increasingly interdicted by the activities of the company. But there was more than one opposition voice: some wanted to destroy the power of the company; others hoped to amalgamate with it; still others hoped that the strength of the African middlemen could be undermined by company or consular action so that they could imitate the company's strategy of trading directly with the producers.

One intriguing sidelight on the cut and thrust of commercial conflict in the delta area has been revealed by Professor J. E. Flint. Apparently King Ja Ja of Opobo "from the 1870s had cherished ambitions of competing in the seaborne trade by shipping oil direct to Liverpool. Though his fingers had been burned by dishonest brokers in England, he was intelligent enough to see that this should be his ultimate ambition. Thus did the greatest African middleman of all time plan to remove the European middleman!"

It was under the pressure of these two factors that the Foreign Office reluctantly agreed: (1) to declare the Oil Rivers Protectorate in 1885, blocking French or German intervention and particularly guarding against the imposition of the French system of protective tariffs; (2) to separate Lagos from the Gold Coast, giving Lagos its own governor and extending its authority along the coast and into the hinterland; (3) to proclaim all the territories in treaty relationship with the company another protectorate; and (4) eventually to make an agreement with the alafin of Oyo, who promised not to interfere with trade, to levy duties without permission, or to cede territory to foreigners.

The proclamations of protectorates had various consequences. Much depended on the attitudes of local men—traders and consuls—for the Foreign Office itself seemed to have little coherent policy toward them. In certain cases, use was made of the new power acquired by British officials to further the interests of British merchants, as was being done in the Gold Coast. Always it was the internal trade routes that were at issue. So long as the middlemen of the hinterland or the coast, whether it be the Ashanti, the peoples of the Niger, or those of the delta towns, were in a position to enforce their will by cutting commercial paths or banning trade, merchants from Britain felt that they were at the middlemen's mercy. Moreover, the mid-1880s saw a fall in palm-oil prices, which made those in the trade even more anxious to cut their costs by eliminating the middlemen between them and the producers.

In 1886 the first serious effort to eliminate the middlemen was made by a British consul. Taking advantage of civil conflict in Bonny, where the heads of the most important trading houses had usurped the power of the king, the consul stepped in to create a council the laws of which he claimed the right to veto. Since taxes provided adequate revenue, the British government did not object, although the action clearly contravened the definition of protectorate status presented to Ja Ja only two years earlier. Indeed, Ja Ja himself suffered from the next move.

Ja Ja's power and prestige had been a source of envy to British merchants for some years. By skillfully playing off one British firm against another, he had maintained his paramount position. Thus although he had antagonized the Liverpool merchants when he had allied himself with a Glasgow company, when he signed a treaty of protection, he was strong enough to insist to the consul that the clause in the treaty providing for free trade should be deleted.

Nevertheless, the intrigue to get rid of Ja Ja continued. The immediate cause of dispute was characteristic of the temper of the time. It arose out of a disputed market, which Ja Ja claimed to be reserved for Opobo, but which was penetrated by one of the Liverpool traders. Ja Ja appealed to the Foreign Office, quoting the protectorate definition given him in 1884. The Secretary of State answered that no chief on the coast could obstruct a policy designed to promote the welfare of the people as a whole; the people should be assured of trade and intercourse with the Europeans.

In short, the British government was now completely changing its former principle of protection by arrogating to itself a right superior to that of any ruler to determine what was good for his people. The change in attitude was underlined when, immediately after this incident took place, Harry Johnston, the vice-consul, assumed authority on his superior's return home on sick leave, for Johnston was determined to remove the menace of Ja Ja. Johnston's first move was to ask the Foreign Office to sanction the deportation of the monarch. Although the reply did not give him this authority, Johnston chose to interpret it according to his wish. He lured Ja Ja onto a British warship under safe-conduct and then offered him the alternative of being deported or of facing war. Ja Ja chose to be deported; he was sent first to the Gold Coast and then to the West Indies. Although the Foreign Office disapproved, it did not countermand Johnston's action. Johnston therefore was able to press home his advantage by sending the navy up the rivers on a display of strength, imposing his own administration, first on Opobo, then on Bonny, and collecting the king's customs dues for his own treasury. Again the Foreign Office admitted that Johnston was acting illegally but allowed him to proceed without hindrance.

Johnston's own account of this event is of some interest, for it illustrates the attitude of one of Britain's first convinced imperialist officials. In his book *The Colonisation of Africa,* first published in 1899, Johnston wrote:

> . . . these consular administrators were obliged to face a serious difficulty in the determined opposition of certain coast chiefs to the carrying on of direct trade with the interior. . . . Foremost among these obstructive individuals was Jaja. . . . As Jaja at last went to the length of forcibly opposing trade between the British merchants and the natives of the interior, Mr. H. H. Johnston [the author], then acting consul for the Oil Rivers, removed him to the Gold Coast to be tried before a commissioner. . . . With the exile of Jaja the principal resistance of the middlemen was broken.

In short, Ja Ja was exiled because he insisted on determining his own policy in the country that Queen Victoria had promised should remain "still under your government."

The final words of Johnston's book are so revealing as also to warrant quotation:

> No doubt, as in Asia and South America, the eventual colonisation of Africa by alien peoples will be a compromise—a dark-skinned race with a white man's features and a white man's brain.

The power of the middlemen might be seriously reduced by the deportation of Ja Ja, but this reduction in power did not leave the Niger Company in command. There was still opposition to its activities from the Liverpool firms, which now formed their own association and hoped to secure a charter of their own. The companies did not succeed, but these continuing conflicts induced the British government to try to sort out the confusion. The government sent a special commissioner to examine the position in the oil rivers and report to it on the best solution. The commissioner, Claude Macdonald, was ready to hear all sides. During his investigations it became obvious to him that the regime of the Royal Niger Company, which the government had hoped would remove from it all responsibility for administration, was unpopular with almost everyone. Most of the African rulers, it became clear, would have liked the kind of British protection outlined in the queen's assurance to Ja Ja, which would have left them with their traditional forms of government and trade virtually unaffected. The missionaries, especially the Africans, would have liked a colony to be established, if only because this would have outlawed slavery, which was illegal in British colonies.

In the event, the British government decided to establish a cross between a colony and a protectorate, so that, although an administration would be created under British control, the area would not legally fall within the empire and consequently the difficulties surrounding the abolition of slavery would not have to be faced. Macdonald was appointed consul-general and charged with creating an administration. This he achieved with tact and humanity, but it was now clear that Britain was taking control of the area in the official manner that governments had previously tried to avoid. Customs duties and military forces were taken under official authority; rulers were given subsidies from the central revenues, a sure sign that they had lost their independence.

This new arrangement did not end the conflicts over markets. In 1894, in the absence of Macdonald, his deputy invaded the country of the Itsekiri people, who had been obstructing open access to oil markets they considered to be their own, and exiled the Itsekiri chief, Nana. In 1895 the people of Brass revolted against the company, which was excluding them from their particular markets, and destroyed its headquarters in Akassa. An expedition was sent to punish them. In both cases, the British navy was used to destroy the centers of resistance.

By now the involvement of the British government in the affairs of the whole area could not be ignored. The Foreign Office was concerned not only with the activities conducted by its consuls but with the constant threat of conflict with the French, who were maneuvering on the borders and preparing to destroy the barrier to the coast represented by the kingdom of Dahomey. As a direct result, the British government began to negotiate with France in order to avoid a clash. In 1889 the two governments agreed on a frontier to the west of Lagos. The following year another agreement was signed in which the northern frontier, between the Niger and Lake Chad, was defined. The empire of Sokoto thus fell within the British sphere, the French quite falsely believing that the British had established authority over it.

These agreements did not remove the mutual British and French suspicions that their rival's ambitions might lead to intervention in their own territories. When the French defeated Dahomey in 1892–1893, the British feared that the French might follow earlier Dahomean custom and invade Yorubaland. Civil wars had gravely weakened the Yoruba states; they would certainly not be able to resist a French attack and might be persuaded to make some sort of agreement with the French; indeed, some Frenchmen had attempted to gain a foothold in Abeokuta in 1888. In addition to the incentive provided by British fears of French ambitions, officials and traders in Lagos had been pressing the British government to intervene in Yorubaland for some years because the

Yoruba wars had greatly interfered with trade. Hitherto their pleas had usually fallen on deaf ears, but the bitterness that had grown up among Yoruba towns following the pressure of the Fulani from the north, the reduction of the slave trade, the antagonism felt toward the new power of Ibadan, and the collapse of Oyo—aggravated by personal and political rivalries—was held by increasing numbers to present a very dangerous situation and grounds for British intervention.

French control of Dahomey introduced too potent a factor for the British government to fail to act. The governor of Lagos was given authority to show the flag in Yorubaland, to persuade the chiefs to sign treaties that would enable Britain to intervene if it became necessary. Exhausted by the wars, with government often in chaos and security destroyed, most ordinary Yoruba welcomed the appearance of British authority, in which attitude they were encouraged by African missionaries.

The main exception was the Ijebu, who straddled the most important road from Lagos to Ibadan and the interior and whose ruler had excluded the missionaries from his kingdom. Ijebu resistance, however, was quickly reduced by a military expedition. A minor revolt in Oyo in 1895 was similarly dealt with. To protect their interests the British stationed garrisons in several Yoruba towns; it did not need a declaration of protectorate or of colonial status to ensure that British interests were thus safeguarded. Moreover, with the British presence now firmly established, interference with trade almost ceased: trade in Lagos rose by more than 50 percent during the next four years and the revenues of the colony nearly trebled.

By the late 1890s it was clear that most British inhibitions over colonial acquisition had been discarded. The change was marked by the retirement of Gladstone, his replacement by Rosebery, a declared imperialist, and then by the advent of the leader of the imperialist lobby, Joseph Chamberlain, as colonial secretary. A new era of unashamed and positive imperialism opened, and its effects were quickly visible in the Niger territories. On the constructive side, plans were made for the construction of a deep-water harbor in Lagos and the undertaking of a survey for a railway from Lagos to Ibadan. Moreover, since imperialists were now in office in Whitehall, the threats from the French were taken more seriously and the expansionist ambitions of officials in Lagos given greater support.

In the circumstances, the changed approach was necessary, for the French had again begun to put pressure on the company's territories by moving into Borgu and leaving garrisons in its towns. The French object was to occupy the bend of the Niger, from where they could penetrate into the northern Fulani empire. When the Royal Niger Company tried to forestall the French plans by employing Frederick Lugard to make treaties with the Fulani emirs, the French made it plain that paper agreements would not be acknowledged as an equal claim to that presented by the presence of soldiers.

At this point, Chamberlain revealed the new temper of the British government: he commissioned Lugard to raise a British African army capable of resisting French expansion. Thus the British government had completely reversed its former attitude toward colonization; it was now financing operations designed to extend British territories and to protect the interests of a commercial company. One corollary was obvious: as the British became more active officially, the company, the main purpose of which had been to relieve the government of just such responsibility, began to live on borrowed time.

As Lugard advanced with his new forces into Borgu, it seemed that war with the French was possible, especially since at the same time British and French forces were facing each other at Fashoda on the Nile, while British and Boer armies were approaching war in South Africa. However, if the British were prepared to risk war with the French, they certainly were not willing to tolerate obstruction from Africans. Thus continued resistance to European trade by the ruler of Benin, resistance that involved the killing of British officials and of African militia, was met by a military expedition against the kingdom, its defeat, and the now customary exile of its king. Further campaigns, this time undertaken by the company, brought Nupe and Ilorin to the British heel. Consequently, only Iboland and the north remained to be brought under some form of British administration.

The armed intervention of Lugard did not, in the end, precipitate war between France and Britain. As at Fashoda, negotiation was chosen as an alternative to a trial of military strength. In 1898 an agreement was concluded between the two countries that defined their respective boundaries in west Africa. Borgu was divided between them. The agreement appeared to recognize the paramount position France had gained in the region through its more consistently aggressive policies (the extent of its territories far exceeded that of Britain or Germany, France's only two rivals). Yet appearances were illusory: by the treaty Britain carefully protected the commercial interests of its west African traders by protecting all the recently acquired territories that had expanded the areas of current trading activities and provided opportunities for the future. France might have secured the larger territories, but Britain had many more people who would buy and sell within those areas it was agreed the British should control.

The developments of 1899 were inevitable: the Niger Company surrendered its charter to the crown. Then, in 1900, the government took over the administration of all company lands. Territories in the south were added to the Niger Coast Protectorate to form the Protectorate of Southern Nigeria; those for which the company had made treaties with northern rulers were formed into the Protectorate of Northern Nigeria; Lagos remained a colony; treaty obligations bound the Yoruba states.

To some extent the proclamation of these protectorates was

a huge bluff. As we have seen, certain states in the south had been invaded by British forces and could be considered to be conquered territories, but these states did not include much of the land designated as lying within protectorates. In particular, the lands of the Ibo and huge areas of the northern empires were far from being under de facto British control. The bluff could only succeed if the British government proved willing to supply the money and arms to force the "free" territories into accepting British rule. However, since Chamberlain was now at the helm and his country was seized by a wave of hysterical jingoism in the midst of the Boer War, the government was prepared to provide the means if the officials sent to administer the territories proved sufficiently insistent.

When Ralph Moor, the man who had deported Nana of the Itsekiri in Macdonald's absence, was made high commissioner of the southern protectorate, and Lugard of the northern, it seemed likely that aggressive attitudes would be exhibited within the territories, though the two protectorates posed very different problems of administration. The northern was more than twice the size of the southern; its communications were rudimentary; and its great Fulani empire, based on Sokoto and Gwandu, formed the second largest African state south of the Sahara. To the east the rival Bornu empire was almost as large.

Many of the Fulani emirs had signed treaties with the Royal Niger Company, the authority of which was now taken over by the protectorate, but the company had exercised hardly any power over the emirates. It was a vastly different proposition to claim that all emirs should be subject to British authority. Moreover, the fragility of communications and the long delays frequently experienced meant that British representatives would have to be cautious; in the event of trouble they could not expect to secure reinforcements quickly. The death of Charles Gordon in Khartoum was sufficient example of the dangers faced by Europeans who antagonized the inhabitants they claimed as subjects. Above all, northern Nigeria had very little economic activity on which British officials could count to supply revenues to pay for their administration. The height of the trans-Saharan trade had probably been reached around 1875; since then it had declined. Internal trade still continued, both across the Sahara and to the south, but it was hardly of a nature to produce revenue from duties. Moreover, since there was no sea coast, the usual colonial revenues accruing from customs duties were also unavailable.

In the southern protectorate the situation was vastly different. The growth of the palm-oil trade had been sufficient to attract European merchants for some seventy years. Lagos and the delta ports offered a rich harvest in customs dues. Throughout Yorubaland and Iboland market economies had formed the keystone of social life for centuries. The inhabitants were highly individualistic, competitive, commercially minded. They could be expected to seize eagerly any new opportunities to produce or market that the British administration might offer. It could therefore be anticipated that expanding revenues would be available to the administration of the southern protectorate for the future.

The contrast between conditions in the two protectorates might have been expected to provoke thought and discussion in British governing circles. It did not do so; the two areas were left to work out their salvation separately, except that the south was expected to help to pay for northern deficits. In any case, at first both faced a similar problem: establishing authority. In the north some emirs were prepared to welcome the suzerainty claimed by Lugard in return for his support. In Bornu, which by the Anglo-French convention of 1898 had been divided between France, Britain, and Germany, a French invasion, interference with the ruling family, and demands for an indemnity provided an opportunity for Britain to act the role of protector, supporting the ruler in Maiduguri with a garrison on condition that he accept British authority.

The Royal Niger Company had already defeated the emirs of Nupe and Ilorin and, aided by a government subsidy, established the West African Frontier Force; indeed, it had been the existence of this military unit that had strengthened the company's hand in negotiations with the French when the northern and western boundaries were agreed in 1898. Once the protectorate was established, the force could be used by Lugard, and despite Colonial Office misgivings and the small numbers at his command, Lugard determined to use military force to impose his fiat on the whole of the north. It took him all of his first administration, 1900–1906, to compel the emirs to bow to British authority or to replace recalcitrant rulers by rivals of a more subservient nature. But in 1900 British authority in northern Nigeria was a fact.

In the south, theoretically, the Oil Rivers Protectorate, proclaimed in 1885, which became the Niger Coast Protectorate eight years later, stretched as far as the Benue, but for many years little British authority existed over large areas of it. We have seen how British gunboats were used to destroy the independence of the delta states, where most of the external trade was conducted, but although frequent attempts were made to break the power of the trading communities along the Niger, the main producers in the scores of Ibo villages remained for long out of reach of the British authorities. The new protectorate government of 1900 had to penetrate deep into Iboland before it could exert its authority among these economically important communities.

The main difficulty faced by the British in the southern protectorate was the absence of powerful kings and chiefs among the Ibo, the Ibibio, and neighboring communities. In Yorubaland it was possible to undertake some form of negotiation with a leader who could represent his people. Even in

the north negotiation or intrigue played some minor role, alongside threats or actual force. But, as we have seen, the Ibo were a village people; the village, or group of villages, formed the political unit. Large centralized states did not exist. No one could therefore negotiate on behalf of any considerable number of people.

The Aro, the main traders, represented a particular case in point. They were considered by the British to form a monopolistic element obstructing the trade routes to the interior. At the end of 1901 an expedition of nearly two thousand men was sent to crush them. It succeeded in its main purpose—in fact, it destroyed the Aro Chukwu oracle, the single centripetal influence among the Ibo—but victory was not succeeded by the anticipated results. The oil-producing villagers did not think that they had been liberated from oppressors, as the British had assumed would be the case. Rather, they resented the intrusion of Europeans into their affairs, and it soon became obvious that the imposition of the degree of authority required if there was to be a real administration in the area would require the use of military forces throughout the area. Nothing short of force would bring the villagers to accept the British as their rulers. The process took many years to complete, in some of the more remote areas only being completed by the outbreak of World War I.

The power of Benin had been destroyed in 1897 when its opposition to British traders, its refusal to abolish human sacrifice, and its killing of a British mission had been punished by a joint military and naval expedition. The city was burned, the oba deported, and many of the famous bronze treasures taken from the palace. Thus the eastern areas on both sides of the Niger were brought under British control.

During this period of about twenty years, a decade on each side of the turn of the century, Britain, through the company, its consuls, and then the protectorates, imposed its authority on almost all the territory now within the frontiers of Nigeria.

Britain accomplished the task through a combination of diplomacy, political and commercial intrigue, and force of arms; it was the latter weapon that was decisive. Throughout the period the ability of the British to call on the services of the navy or to mount military attacks lay behind all other methods of enforcing authority.

The major factor in Britain's military superiority was the new firepower it had acquired as its manufactures became increasingly sophisticated. Often the African armies defeated during these campaigns outnumbered the British forces by as much as ten to one. Very few Europeans were used in the British forces, usually no more than a handful of officers leading several hundred African soldiers, but the soldiers in the British armies had modern weapons, particularly the Maxim gun. The navy had its shells, the army its cannon, either of which could reduce mud-hut villages to shambles within a few minutes. The African forces were usually fighting with antiquated firearms imported from Europe many years earlier, for the import of arms had been forbidden at the time of the Berlin conference in 1885. To use these obsolete rifles or the traditional cavalry against the repeater-action weapons of the British armies invited mass slaughter. Given agriculture-based societies, living in mud-walled huts, sometimes within mud-walled towns, facing the massive resources of the greatest industrial empire the world had ever known, it was not surprising that it required only a tiny portion of those resources to destroy African resistance, though it took many years before resistance was finally overcome in every part of the huge country.

One significant feature of African attitudes at that time is revealed by the dependence of the British armies on the recruitment of African troops. It might be supposed that Africans would not be prepared to fight against their fellow countrymen. But it was not their fellow countrymen against whom they were fighting. The concept of belonging to a country was entirely European, alien. Africans did not regard the white men as being more alien than the citizens of rival states, towns, or villages. Thus the intervention of the white men was seen as nothing more than a new—and often welcome—factor in their traditional intercommunal conflicts. The notion of nationalism was rare and weak. It may have been present in a few west African societies, perhaps among the Ashanti and in Dahomey; it was almost totally absent in Nigeria. There was some fear that the new foreigners might undermine Islam in the north or traditional cults and customs elsewhere, but when it became clear that they did not intend to do so, resistance usually quickly crumbled. When the Europeans wished to crush a state, there were always Africans from opposing societies ready to assist in terminating the resistance of their rivals.

Yet though in the decade following the opening of the century most of the inhabitants of west Africa submitted to European authority, the problems facing European administrators were not solved. European officers and African troops might impose and maintain European power, but the issue of how government was to be organized and staffed remained to be solved.

To a considerable degree the solution was determined by manpower, as was foreshadowed to some extent during the military operations. Where military forces were scarce, as in most of the Yoruba and northern campaigns, every opportunity was taken to preserve the authority of existing rulers, or at least to choose a successor from the ruling family. Thus, defeat of the Ijebu was followed by confirmation of the ruling oba; the Egba and Ibadan retained their local forms of government; Zaria accepted Lugard's terms; after occupying Sokoto, Lugard quickly installed another emir. Even in Benin and the east attempts were made, following the military campaigns, to identify new rulers.

In each case the object was to preserve a local form of authority that could be used under British direction, for the British administration did not have a tithe of the personnel that would have been needed to govern directly. The British, therefore, had no alternative but to adopt the policy that has come to be known as "indirect rule." Indirect rule took various forms in different parts of west Africa, according to local circumstances and the methods by which the people had been brought under British authority. But essentially it was based on the impossibility of governing any substantial area of the region without local help. It was vital to secure the support of individuals and groups in as many areas as possible in order to use their services to sustain the administration.

Superior firepower had imposed British authority over Nigerian societies; it would require much greater thought and skill to apply that authority to the organization of a colonial society.

10

BRITISH ADMINISTRATION

THE PARTITION of west Africa among the European imperial powers was part of a wider movement that placed almost the whole continent under European rule at about the same time. Much of South Africa had been governed by Europeans for many years. The original Dutch settlement of the seventeenth century had progressively extended its frontiers; from the beginning of the nineteenth century Britain had possession of South Africa and later added Natal to its Cape colony. The Portuguese had been on the west and east coasts since the fifteenth and early sixteenth centuries. The French had seized Algeria in 1830 and pushed their way up the Senegal River. A few coastal stations were occupied by France, Portugal, and Britain. The rest of the continent was ruled by Africans. This was the position in 1880; twenty years later, with the exceptions of Ethiopia, Liberia, and Morocco, the whole continent was under the government of Europeans: Britain, France, Germany, Belgium, Portugal, Spain, and Italy.

The explosion of European industrialism had burst on Africa, dividing its lands and peoples haphazardly according to Europe's ambitions and the relative strength of its major states. Apart from the gold and diamonds of South Africa, the rubber of the Congo, and the crucial strategic location of Egypt, there was little important economic advantage to be gained from the seizure of these lands, but at the end of the nineteenth century power in Europe demanded the possession of an empire and Africa was the last of the continents available for colonization.

The partition arranged by the Europeans paid scant attention to the realities of African life. As we have seen in west Africa, the frontiers frequently were decided by the military maneuvers of European armies. They cut through established African communities, ignored geographic factors, and divided economic units. In west Africa the only colonial territory created by the Europeans that had existed as any kind of political unit before colonization was Dahomey, and even its boundaries did not coincide with those drawn by the French, British, and Germans.

The two Nigerian protectorates and the colony of Lagos thus represented an example of what was happening throughout the continent. The British, long before the days of experienced social analysts or anthropologists, tended to regard all African societies alike. Some of the earlier "ruffians" in the delta, despite their ruthlessness, and "ungentlemanly behaviour," had known the Africans they dealt with personally. Some of the educated Africans, in church, commerce, and government service—particularly those in Yorubaland influenced by the Sierra Leone immigrants—had been accustomed to social contact with Europeans. But the days of the delta "ruffians" had given way to more sophisticated commercial organization, and the educated Africans quickly lost influence once the imperial era opened. Europe adopted a new arrogance toward Africans, reflected in church, business, and government. The European administrators who were now recruited to the service of the protectorates assumed a superiority that, in place of the partnership that had existed during much of the nineteenth century, *gave* them the right to rule.

Thus when the Colonial Office took responsibility for the whole of Nigeria in 1900, no one realized the significance of the act. Two years earlier a Niger committee, consisting of Lord Selborne, the colonial under-secretary, as chairman, and representatives of the company, Goldie, the Foreign Office, and the Colonial Office, together with the governor of Lagos and the commissioner of the coastal protectorate, had been set up and had recommended that existing African states, with their officials, should be employed as the bases of the new administrative structure. This system would overcome the problem of shortage of trained personnel and would limit expenses, but it was based on the assumption that Nigerian societies—the Yoruba urban kingdoms, the Fulani-governed emirates, the pagan communities such as the Tiv, the village units of the Ibo, as well as the commercial ports of the delta, and the mixed society of Lagos—could all be fitted into a single pattern. As we have seen, differences within these societies, in addition to those between them, had always been deep. To assume that they could simply be thrown together and governed under one policy revealed a total lack of insight into the realities.

It is important to examine and understand the attitude of the British rulers, for it has been a major factor in all subsequent developments in Nigeria. The initial absence of knowledge about the complex nature of the societies in Nigeria meant that colonial rule was imposed without any understanding of its implications, any vision as to its consequences, or any plan for the future of its people. Therefore policy had to be devised ad hoc by the men on the spot, making decisions in the light of current circumstances and according to their own personal attitudes. As we shall see, despite the fact that British rule started from the assumption that a single basic principle could be applied to the whole country, differing conditions, along with the contrasting personalities and preconceptions of those in authority, produced deeper gulfs between different parts of the country than any that had ever previously existed. The consequences are visible today.

The most important single social factor to result from the imposition of colonial rule was the breach between Europeans and the African elite. For most of the nineteenth century it had been a primary aim of Britain, expressed through missionary work and government, to create a Europeanized African middle class. Bishop Crowther was only the most distinguished of many African clergy. Africans had taken part not only in their own commercial operations but within European firms; before the middle of the century they had been included in governmental councils and employed in government institutions. Social contact between Europeans and Africans therefore had become customary, if never widespread.

Toward the end of the century relations began to change. White clergy became increasingly hostile to the appointment of Africans to posts of responsibility—a change in relationship that led to African moves to create their own separate churches. Commercial firms brought out Europeans rather than appoint Africans to higher offices. In government the concept of partnership was replaced by that of ruler and ruled. Not the least important reason for this changed relationship was the improvement in Europeans' health conditions. At the end of the century mosquito-control was instituted effectively for the first time. European officers were therefore enabled to bring out their wives; the appearance of white women had the same effect as elsewhere in Africa: it increased the tendency toward segregation. The wives wanted to live something approximating European life, so their houses were built outside the towns or villages, usually on airy hillsides, where all their neighbors were also European. Social contact between black and white therefore declined, and residential segregation became the standard pattern. The psychological consequences of this change and their political influence cannot be specifically measured, but everyone in Africa was, and is, aware of them.

The division of the country from the start of the twentieth century into three separate administrative units—northern and southern protectorates and Lagos—to some extent modified the impact of the breach in the partnership between educated African and European that had been characteristic of the nineteenth century. There were major contrasts between the three areas and in their administration, as well as deep differences within each of them. Thus no concept of united opposition to the imposition of British rule could emerge, even if the separate states and communities had been prepared to forget their histories and unite against a common foe. Such a vision of common destiny was only likely to appear among the elite, for the mass of people simply regarded European rule as one more in the line of imperial regimes demanding obedience and taxes from its component communities. However, the educated Africans were divided between the three units of government and found that the attitude of each differed in important respects.

It was in Lagos and Yorubaland that in the early years of the century educated Africans retained the highest degree of their former influence, and, of course, it was there that they were most numerous. During the period in which the British consul, after displaying British power in a tour in 1893, was making treaties with the Yoruba states, there were sufficient educated Africans to understand fully British policy and motives and to negotiate with equal skill. The African leaders were therefore able to retain a considerable degree of internal autonomy, which allowed them to retain much of their former position. Indeed, with British authority firmly behind them, there were some who found it possible to increase their influence. In the Egba state, for instance, the aleke was able to claim the powers of a king, despite traditional Egba republicanism, because British rule presupposed that each community must have a chief with whom Britain could deal. In fact, on two occasions, in 1901 and 1903, British troops helped the aleke to suppress revolts against his rule.

This continuation of a measure of partnership between the British consul in Lagos and the Yoruba also facilitated the replacement, without serious economic dislocation, of many traditional trading routes through Yorubaland by a railroad. The railway from Lagos to Ibadan, which was completed in 1900, could have fatally undermined Yoruba states by removing their revenues, which depended on duties imposed on trade passing through their territories. Many British traders, indeed, hoped that the coming of the railway would be used for just this purpose, for they aimed to remove the taxes that were imposed on them. But the consul had no intention of allowing the states to collapse, and for his pains in negotiating constructively with their rulers he incurred the hostility of many traders.

The consul, William MacGregor, remained on easy social terms with the African elite, several of whom he appointed to government office and to the advisory Lagos legislative council. Consequently, it is clear that his interpretation of indirect rule, through African states, their rulers and officials, had a liberal strain that retained some sympathy among educated Africans. MacGregor's objective was to extend this enlightened attitude to the whole country by means of the railway, which he expected to be extended beyond Ibadan into the northern territories and to be the economic spine around which to build a body of civilized administration.

MacGregor's policies, however, were the exception; they were certainly not approved in the neighboring southern protectorate, where military force, which had destroyed Benin and gradually crushed Ibo resistance, characterized the administration. The same Ralph Moor who had invaded the Itsekiri country to destroy their middlemen role and to exile Nana was commissioner, and Moor used military forces to crush the Aro and gradually occupy Iboland. On the coast the kingship and house system was too strong to destroy, while the educated community in Calabar and other coastal towns was generally prepared to work with the commissioner in order to secure some benefits for themselves. But in the interior, where the British mistakenly assumed social organization to resemble that of the coast, attempts to rule through appointed chiefs, to support Africans favorable to the administration, and to create courts under such arbitrarily selected people resulted in strong resentment. Although superficially Moor's policy was commensurate with "indirect rule," in practice it involved the imposition of British authority through African agents who would cooperate with the commissioner's administration. Inevitably, the new administration challenged the established systems of authority and was bitterly resented by those who had been accustomed to share in the decision-making, as well as by the Lagos elite, who foresaw, with foreboding, the imposition of an authoritarian regime in neighboring territories.

By 1906, however, the tension between Lagos and the southern protectorate was bridged by amalgamating the two as the Colony and Protectorate of Southern Nigeria; Lagos was recognized as the administrative capital. The legislative council, composed of ten government officials and three European and three African representatives of non-official communities, became responsible for legislation and taxation. Moreover, though the small representation of Africans, in proportion to their number, quickly became a focus of protests, the amalgamation was seen as a means to strengthen southern ambitions by extending the south's influence to the north and thus bringing the whole country within its form of administration.

Any expectation that this ambition might be realized would

have been abandoned if the southerners had been aware of the caliber of the man in charge of the north and of the strength of the system that he was building between 1900 and 1906. Frederick Lugard had to face the same basic problems that beset the south—lack of trained personnel, small revenues, an absence of specific directions from Whitehall—but he also had a problem that hardly applied to the south: he had very little trade or cash production and no ports to provide him with sources of taxation the growth of which would enable him to increase his revenues. Thus Lugard really had no choice but to rely on indigenous rulers. If he had had the greater diplomatic skill and understanding of a MacGregor, Lugard might have saved himself the extra expense he incurred by his military methods. Yet indirect rule was always Lugard's first choice. He had already demonstrated his belief in the method in Uganda; northern Nigeria offered him still greater opportunities.

By 1900 the Fulani emirates, which had now been in existence for almost a century, had become feudal oligarchies governing their Hausa subjects, although a considerable amount of intermarriage had taken place and was to continue. Indeed, though most of the ideals expressed in Fodio's jihad had been laid to rest, its administrative structure remained: each emir had a bureaucracy, founded on a common adherence to Islam, responsible for the collection of taxes, the maintenance of order, and the administration of justice. Lugard was thus presented with a comparatively well-established structure that he had only to convert to his own purposes. His policy, therefore, was to impose his authority on all the emirs, coercing with military force those who resisted, and then to use their systems of administration and their officials as agents of Britain.

A British resident was stationed in each emir's court, but he interfered only to a minimal degree, unless he happened to be an enthusiast, as sometimes occurred. Muslim law and its courts were retained, but the complicated system of taxation was reduced to a single tax on villages. The tax was still collected by the same officials, though, and all of it was paid into the emirs' treasuries. Once it was in the treasury, at first a quarter and later a half was transmitted to the central treasury of the protectorate to finance projects concerning the whole region—agricultural schemes, health facilities, or railways—and the general expenses of the British administration.

In effect, British rule helped to perpetuate the power of the emirs. To many inhabitants it simply appeared that Lugard had assumed the role previously played by the most powerful emir—a man such as Bello, for instance—and was claiming obedience and dues from tributary states. But the power of Britain that Lugard represented was far greater than that of any former overlord, and it was concentrated on the British-stabilized Islamic feudal hierarchies. Nor, in contrast to the south, were there many counter-influences to this ossification of the power structure. There was a little Christian influence from the CMS mission, but it was limited, and the British administration deliberately prevented it from expanding, for Lugard did not want any potentially subversive influences to undermine the admirable status quo. The trans-Saharan trade had sharply declined during the later years of the nineteenth century, thus tending to isolate Fulani society from modern Islamic ideas, as well as reducing its revenues. Finally, the trade that used the main Niger as its channel was insignificant compared with that on the southern reaches of the river.

Other societies than the Fulani emirates existed within the northern protectorate: many pagan societies and a few Christian communities, where Fulani rule either did not extend or was not in full control. In these areas, Lugard's policy was not so successful, but these areas were the exception: the main character of the protectorate was formed by the emirates and the partnership entered into with them by British rulers.

Many men from Britain during the nineteenth century were attracted to Africa as a refuge from the destruction of traditional rural aristocratic values by the insistent clamor of individualism, competitiveness, and populism associated with industrial society of Europe. After the turn of the twentieth century northern Nigeria became the natural haven for such men. There they found an aristocracy they could identify, rooted in a religion simpler, more manly, and much less individualistic than Christianity had become under the influence of industrial capitalism. Life could be lived in a pastoral atmosphere, for though there were markets and much local commerce, it was confined to the lower orders, who could be ignored except as their liability to pay tax arose. In the north there was little of the commercialism among rulers notorious in the south. Moreover, as the emirs continued to administer their territories while the residents simply advised them and assessed taxes (and therefore remained influential over their policies), the young British men appointed to positions of authority could become almost independent of the commissioner's control. They knew their districts, emirs, and bureaucrats; they could and did build little empires for themselves. Thus the scope for men who wished to exert their own initiative rather than accept a niche in the increasingly depersonalized industrial system of Europe seemed almost unlimited.

A mystique about northern life and indirect rule consequently arose among many administrators who served there. Indeed, it became a kind of northern patriotism and was wedded to the ambition of extending northern government to the south, an ambition that complemented that of southerners in the reverse direction. It should be noted that this conception of rivalry between north and south Nigeria was a boon to the British, who in any case originally divided the country between these two regions.

The rivalry between northern and southern administrations was revealed over a very practical issue. In the early years of the imperial period railway building was seen as one of the most common methods for economic development, one that was used, of course, much more extensively than just within empires; British-built railroads supplied a framework on which economic power extended over the six continents. It was natural, therefore, that a method that brought such rich dividends elsewhere should be employed in African territories under British rule. In Africa railways were built up the Nile, across the Cape into Natal and the Transvaal, from the Indian Ocean to Lake Victoria, and from the west coast into the hinterlands. Disputes over their routes, finances, and tariffs form an important aspect of colonial history.

In Nigeria the first railway was built from Lagos to Ibadan, tapping the markets of the Yoruba towns and stimulating overseas trade in Lagos. It was expected that, once it reached Ibadan, the track would then be extended northward to cross the Niger and be used by the commerce of the huge northern protectorate. Plans were actually accepted for the track's extension as far as Ilorin. But then the northern commissioner, successor to Lugard, proposed that the north should have its own railway, from Kano to the Niger. This new railroad would enable northerners to import and export produce by rail and river, bypassing Lagos, which would consequently lose the anticipated customs revenues. To add insult to injury, because of the north's scanty revenues, a loan was raised for the project against the security of southern revenues.

As the railroad quarrel became more intense, rivalry between north and south became acute, marked by contempt among northern administrators for the commercialism of the south and derision among southerners for the ossified feudalism of the north. But however much the northerners might despise southern commerce, they had to rely on it to subsidize their own activities. From the first year of the protectorates the south was called on to contribute to northern finances.

For the first three years the annual subsidy amounted to some $80,000; after 1906 the sum more than doubled. Yet this sum could do no more than marginally help fill the yawning northern deficit. The imperial government had to bear the major burden and provided a grant-in-aid, which rose from $201,400 in 1900 to $972,000 four years later and had only declined to $660,000 by the end of the decade.

The effect of such government expenditure in a dependent territory was to raise severe Treasury criticism, and this criticism in turn induced the Colonial Office to revive consideration of the proposal to create a united Nigerian administration in order to pool revenues and costs. There were many arguments in favor of the idea. Southern trade was booming; between 1906 and 1912 imports, exports, and revenues all doubled. Amalgamation would allow the surpluses acquired in the south to be used in the north, thus reducing British Treasury responsibility. Railway building was well under way: the line from Lagos was extended to Ilorin and then to Jebba on the Niger; it was then taken on to the Kaduna, Zaria, Kano, and Nguru. The tin mines in the Bauchi area were now connected to the main line. The obvious next step was to build a track into Iboland, to the heart of the oil trade, and to utilize the coal discovered in the same area. (In fact, this line was not completed until 1926.) Coordinated planning of such expensive projects would obviously be assisted by amalgamating the two protectorates.

However, once again an enormously significant policy was undertaken without recognition of the issues involved or any vision as to future objectives. It was sufficient in Whitehall that the scheme seemed to make good financial sense, irrespective of its impact on the many millions of people involved. The contrast between northern and southern administrations had been so sharp that one might have assumed that someone in the Colonial Office would have asked which administration was to be applied in the amalgamated state. Was the resident system of advising and supporting feudal rulers while using their officials to be extended from the north to the south? Or were the more commercial considerations prevalent in the southern protectorate to be applied to the north? What would be the effect of uniting the Fulani emirates—with their comparatively static, traditionalist outlook—with the thrusting, competitive, individualistic society of the south, now acquiring knowledge from a growing number of mission schools, which were making available an expanding clerical class. How would societies that only a few years earlier had been rival and often hostile states live together under one administration? Should they form a single nation? If so, how could a single allegiance be created? In any case, what was the central objective of British policy? Was it to build an empire permanently subordinate to Britain, to act as a trustee for some shadowy African future, or to encourage a national spirit leading to ultimate self-government? Not only did no one appear to know the answers to such questions, but the questions do not seem to have been asked.

The early future was determined in much the same way as it had been in the first protectorate days. When Lugard was sent back to Nigeria to effect the amalgamation, it was certain that he would try to apply the policy that he had instituted in the north and that he believed in as a basic principle of government for Africa. He appears to have acquired not only a puritanical abhorrence for the revenues taken in the south from the taxes on alcohol but an eighteenth-century aristocratic distaste for all commercial activity. He consequently condemned the southern administration for its encouragement of economic life and commerce and contrasted it with the purely administrative function of government in the north. His antipathy to educated Africans, whom he sneeringly described as "trousered blacks," exposed his unwillingness to conceive of his mission as one of building a modernized, self-governing state.

The result of these attitudes was that Lugard proposed to the Colonial Office a scheme that kept the northern administration virtually entire and concentrated on securing the finances needed from the south to sustain the north. It is significant that the only departments Lugard proposed should be fully merged were those for railways, marine, and customs—all mergers designed to make southern commercial enterprise pay for the northern structure. In other fields of government, such as posts and telegraphs, medicine, and the West African Frontier Force, separate southern and northern departments would be preserved, but with a joint head. Over the whole administration there would be a governor-general, but the separate administrations would continue under him, and each region would be responsible for its budgetary contribution to the central revenues.

Lugard's antagonism to the south was best illustrated in the reforms he proposed in its administration. He obviously believed that the nearer the south came to the practices of the north, the better it would be governed. For instance, he thought it would be possible to find and train chiefs who could be made into the feudal autocrats whom he had been accustomed to use in the north. He suggested that the region be divided into provinces, with district officers exercising judicial and executive powers, as was customary in the north. He believed that the spread of British forms of law, many of which were being gradually accepted in the south, should be halted, for the introduction of British common law indicated, Lugard thought, a step toward a modernized and Europeanized society.

Above all, Lugard criticized Lagos. In particular, he thought the city should never become the capital of Nigeria, for since it was inhabited by so many Africans, it would be impossible to apply a policy of segregation! Instead, Lugard proposed that Lagos should be separated from the southern region and administered on its own—an obvious attempt to limit its power. Lugard's proposal for Lagos would enable him to reduce the influence of the legislative council so that it would legislate only for the city. As the council represented the embryo of a genuinely representative system, with African members having powers to make laws for the Yoruba territories as well as for Lagos, this attack was a blow not only to Lagos itself but to the whole concept of democratic progress. It is significant of Lugard's outlook that he proposed a substitute Nigerian Council, to which prominent men would be nominated by the government. The Nigerian Council would be confined to a purely advisory function and then allowed to sit for three days each year—scarcely an important body.

In 1914 Lugard's ideas prevailed in the Colonial Office. All his proposals were implemented, and the two protectorates were amalgamated along almost identical lines to those he had suggested. The northern conception of the form and purpose of British rule emerged victorious. Henceforth, the objective was to be neither the nineteenth-century ideal of British-African partnership in modernizing, educational, and missionary endeavor, nor the active encouragement of a capitalistic modernizing process, nor yet the building of a new nation-state. Rather, the objective was to preserve traditional aristocratic feudalism where it existed, to reduce the power of southern states, to avoid having the commercial entrepôt of Lagos become the focus of Nigerian society, and to halt the spread of British practices except where they were conducted by British officers (where aristocratic chiefs were not visible, they had to be found).

Thus, for the first time in history, a country called Nigeria was created—the name had been suggested by Lugard's wife in 1897—composed of assorted elements, including Muslim feudal emirates, pagan states, Christianized states, large market and port towns, and many interlaced villages and small, noncentralized communities. Many of these elements had a history of hostility to each other, sometimes to the point of warfare. There was little of common language, religion, tradition, or custom. The separate units had been joined to save Britain expense and were to be governed under a system based on one special set of customs by a man who believed in the traditional aristocratic virtues rather than the influence of modernization.

The most profound and far-reaching aspect of the policy adopted in 1914 was the continued separation of north and south. Instead of having the two sets of societies interact—which would have resulted from full amalgamation—they were to be deliberately kept apart, thus continuing the isolation of the north from the impact of southern economic activity, educational progress, and Christian influence. Moreover, the imposition of British rule in the north had increased the tendency, already visible toward the end of the nineteenth century, of Nigerian Muslim society to lose its contact with the rest of Islam, for British rule hardly encouraged expansion of the trans-Saharan trade, which had been the main channel of communication. In fact, the north was deliberately kept in an isolated, semi-feudal state, while many of the modernizing influences of the south were purposely retarded. Although the south could not be long insulated from outside influences because of its commercial position, the continued division of the country largely prevented these influences from being transmitted to the north. Meanwhile, the peoples of north and south, who had never known each other intimately, remained separate, although nominally under the same government.

The divisive influences of Lugard's scheme also affected societies within the two protectorates. The bolstering of traditional rulers by residents may have been applicable to Fulani emirs; it was much less suitable for the pagan societies on the fringes of or outside the area of Fulani domination. In such societies, because the need to protect Muslim society did not apply, Christian missionary work was permitted, and as a result of the effects of mission schools, many of the outlying-area people became well educated and progressively minded. Thus a social division grew within the north itself. Later, too, since education within the Muslim areas was almost entirely confined to Islamic schools, and since these schools did not prepare their pupils for modern professions, when the administration began recruiting local staff, when postal, telegraphic, and railway services needed workers, and when commercial firms required clerks, the workers had to be drawn from the south or from the non-Muslim northern population. Consequently, northern Muslim society was by this means again insulated from modern trends and separated from the rest of Nigerian society.

In the south the new system intensified centrifugal tendencies. Among the Yoruba the causes and outcome of nineteenth-century civil strife were ignored. In the obsession for discovering autocratic chiefs on whom to base the administration, the British tried to return to eighteenth-century conditions. In particular, they attempted to restore the supremacy of Oyo, opposition to which had been a principal cause of the civil wars. Moreover, Ibadan and Abeokuta, which had, in their different ways, replaced Oyo as centers of commercial and political power, were strongly influenced by the new educated class. As a result, if British administration was to be based on traditionalism, the modern towns would have to be subordinated to the older, more conservative authority of Oyo, and consequently the spirit of conflict, which had died down after the nineteenth century, was revived among the Yoruba.

At the same time, lack of understanding of Yoruba political realities caused further dislocation. On the assumption that an oba in Yorubaland resembled an emir in the north, the British tried to govern by controlling the obas as they did the emirs. But the Yoruba oba was not an autocrat; he shared power with a number of chiefs and was often dependent on their approval for the maintenance of his power. When the

British tried to ensure that the chiefs selected were favorable to their policies, they found that a complex system of lineages was involved. And their subsequent attempts to bribe and bully the lineage groups so as to reward friends and punish opponents produced further confusion, resentment, and conflict.

If the policy of indirect rule imported from the north was unsuitable and often disruptive in Yorubaland, among the Ibo it was even more alien to existing political structures. The core of the Ibo system was the village assembly. It might well have been possible for imaginative, progressive British officials to adapt this popular form of government to British methods of local government; from there it might have been developed into a pyramidal structure of regional or state representative government. But Lugard's notion reigned supreme. It was therefore considered essential to discover traditional authorities among the Ibo, as elsewhere.

Lugard sent an officer from the north to make this discovery, and he identified the lineage elders as the local repository of authority, despite the fact that the elder was usually no more than the spokesman for the village meeting. The elders were therefore invested with powers of government and justice that they had never before possessed. Inevitably, therefore, they came to be regarded by the local people under their power as tyrants representing British rule rather than as representatives of their own communities. Resentment turned to anger at their activities, and whenever discontent arose, it tended to be concentrated on these "warrant chiefs."

Meanwhile, another social development was beginning to provide the means to express opposition to British policy. The Ibo soon recognized that their Yoruba neighbors possessed in European education an institution capable of offering the means to social advancement that might offset the economic problem of a dense population without substantial natural resources. At once the local strength of the Ibo village-clan system came into operation to build schools, find teachers, use the services of as many missions as would help, and thus create one of the strongest and most extensive education systems in the whole country. Eventually, the Roman Catholics emerged as the most helpful in this endeavor, thereby securing a paramount place in Ibo society, but, in any case, educational development was the product of Ibo local organization, not of the British administration. The Ibo system was to supply the kind of educated men and women who would be capable of expressing the resentments felt against the imposition on Ibo society of Lugard's ideas through the British administration. The seeds of deeply planted conflict were being sown.

Finally, there were the large coastal towns: Lagos, Calabar, Port Harcourt. At first, it appeared that the trading house heads would admirably suit the purposes of Lugard's policy. They were often autocratic and always controlled large communities of agents, workers, and followers, along with the lesser merchants who owed them obedience. Yet this was a short-term, superficial view. To a considerable extent, particularly in Lagos, the inhabitants were detribalized immigrants from many different societies. They might form enclaves among their own people in their new habitats, but they were not accustomed to the rule of house heads, whose influence had been built on commerce rather than on any kind of lineage, clan, or communal allegiance. In any case, the house system was scarcely known in Lagos, and the towns where it had become common practice, with the exception of Calabar, were declining in importance in comparison with the newer urban centers. Given these many problems, it soon became clear that the major towns of the south and east could only be satisfactorily governed by the introduction of some form of municipal government based on European models.

On almost every count, it is clear, the system of indirect rule and the form of amalgamation based on separation that accompanied it were unsatisfactory, and their application lit a set of fuses that could end only in a series of explosions that would detonate not only the accumulation of resentment against British rule but the growing suspicions, frustrations, and antagonisms of African community against African community.

In the immediate event, however, much of Lugard's objective was undermined by the outbreak of war in Europe in 1914. The involvement of Nigeria in World War I could not be avoided, and this meant that many Africans were taken out of their traditional societies and thrust into the rough experience of serving as soldiers. Traditional authority could not retain the allegiance of men who were mixing with so many different nationalities, seeing so many contrasting ways of life. As in Europe and Asia, war was bound to stimulate powerful forces of nationalism in Africa.

The fact that the German Cameroons lay along the eastern borders of Nigeria inevitably involved Nigeria in war strategy. In the first place, war brought a major shift in trading patterns. Before 1914 Germany had imported 44 percent of Nigerian exports, largely palm oil; the war first cut this trade and then transferred it to Britain, which could take all the oil Nigeria could provide, with a consequent boom in production and commerce.

Apart from certain minor disturbances, mainly in the delta, the embarrassments of Britain resulting from the exigencies of its war efforts were never used by Africans as an occasion for revolt against imperial rule. The Leninist strategy never appealed to Africans in either world war. They fought on both sides for their colonial masters; the only major revolts were those of the Afrikaner whites in South Africa.

The Nigeria Regiment served in Togoland and the Cameroons, along with French Senegalese, Gambians, Sierra Leoneans, and Gold Coasters. German resistance in Togoland was quickly suppressed, but in the Cameroons it took until

February, 1916, to defeat German forces completely. Then many Nigerians were sent to east Africa. On both sides of the continent Nigerians learned to use modern weapons; perhaps even more significantly they fought and killed Europeans: the aura of white invincibility, of inherent superiority, must have been gravely shaken.

The practical effects of the war experience were seen immediately after 1918 in the growth of nationalist sentiment and consequent actions; they will be described later. But the dislocation caused by the war also had its impact on British policy. Lugard's policy represented an attempt to reverse the conventional colonial principles that had emerged from Britain's experience in its American colonies. From the eighteenth century Britain had found that the inhabitants of its colonies, largely British or other European immigrants, demanded an increasing share in the determination of their lives. This demand had especially centered on the ancient British principle of "no taxation without consent"; in other words, if they were expected to contribute through taxation to the administration of their countries, the colonists insisted that they be allowed to participate in the process whereby the purposes for which revenues were used were decided. Following the American revolution the principle of self-determination was recognized in Britain as a first necessity of colonial government, and, reinforced by Lord Durham in his report of 1839 on the dangers of discontent in Canada, the principle was also consistent with Britain's desire to reduce the expenses of its colonial administration to a minimum.

Accordingly, as Britain began to acquire colonial territories on the coasts of west Africa during the nineteenth century, the question arose as to whether the concept of representative government, which was being applied to the white-settled colonies, was also suitable for those in Africa. The French were much more single-minded over this issue: to them, colonies were essentially an extraneous part of greater France;

they were therefore given centralized governments dependent on Paris. The British attitude was always more insular, and a deep dichotomy existed between the claims of metropolitan and local responsibilities.

From an early stage it was clear that each British colony would have a considerable degree of autonomous responsibility, varying according to local circumstances and the personalities of the officials concerned. Moreover, the acceptance of this necessity led to the creation of the kind of embryonic councils that had formed the foundations of representative institutions in the other colonies. Thus, during the middle years of the nineteenth century, executive and legislative councils were established as part of the British governmental structure in Gambia, Sierra Leone, the Gold Coast, and Lagos.

These councils did not develop along representative lines, as had those of the other colonies. They consisted of officials and certain laymen nominated by the government. It might have been expected that a representative system would have developed out of this infancy. It did not do so, first, because of the trend against the appointment of Africans to positions of responsibility that occurred toward the end of the century, and, second, because of Lugard's antipathy toward African representation. Yet even Lugard's demotion of the Lagos legislative council through his removal of its power to legislate for the territories of the hinterland could not prevent the halting progress toward representative institutions that started again after the war.

It has been suggested that the legislative council constituted in 1922 was the product of nationalist pressure, but this is unlikely, for the governor had been very scathing in his reference to nationalist activities as recently as the end of 1920. Moreover, the electoral system had been introduced for the town council of Lagos in 1920, before the nationalists had made their presence felt. However, since the legislative council was to include the first directly elected Africans in British

Africa, the new constitution certainly represented a dramatic change in the governor's sentiments toward the nationalists and from Lugard's policy. This change probably resulted from two interrelated causes. First, the war, with its propaganda about "freedom" and its conclusion in Woodrow Wilson's euphoric rhetoric about "self-determination," had affected the climate for colonial policy. And second, the changed climate of opinion had also influenced the British Parliament and governments over the need for some form of representative system in the colonies they governed. As Aneurin Bevan later told Tom Mboya of Kenya, the British representative and elective system is of such a character that pressure for representation from colonial peoples must always finally succeed, eventually approximating to representation proportional to their inhabitants.

Whatever the cause, the constitution of 1922, which introduced the legislative council, marked a new stage in Nigerian political development. The Nigerian Council, on which twelve of the forty-two members had been Africans nominated by the governor, had never been more than a phantom institution, dominated by the government, its Africans selected for their quiescence, its function purely advisory, and its meetings rare. The new council was a totally different kind of body. It was to consist of forty-six members, the governor, twenty-six officials, three members elected for Lagos and one for Calabar, together with not more than fifteen nominated members. The fact that direct elections were to be held in Lagos and Calabar was the constitution's most momentous feature. The elected members would only number four out of forty-six, but the electoral principle was being established and elections always provoke the organization of political parties. All male British subjects or protected persons possessing an annual income of at least $240 and resident for a year in either town were to be eligible to vote. The property qualification would certainly restrict the electorate in a country in which few had an income of even $60. Nevertheless, there would be an electorate, largely composed of educated Africans, to woo. It is also true that the council would only be able to legislate for the colony of Lagos and the southern protectorate; the governor would still have power to proclaim laws for the north. Yet the significance of the electoral principle outweighed all reservations: it was at the proclamation of the constitution of 1922 that modern politics were born in Nigeria.

The actual elections, which took place in 1923, 1928, and 1933, were less important than the outlet they provided for political activity. All the seats were won on each occasion by the party of Herbert Macaulay, a member of Bishop Crowther's family who had taken a leading role in nationalist criticism of the colonial government from before the war. The fact that the governor's promise that the electoral process would extend to other areas showed no sign of fulfillment provided a focus for political agitation. Yet, since the elections continued to be confined to Lagos and Calabar, most political activity remained within the two towns.

It was not, however, from Lagos and Calabar that the most serious form of protest arose; the 1922 constitution remained virtually unaltered until 1947, and normal political activity took place within it. The consequences of administrative policy continued to arouse their own quota of hostility, and the most significant element in this anger was the resentment caused by the policies applied in the east. As has been seen above, the attempted introduction of indirect rule into the societies of the Ibo and Ibibio, and particularly the powers given to warrant chiefs and native courts, were bitterly resented; indeed, the unpopularity of administrative measures was constantly reported by investigators and officials. Moreover, when, in 1926, it was decreed that a poll tax of 2.5 percent should be levied on those males who did not pay tax, hostility gathered momentum. During the process of tax assessment in the following year disturbances occurred in the Warri and Kwale districts. Armed police had to be rushed to the area. Two years later, when it was feared that the tax was going to be extended to women, resentment burst into violence while tempers were exacerbated by low produce prices. It is significant that most of the rioting occurred among women, demonstrating both their important role in production and markets and the strength of their social organization through age groups.

The 1929 violence began in the Aba and Owerri areas in the east, from where it spread to Calabar and Opobo. The violence was concentrated against administrative buildings—such as native court houses—unpopular warrant chiefs, and certain stores symbolic of the economic grievance. In December, 1929, the violence became so ferocious that the police fired on the crowd, killing thirty-two people and injuring another thirty-one. In the subsequent inquiries two African barristers were appointed to a commission studying the causes of the riots; the fact that black Africans were able to examine British officials attempting to justify their actions assuaged some African hostility toward the administration and foreshadowed a change in relations between the government and educated Africans. The whole affair conclusively proved that the administration of the east and of those western areas bordering the east would have to be drastically changed if further violence was to be avoided.

It was at this moment that Donald Cameron arrived in Nigeria from Tanganyika, where he had tried to apply Lugard's principles. He faced the much more complex problems of Nigeria. Cameron quickly recognized the dangers presented by what had become administrative protection of feudal monarchy in the north and decided to separate the northern pagan areas from the administrative policy followed in the emirates. He also saw the folly of trying to turn back history by restoring the vanished glories of Oyo and allowed

Ibadan to develop free from subservience to the older capital. Moreover, Cameron suggested that educated Africans should be included within the native authorities, thereby removing one of the main sources of political agitation.

In the east attempts had been made by the administration to secure reliable anthropological reports on which new administrative approaches could be based. As a result, it had had to be admitted that real authority was concentrated in much smaller units than had been previously recognized. Efforts therefore followed to reestablish the native authorities of the village groupings that had formed the traditional political structures. Cameron then abolished the provincial courts and reduced the power of native courts, thereby doing away with the bitter criticisms of the administration of justice that had been a major factor in popular resentment. And since he instituted a High Court to sit for the whole protectorate and allowed lawyers into the magistrates' courts, he went a long way to appease the local elite. His abolition of the system in which north and south each had a lieutenant-governor under the governor-general not only pleased educated Africans but went a little way toward reducing the separation of the two regions.

Few other changes were made in the administration of Nigeria before the end of World War II. Basically, the country remained a collection of separate communities linked together by nothing more substantial than British rule. Nevertheless, beneath the surface elements were developing that were to have an influence for change. Even though some aspects of British rule had persistently separated rather than drawn together the various communities, colonial government had in itself produced a single political unit for the first time. Although often all but invisible, an element of national identification was thereby induced. The colonial government needed to recruit clerks, teachers, entrepreneurs, clergy, doctors, and lawyers. But preparation for such jobs involved a considerable degree of detribalization, while English education provided a lingua franca. Educated Africans looked toward the central government either for their employment or for participation in decision-making—or for both. They consequently began to develop a common consciousness, irrespective of their communities or origin. Gradually, some little sense of national identity began to appear, at least among the tiny minority of educated elite.

It would be a gross exaggeration to suggest that Nigeria showed signs of becoming a modern nation-state in the period, but between the two world wars colonial government was unconsciously providing a catalyst around which resentments, ambitions, hopes, and ideas could fuse into a common, if variegated, body of opinion on the future of the country.

11

ECONOMIC UNDERCURRENTS

BENEATH the surface of administrative and political policies there always lay strong undercurrents of economic influence. Before European political control was imposed, African economies were dependent on the export of commodities the prices of which were determined by the purchasers—with a few temporary local exceptions during times of shortage—often according to powerful forces that the individual trader or agent himself could not influence. In west Africa the export of slaves and subsequently of palm oil dominated economic life; the export trade therefore had a crucial impact on political decisions and on social development.

This position was not altered by the arrival of imperial rule. Certain new economic features appeared in the African colonies, but the basic fact of economic dependence was not altered. In some ways, indeed, it was strengthened. As colonial governments were commanded by the metropolitan powers to pay their own administrative expenses, thereby encouraging the production of cash crops to provide export revenues, so not only commercial profits but government revenues themselves came to depend on prices determined outside the continent. Moreover, as political power involved control over economic legislation and regulation, colonial governments, often under orders from their own masters in European capitals, could subordinate the interests of their subjects to those of the merchants, manufacturers, and financiers of Europe.

It was no objective of colonial rule to undermine the foreign dependence of colonial economies or to replace it by independent, self-propelling economies. The only part of the African continent in which independence was tolerated was in South Africa, and there the process was accomplished only after World War II as a result of an alliance between British, U.S., and white South African industrial finance. Elsewhere, while economic activity was often stimulated, the purpose of encouragement was either to assist the economy of the imperial power, or to promote the activities of its companies, or to swell the treasuries of colonial administrations. The methods of economic stimulation therefore had to fit these purposes.

When the British government was first persuaded to use its diplomatic and military weapons in order to establish political control over Nigeria, a number of economic factors influenced the decision. It can be argued that the politico-strategic issue of preventing Germany and France from gaining ascendancy in west Africa formed the dominant influence. Yet even this issue had its economic aspect: the Germans had become Britain's primary European trading rival, and French inclination to regard their colonies as closed markets was always considered to be inimical to British interests. But whatever the importance of this inter-European rivalry, specific British economic interests also were concerned.

The partition of Africa took place during a period of falling commodity prices, and the price fall intensified the competition to secure a dominant role over the producers, middlemen, and export trade. The outcome was inevitably a drive toward monopoly, as Goldie's adventures illustrated, and monopolists usually sought their government's intervention to protect their supremacy. At the same time, depression and increasing competition were gravely threatening British exports, on which its capital accumulation and therefore its economic paramountcy had been built. The west African market had been established for several centuries; during the second part of the eighteenth century it was thought that it might be substantially expanded although the difficulties of doing so without a radical transformation of economic and political policy were not recognized. Thus the dual pressure exerted by west African merchant companies and exporting interests played an important part in converting British ministers to the new policy of imperial expansion, in the form reflected in the government's original policy of leaving administration and economic policy to Goldie's company and subsequently conducting its own administration at minimum expense.

Once the government took over responsibility for administration from the company, it acquired its own incentive to promote economic growth. Only by an expansion in cash crops, trade, and import-export activity could the colonial government create those sources of wealth able to provide it with revenue from taxation. From the turn of the century government control also coincided with increased commodity prices, and the rise in prices, with the addition of wartime stimulation, continued beyond World War I. The increase in prices naturally led to a desire on the part of British manufacturers to gain greater control of raw-material production in order to reduce costs to a minimum. The textile interests hoped to promote cotton growing within the empire, especially seeking to develop Egypt, Uganda, and west Africa for this purpose (they had, in fact, very little success in west Africa). The soap and lubricant manufacturers, led by the major firm of Lever Brothers, also sought to gain greater control over the producers. Cocoa had been introduced into west Africa during the last quarter of the nineteenth century; its cultivation spread from the Gold Coast into Yoruba areas, brought there by African clergy and merchants. Kola nut and groundnut production could be increased both for internal and export trade. Tin could be mined around Jos and coal outside Enugu. Yet all these opportunities for producing commodities not only profitable but essential to revenue collection depended on one central factor: the system of communications. If trade was to grow, communications would have to be radically reorganized and expanded.

Thus the assumption of responsibility by colonial government coincided with the need for capital expenditure on a considerable scale. However, the presence of convinced imperialists in Whitehall, led by Joseph Chamberlain, made it possible for the government to modify its traditional policies, incur expenses drawn from contributions from its own taxpayers, relax its insistence on self-sufficiency for colonial governments, and agree to invest in expenditure designed to promote economic development. The "businessmen's governments" in London were now prepared to regard the colonies, to some degree, as "undeveloped estates." And it seemed quite all right that the infrastructure for economic activity should be largely provided by government initiative, financed by taxes on existing commerce, by direct and indirect personal taxes, and by loans from Britain.

Railway and road building therefore became a feature of colonial governments during the inter-war period. Lines were built from Lagos to Ibadan and through to Kano, from Jos to the main line, from Enugu to Port Harcourt, eventually to Maiduguri. As late as 1926 the southeastern section was linked to the northern. At the beginning of the century Carter Bridge linked Lagos and Iddo Islands; Denton Bridge, Iddo and the mainland. Electric lighting was introduced to Lagos and swamp drainage begun. Meanwhile, district commissioners were using what funds they could lay their hands on to build every type of road, from the modern metaled highway to the dusty laterite track, facilitating both administrative communication and the movement of goods. Telegraphs and postal services were added to the network. In 1913 deep water berths had been opened in Lagos; thirteen years later some were opened in Apapa. It is significant that this web of communications possessed one common feature: their respective lines all took paths from areas of production to ports on the sea. In short, their object and their function was to facilitate the transport of produce from the producers to the ships that would take it abroad. The export trade was all-important to this policy, for it emphasized the dependent nature of the economy, the intensification of dependence through colonial policies, and the subordination of the interests of the indigenous inhabitants to the exigencies of a colonial economy.

One of the most important illustrations of Nigerian economic dependence and its aggravation through colonial policy was seen in 1912, when the West African Currency Board was established. It was necessary, of course, for the purposes of modern trading activities to introduce a coinage system to supplement and eventually to replace the traditional currencies of cowries, manillas, iron bars, and the like. But the currency policy adopted was based on a standard of 100 percent sterling exchange. This system meant that the currency issue must always be entirely covered by reserves, in turn implying that all imports must be paid for by current exports. In other words, internal development could never be financed by reserves, all of which were needed to support the currency, which itself must be limited to the existing reserves. So not only was the supply of money circulating within the country kept low through lack of large reserves, but it could only be increased by expanding exports at the expense of imports in order to create a "favorable balance of trade" the profits of which could be used to raise the reserves. Such a policy in a developing country must always limit domestic development and improvements in living standards—the price for attracting foreign investment through an absence of inflation.

When one thinks of a *national* economy, instead of one devoted to the welfare of the inhabitants, Nigeria certainly benefited enormously from colonial investment and guidance. The railways allowed groundnut exports from the north through Lagos to increase considerably, coal and tin to be mined successfully, and cocoa to be developed into a substantial export crop. The commercial organization that had grown from the days of slave trading through the palm-oil period could be adapted to the new needs. The overall expansion in trade can be measured by the increase in export figures: from $4.4 million in 1900, when colonial government was established, to $21.8 million in 1921, and $39.7 million in 1926.

Nor can it be denied that some advantages were gained by the local inhabitants. The main Nigerian cash crops—groundnuts, cocoa, and palm products—could be, and almost always were, cultivated alongside food plants, although the latter largely remained on a subsistence basis, and therefore the increased export trade served largely to supply many rural Nigerians with some cash. Then, despite the emphasis on exports, the railways and improved roads allowed increased internal trading. Kola nuts and palm oil, for instance, were sent to the north, which in return sent cattle to the south. Moreover, the increased revenues allowed the government to make some small provision for educational and other social amenities, although education continued to depend largely on mission efforts and never measured up to the needs of a population expanding from something over 20 million to over 30 million. Moreover, the education offered was always based on the British model—basically a literary training. No thought was given by British or Nigerians to the use of education in agriculture or technology, although it was in these pursuits that the vast majority of Nigerian children would spend their lives.

One colonial measure that had a profound effect on the future of Nigeria was the prohibition of alienation of land to Europeans outside a few coastal areas. This policy contrasted sharply with what was happening in east Africa, central Africa, and some French territories. The production of export crops could be accomplished by African farmers, but there were always voices to be heard asserting that production could be increased by using the plantation methods employed in places such as the Congo basin. Lever Brothers were trying to persuade the colonial government to allow them to buy land as early as 1907. As late as 1924 Lord Leverhulme was telling the Nigerian governor "that the African native will be happier, produce the best, and live under the larger conditions of prosperity when his labour is directed and organised by his white brother who has all these million years' start ahead of him"! But the Colonial Office stood firm. It had the example of the Congo, where Lever Brothers had vast plantations, before it. Not only had Leopold's brutal depredations in the Congo shocked the world and forced the Belgian government to take over control from their king before the outbreak of World War I, but whether it was in the Congo or in Nigeria's neighbor, the German Cameroons, or in east Africa, plantation economies always involved the colonial government in forcing its subjects to labor for companies or private European farmers. The consequent resentment and hostility shown to the government were warning enough to any government anxious to avoid the expense and trouble of military defense of its policies. Thus, in Nigeria, the expansion in output, except for the mining activities that required external capital and technology, was almost entirely a product of African enterprise. And this meant that Nigerians, once they regained control of their own government, enjoyed a great deal more scope for choice than those peoples among whom foreign farmers and plantation owners had settled.

Nevertheless, subservience remained the chief characteristic of the economy, especially during the years between the two world wars. Two major illustrations prove the point. Fluctuations in commodity prices drastically reduced national revenues; the effects of the world recession on Britain halted internal development in Nigeria and intensified the emphasis on its exports. Both features directly influenced British policies, which, during this period, seem to have exhausted their constructive progress.

Until the middle 1920s commodity prices continued to soar. Wartime shortages had produced the usual boom conditions for suppliers of raw materials; for nearly two years after the end of the war the demand for commodities continued to spiral upward as the victorious countries sought to catch up with lost years. But economies were not equipped for such a process. Low wages curtailed purchasing power, and when the workers tried to raise their standards by combination, they were met with lockouts. The boom bubble burst; what had seemed an unlimited demand for tropical products suddenly halted; prices fell. For the rest of the interwar period booms and slumps alternated, with the prices of commodities swinging up and down before descending steeply in the early thirties; no period of regularly rising prices such as that between the last years of the nineteenth century and 1920 counteracted the descending trend.

So long as prices remained high, ambitious schemes for colonial investment and development were publicly discussed in London. Once the prospects of profitability disappeared, however, interest evaporated. A few of the projects, especially railway construction, were completed, but little further serious interest in colonial development reappeared before World War II.

The second aspect of economic dependency, the impact on Nigeria of Britain's part in the world recession of the early thirties, can clearly be seen from bare statistics. Total import-export trade in Nigeria reached a figure of over $43 million in 1921, immediately after the end of the boom years. The effect of improved communications allowed this figure to rise steadily, despite fluctuations in prices and demand, until in 1929 it passed the $72 million mark. Yet in the last full year before war broke out in 1939, trade figures had fallen below the figure for 1921. Government revenues rose from $9.6 million in 1918, to $12 million in 1920, and to $19.2 million in 1925. In 1925 the population was estimated to be about 20 million; in 1938–1939, when the population had risen to around 25 million, the revenues were under $14.4 million. One example of the catastrophic price fall will suffice: in 1925 cotton farmers received three cents per pound for their product; in 1930 the price was one-half cent per pound.

Prices and revenues might fall; interest charges did not. Consequently, the cost of financing projects previously completed bore more heavily on the national economy. By the 1930s about 30 percent of the nation's revenue was being spent on interest charges and the pensions of retired government officials. Inevitably, with the fall in revenues and constant difficulty in balancing budgets, the government emphasized the importance of exports, even though their prices had fallen. A favorable balance of trade was achieved from the early 1920s, but this status simply indicated that this country of poor people—an average income of around $48 a year—was sending more goods abroad than it was buying for their own use.

These were years of general goverment uninterest. Some small advances were made, either through concern for Britain's parlous economic position, or from parliamentary pressure at Westminster, or in order to supply the increasing needs of colonial administration and commercial firms for educated employees. Thus the Colonial Development Act of 1929 allowed some little money to be spent on actual economic development in the colonies and created an advisory committee to combine colonial development with the needs of the British economy. Rudimentary social services also were provided by the colonial government, at the rate of approximately eight cents per head per year in 1935. The government allowed an increase in health provision so that 16 dispensaries in 1920 grew to 350 twenty years later, 18 hospitals with 569 beds to 85 with 4,135 beds during the same period. Education still remained almost entirely dependent on the missions: fewer than one out of every ten children was at any kind of school, and secondary education was available to no more than a fraction of 1 percent.

Out of these circumstances of declining trade, low revenues, and reduced prices arose one feature of economic life that was to be crucial for the future. As markets declined, so competition sharpened. In the bitter rivalry for less extensive and more profitable trade the small merchants and firms were eliminated. Those companies with sufficient reserves to allow them to undercut their competitors concentrated the bulk of commerce under their control. By the end of the interwar period it is estimated that two-thirds of the total trade in west Africa was controlled by seven firms, and that one of them, the United Africa Company, handled 40 percent of the import-export trade. The small firms were simply unable to meet increasing overheads or bear the strain of continual fluctuations in prices, and most of the small firms were those owned by Africans.

The United Africa Company was formed in 1929 by a merger that in itself illustrates the trend toward larger units during this period. It consisted of the Niger Company, which had continued its commercial activities after its charter was revoked in 1900 and had been bought by Lever Brothers in 1920, and the African and Eastern Trade Corporation, the product of another set of mergers between old west African trading companies. The UAC share of trade became so large that it had some considerable influence in fixing prices paid to producers and those paid to it for produce. When, as happened from time to time, the UAC entered into agreements with brother firms, such as the Compagnie Française de l'Afrique Occidentale and the Société Commercial de L'Ouest Africain, to fix prices and divide the market, real monopoly was established. Even when such agreements did not pertain, the power of such companies excluded smaller competitors, though occasionally an exceptional man could force his way in, as was seen in the instance of A. G. Leventis, a Greek businessman.

Monopoly or near-monopoly allowed the great firms to ignore African needs and avoid the expenses of modernization that would have become necessary factors in conditions of genuine competition. It also made it possible for these companies to repatriate most of their profits, which colonial governments avoided taxing, to their respective European countries, and the only defense that African producers could raise to such concentrated commercial organization was to form farmers' unions. Farmers' unions appeared in both the Gold Coast and Nigeria, and in 1938 they had some effect in holding up supplies of cocoa in the Gold Coast. But, generally, the unions' efforts were puny beside the power of the great colossi that came to dominate the economic life of west Africa.

One other consequence of the Euro-American depression provided further illustration of the effects of economic dependence on life in Nigeria. Usually, Britain had observed the principles of free trade in its relations with its west African colonies, largely because traditional trade links and the natural inclinations of its administrators were sufficient to preserve Britain's supremacy, and there was no barrier to foreign firms' trading in British colonies if they wished to do so. However, this principle was discarded whenever need arose among British concerns. After World War I, for instance, discriminatory tariffs were placed on palm oil exported to Germany in order to ensure that British processing firms received the supplies they required. When the depression hit the financial-industrial world during the 1930s, the priority of British interests was again exposed. The Japanese had begun to compete successfully with British firms in selling cheap cloth and other manufactured goods. This competition was directly damaging the interests of the Lancashire textile industry, already suffering from slump conditions with mills closed and thousands unemployed. Under this pressure the principle of competition soon gave way to one of self-interest. In 1934 discriminatory duties were placed on Japanese imports into each of the four British west African colonies: their inhabitants were not to be allowed to enjoy the cheaper clothing and other goods offered by open competition; the welfare of British firms and Britain's economy took precedence.

By the beginning of World War II, therefore, forty years of direct colonial government had produced a veneer of social services, some expansion in production for cash, a small communications network principally designed to carry produce to the coast for export. But the vast majority of Nigeria's inhabitants had no contact with education or medical facilities, though control of some epidemics and greater knowledge of hygiene were causing a rapid increase in population growth. Most Nigerians remained on their farms, smallholdings, village lands, growing their food by the same methods as their ancestors had used for centuries past, with primitive technology and low productivity. Industrialization was noticeable only by its absence, manufactures being almost entirely confined to those bought from Britain. Social organization was scarcely altered by the impact of British rule, the minor scars that had been caused by administrative ignorance being quickly healed through local ingenuity. Migration into the towns had begun, but it was still a small stream compared with the floods that were to follow. Even in the towns most immigrants continued to retain their links with their rural home societies.

In general, Nigeria slumbered. The one omen presaging future radical change was the return of the few Nigerians who had sought education abroad. In association with some members of the local elite these men had begun to talk politics in public, address their fellow countrymen through newspapers, and seize on every economic grievance as a weapon with which to belabor the colonial government.

12

AFRICANISM

During the nineteenth century European—particularly British and French—culture made serious contact with African society for the first time. Throughout the century relations between the two continents became closer. Their beliefs, assumptions, techniques, customs, and commercial practices sometimes clashed, at other times merged. Occasionally, one absorbed the other. From the days of their first contact with Africa the Europeans assumed that theirs was the stronger culture, the higher body of knowledge, spiritual values, social organization. They began with an attack on the slave trade, continued by outlawing slavery itself and trying to abolish many cruel practices such as human sacrifice and infanticide. In the early years it was assumed that once Africans had accepted the higher forms of morality and taken advantage of European social facilities they would become equal members of an enlightened community. By the end of the century, however, this assumption had been laid aside; it was now asserted that Africans were actually less capable of participating in "civilized" life than Europeans, irrespective of their qualifications or performance. Opinion in Europe was divided between those who would use Africans to further the ends of European states and economic interests and those who considered that African society should be protected from external influences by barriers of European colonial administration.

The aggressive nature of nineteenth-century European culture was first experienced in west African societies at a time when they were often in a state of confusion or disintegration. Centrifugal forces in the late eighteenth century had undermined the precarious unity of west African states and empires. Muslim jihads had shaken the self-confidence of Islamic society and weakened the structure of both Muslim and non-Muslim states. The abolition of the slave trade had exacerbated the confusion, adding economic to political elements of dislocation. Thus when the superior technology of the Europeans was applied to break into the hinterland of west Africa, in an effort to reach the actual producers of commodities and to establish centers of European cultural influence, there was little real opposition.

Eventually, of course, European political and military rule intensified earlier unofficial attempts to dominate west African societies commercially and culturally. But society in Africa, unlike those of the Americas, never collapsed under the pressures of European cultural contact, though many Africans accepted the assumption of inferiority impressed on them by Europeans, if only because they could not ignore the evidence of technological superiority. In their reactions to this massive ethnic assault some influential Africans accepted the thesis of European superiority and attempted to convert their fellows to European ways. Others defended traditional African culture and tried to protect it against the incursion of Europeans. A third group hoped to use European techniques selectively to strengthen African society by creating an amalgam that would not imitate the Europeans but would nevertheless allow Africans to pursue the advantages of modern life.

The most important group of those taking the first attitude was composed of those Africans who came under the influence of Sierra Leone society, led by Samuel Crowther. This group felt gratitude toward Britain, for many of them were released slaves who owed their freedom to the operations of the British anti-slavery naval patrol. Since they found that society in Freetown, where they were landed, was largely composed of other freed slaves from Britain, Jamaica, and Nova Scotia, and that British institutions were established there, it was natural that they should eagerly accept the opportunities presented to them. Britain had exported its education, religion, and social values to Sierra Leone, which Britain thought offered the best opportunity for converting Africans to its ways of life. Thus Crowther and his colleagues were taken into the strongly Protestant-oriented church; they were offered places in schools and colleges, both in Sierra Leone itself and in Britain, where the language of instruction and the content of education were those of the British educational system. Trade, workshops, and farms offered employment similar to that to be found in provincial Britain. Law, medicine, and the civil service were equally based on British practice and also afforded employment to the educated elite.

As William Fergusson, an African army doctor who actually became governor of Sierra Leone for a year, once wrote:

> . . . a leading feature of the character of the liberated Africans is their great love of money . . . their whole surplus means are devoted to the increase of their domestic comforts and their improvement of their outward appearance of respectability. A comfortable house is the first great object of their desire. . . . their outward observance of the Sabbath-day is most exemplary.

The acceptance of British social conventions was virtually complete.

It was, therefore, with a British-oriented cultural outlook that the Yoruba migrants, beginning in 1839, went back to Badagri, only to find their original homeland in confusion and danger. Thus the new arrivals from Sierra Leone, with their European knowledge and skills, found it easier to influence their neighbors than they might have done in more settled times. They usually settled in Badagri, Old Calabar, Lagos, or Abeokuta, often maintaining communication between each other to form a communal influence on southern Nigerian society. They thus provided a solid foundation for the spread of European missionary activities with the economic and social patterns that accompanied them.

Led by Crowther, who became the first African bishop in the Church of England, this group of Europeanized Africans believed that it was their duty to introduce British customs and attitudes to their neighbors in order to remedy African "backwardness." As a corollary, they pressed Britain to participate to a greater extent in African affairs, convinced, like Buxton, Venn, and Livingstone, that British activities would undermine slavery and brutal traditional practices while bringing "enlightenment" to the continent. It is not surprising that the Crowther group supported Britain's annexation of Lagos in 1861. Crowther particularly abhorred many Islamic and communal customs which he witnessed on his journeys; his remedy was simple:

> The country abounds with produce; labour is cheap; if the youths are only taught to prepare them for European markets our work is done. . . . When trade and agriculture engage the attention of the people, and with the gentle and peaceful teaching of Christianity, the minds of the people will gradually be won from war and marauding expeditions to peaceful trade and commerce.

Few Africans in contact with the British questioned the fact that Britain could offer them some useful contributions to a better life. But by no means all of them went as far as

Crowther in this respect. Some, for example, rather than supplant African by European society, hoped to strengthen African society by adopting, with discrimination, those elements of European mores consistent with African life. Among this group the most remarkable was Africanus Horton, who was born in Sierra Leone, educated there and in Edinburgh, and spent most of his life in the army serving in various west African countries. He became an important political writer, and his work affected opinion throughout the west coast.

Horton's main contribution was to attack the concept of Negro inferiority. He challenged European pundits on their own ground, contradicting their theories by logic, biological evidence, and first-hand experience. Horton's political message was that Africans must build their own independent communities equal in strength and status to those in Europe. He welcomed the help that Britain might offer in this task; he wanted the British to penetrate the interior of west Africa, taking with them educational and economic activities; he believed that western education would provide the key to nation-building and advocated the establishment of a west African university; he also prepared written constitutions for all the west African communities, proposing that Britain should help them to evolve gradually into independent states. When one recalls that Horton was urging these measures at the time of the British parliamentary report proposing Britain's withdrawal from west Africa and of the attempted Fante Confederation, it can be seen that Horton was meeting the challenge of his times, although the withdrawal mood in Britain did not last long. What Horton contributed most significantly to west Africa was the concept of learning from the Europeans without accepting a subordinate role in their society, and thereby of building stronger African societies.

One man who tried to apply Horton's ideas was George Johnson, another Sierra Leone émigré, who became a leader of the Egba in Abeokuta. Johnson had few of the educational opportunities of most other leaders of west African thought of his time, but he had been to England—as a guest of Prince Alfred, who had been entranced by his playing of an African flute! In some ways Abeokuta felt the pressure of European cultural aggression more forcefully than any other area. Not only were the Egba who had settled there always more vulnerable to the dangers of the Yoruba civil wars and invasion from Dahomey, but their insecurity on these grounds was aggravated by the Christian missionaries and their followers from Sierra Leone who taught strange doctrines, by British merchants who tried to trade directly with the Yoruba interior, and by British officials from their Lagos colony who interfered with the commercially strategic position of Abeokuta between coast and Yorubaland, molested their traders, and armed their enemies. To the Egba, therefore, it seemed as though they were under intensive assault from all sides. It was Johnson's objective to use the political lessons he had learned from the Europeans to teach the Egba that only unity could preserve them from these attacks. He tried to construct a centralized government and met Britain's tariff and blockade strategy with counter-tariffs.

In the end, Johnson's efforts failed, for the divisive forces that had led to the civil wars prevented him from creating the political cohesion that alone could have defeated British policy. Egba fury at interference in their affairs turned into anti-European riots that destroyed churches and missionary homes, driving the missionaries from the town for a dozen years. Johnson never succeeded in his political aims, but his use of European methods to defend African societies against European attacks had its effect on the political opinion of his times. It contributed to the growing debate on how the impact of European intervention should be met.

The argument as to the best approach to the new and changing situation was virile and thoughtful. Contributions were made by many different personalities with many points of view. Men such as James Johnson, Bishop Crowther's successor in Nigeria, Samuel Lewis of Sierra Leone, and John Mensah Sarbah and J. E. Caseley-Hayford of the Gold Coast were notable in this debate. Various degrees of cooperation with the Europeans were proposed; different approaches to the acceptance of the new cultural attitudes were discussed; a variety of methods for employing the modern techniques were considered. Clerics, academics, lawyers, and doctors were of course involved. But so were businessmen, traders, market women, for they, too, were affected by the presence of the Europeans and the importation of their customs. And from the resulting wide-reaching debate emerged the ideas and the men of the twentieth century.

One man above all others affected the attitude of west African opinion during this formative period: Edward Blyden. Born in the West Indies, barred from higher education in the United States through color prejudice, and consequently sent by the New York Colonization Society to Liberia, where he attended the Presbyterian High School, Blyden became a brilliant linguist, corresponded with Gladstone about Negro conditions in the United States, and became a minister in the Liberian government. An ordained minister, he visited the Middle East to gain some knowledge of Islam and the Arabic language and eventually, in 1871, went to live in Sierra Leone, where, through the books he wrote and the articles he had published, he addressed himself to Africans as a single racial community.

Blyden differed from his predecessors and other participants in the cultural debate by asserting positively the virtues of African society and its traditions. In doing so he directly challenged the universalist assumptions of European culture. He bluntly told Africans that, far from accepting Europe's belief in the superiority of its entire cultural pattern, they should recognize that each race was making its own unique contribution to God's nature, that Islam offered advantages Christianity did not possess, that African society, with its personal relations, polygamy, mutual aid, communal organization of work and wealth, natural spiritual sense, communion with nature, and awareness of God, displayed virtues Europe could not surpass. Blyden was one of the first writers to claim that Africans had made distinctive contributions to man's history and would make many more. He asserted that those African societies that were developing free from European influences were more healthy than those affected by Europe:

> From the lessons he every day receives, the Negro unconsciously imbibes the conviction that to be a great man he must be like the white man. He is not brought up . . . to be the companion, the equal, the comrade of the white man, but his imitator, his ape, his parasite.

Blyden went to extremes, as was necessary if he was to combat the insidiously growing assumption of white superiority. And his ideas took him into the dangerous paths of opposing miscegenation, advocating the separation of races, urging America's Negroes to seek their salvation in Africa. He selected for emphasis those features of African society consistent with the romantic picture of an idyllic utopia and ignored the harsher, more brutal aspects of African life. But he gave Africans a sense of cultural pride, of security in their heritage, of participation in the kaleidoscopic picture of human society. His contribution to redressing the balance, then tilted so heavily toward the superiority of European culture, was unrivaled; it was a major influence in meeting the challenge of assertive Europe by posing an alternative Africanism.

It is difficult to assess the reactions of the various Nigerian communities to the specific imposition of British rule, especially since British rule was imposed gradually, by various military actions against particular societies, by diplomatic persuasion in the signature of treaties, by taking over responsibility from Goldie's company. Often the British made use of local antagonisms, so that one group would feel that in helping the British to defeat its rivals, it had gained its own victory. Some traders considered that British rule would give them greater protection from competition and produce peaceful conditions more conducive to expanded commerce; others that it undermined the African trader in the interests of his British rival. Many of the clergy and educated Africans believed, at least at first, that British rule would promote the cause of missionary work and advance the influence of the elite; others that it substituted usurping British officials in their natural leadership role. Some saw British rule as a means of modernization; others as an attack on African culture. In short, Africans took many diverse attitudes to the imposition of imperial government. In any case, imperial government took many years to make a direct impact on the majority of Nigerians and was instituted in different ways in the various parts of the country.

There was therefore no single reaction from Nigeria to the declaration of British suzerainty. Some advocated resistance, some compromise, others cooperation. It was not until the end of the century that the debate on the significance of British rule gave rise to anything that can be identified as a concerted attitude.

The resistance that was met by the British as they gradually imposed their authority over the whole country was spasmodic and local rather than national. Military opposition was encountered from communities such as the Ijebu, Brass, Benin, among the emirates, and the Ibo. As late as 1906 Lugard's power was balanced on a knife-edge when one of his companies was defeated at Satiru; it was only the adherence of the sultan of Sokoto to British rule that saved Lugard from having to face a general uprising in the north. Some parts of Iboland were not entirely controlled by the British administration until the end of World War I.

Tentative efforts to bring some direct political pressure to bear on the new situation began at the end of the nineteenth century. A local branch of the Aborigines' Rights Protection Society, which also had been established in the Gold Coast, was formed in Lagos when Britain attempted to take control of all waste land. But the society was London-based; thus it was British members who decided which issues should be raised. In any case, in Lagos society membership was confined to a small elite, who quickly split into conservative and radical groups, and the delegation sent to London charged with the task of making representations over land changes was soon discredited as being unrepresentative.

In 1908 another land issue caused the formation of a People's Union, also in Lagos. The union's object was to protect land in the colony and protest against taxation policy. Again, however, membership was confined to the few, and the union soon became little more than a rich man's club, constantly inclined to defend the colonial government.

Thus, until World War I, the educated, comparatively wealthy elite was divided many ways, while the mass of people regarded colonial government as no more than the latest in a series of authorities commanding their obedience and payment of taxes. As has been seen, resistance persisted only where local customs were directly attacked by the aliens, particularly among those accustomed to popular participation in local decision-making.

A few Nigerians participated in the first Pan-African Conference. Held in London in 1900 and organized by a Trinidadian, the conference was attended by, among others, William Du Bois, a founder of the National Association for the Advancement of Colored People in the midst of the bitter debate among U.S. blacks between Booker T. Washington, who accepted radical segregation and the subservience of the Negro to the white man and advocated the training of Negroes in agricultural and manual skills as the means for the advancement of colored people, and the Du Bois faction. Du Bois directly challenged Washington's philosophy, asserting the right of full equality for Negroes and urging them to resist segregation.

The Du Bois-Washington argument not only stirred the Negro community, it was reflected in west Africa, and the 1900 conference was held more in the context of these conflicting views than in that of the new problems of Africa. At least the Africans who attended were able to see their situation in the wider perspective of the international problems of color.

After World War I political activity in west Africa began to show signs of coherence. Another Pan-African Conference, in 1919, organized by Du Bois and a Senegal deputy, Blaise Diagne, was held in Paris to draw up a Charter of Human Rights for peoples of African descent, though most of its delegates were Africans and Negroes who lived in Paris. Two years later a further conference was held in three capitals: London, Paris, and Brussels. Forty-one delegates came from Africa and were joined by some living in Europe and some Americans and West Indians.

During the 1921 conference Du Bois made the pregnant statement: "The beginning of wisdom in inter-racial contact is the establishment of political institutions among suppressed peoples. The habit of democracy must be made to encircle the world." A perspective of political organization and struggle was beginning to supplant mere rhetoric. Further conferences were held in 1923 and 1927, but Europe and America were still selected as their location. Pan-Africanism had not yet found African hosts.

The meetings with other Africans, U.S. Negroes, and West Indians certainly widened the political horizons of west Africans. They also brought them into contact with some white radicals: Harold Laski, H. G. Wells, and Lord Olivier attended the 1923 conference, which also received an encouraging message from Ramsay Macdonald, soon to be Britain's first Labour prime minister. The Communists were also becoming active, though their tactic in the early 1920s was to discredit what they termed "petit-bourgeois black nationalism," holding that it obstructed communist influence among black people. Africans were beginning to learn that all whites did not think alike, that they might find allies among them. They were also subjected to the intrigues and quarrels among the Negroes on the other side of the Atlantic. Marcus Garvey, with his "back to Africa" propaganda, was engaged in a bitter conflict with Du Bois, who believed in the right of Negroes to live in a state of equality in their own countries of the Americas and Caribbean, and the struggle had repercussions in Nigeria, as elsewhere in Africa.

But the Africans were not content simply to attend conferences organized by others. In 1918 J. E. Caseley-Hayford, a prominent Gold Coast lawyer, took the initiative in forming a National Congress of West Africa (NCWA). The first conference of the organization was held in Accra in 1920. It was attended by six Nigerians, together with three Africans from Sierra Leone and one from Gambia, and a measure of the political interest of the time was the fact that forty of the delegates came from the Gold Coast. It was not only that the conference was being held in their country and therefore that it was easier for them to attend; the greater wealth, educational facilities, and sophistication of the Gold Coast had given its people a head start in political consciousness over their fellow west Africans.

The NCWA achieved little in practice, though it may have lit a small beacon for the future, but it did indicate certain significant political features of west Africa. The NCWA's demands were interesting. They included the creation of legislative councils in each territory, elected Africans taking half the seats, with taxation under their control; chiefs to be subject to appointment and dismissal by their own people; racial discrimination to be abolished in the civil service; a university to be established in west Africa; more specific separation of the judiciary from the colonial administration. The most significant feature of these demands and the political activity that occasioned them was that they were largely confined to the educated elite of west Africa and expressed the desire of this tiny minority to participate more fully within the colonial structure. The congress was clearly an elitist organization, with no pretense of being a mass movement.

This elite factor was utilized by the colonial government in its reactions: the second significant feature. A deputation from the NCWA to London was coldly received by the colonial secretary, while the governor of Nigeria described the delegation as a "self-selected and self-appointed congregation of educated African gentlemen," pouring scorn on the idea that "continental Nigeria can be represented by a handful of gentlemen drawn from a half dozen coast tribes—men born and bred in British-administered towns situated on the seashore." Perhaps even more revealing was the governor's exposition of his attitude to the future of Nigeria, which was provoked by the activities of the congress, activities that he clearly regarded as threatening the British policy of ruling through traditional authorities:

> Assuming, therefore, for a moment that the impossible were feasible—that this collection of self-contained and mutually independent native states were indeed capable of being welded into a single homogeneous nation—a deadly blow would be struck at the very root of national self-government in Nigeria, which secures to each separate people the right to maintain its identity, its individuality and its nationality, its own chosen form of government, and the peculiar political and social institutions which have been evolved for it by the wisdom and accumulated experience of generations of its forebears.

As has been seen, the same governor within two years was introducing a new constitution, which created a legislative council that had certain legislative powers over the whole of the south and to which four Africans were to be elected. Announcing the constitution, the governor drew attention to the scope it offered to educated Africans to examine and criticize the colonial government. Rarely can the inconsistency of colonial policy have been so clearly evidenced from the lips of one man. Despite their modest and limited objectives, the political activities of educated Nigerians obviously were already having some influence on the political decisions of the Colonial Office.

The congress was, equally obviously, not a modern political party, and it soon fell into desuetude, disappearing on the death of Caseley-Hayford in 1930. Even during its active life, the NCWA's exclusive outlook was challenged. Herbert Macauley, grandson of Bishop Crowther, joined issue with its leadership. Although he himself was very much a member of the elite and acted the part of an English Victorian gentleman, Macaulay had the gift of contact with the common people. He was revered by the market women and was never too proud to speak to groups who boasted no social prestige. He had made his name by challenging the colonial government on its own terms. He attacked corruption in railway finances before World War I, espoused the cause of the king of Lagos when he was deposed by the British, and fought the government to the Privy Council over its acquisition of land in Lagos, securing a substantial compensation.

Macaulay's battles with the colonial government and the bitter hostility shown toward him by the governor gave him considerable prestige. His use of the *Lagos Daily News* to maintain constant criticism of the government anchored his reputation and brought new self-confidence to its readers in their attitude toward the government. The fact that his main supporters were "petit bourgeoisie"—market women, chiefs, and ordinary citizens, the very people who qualified to vote—rather than the educated, led to feuds, anger, and jealousies among the politically conscious in Lagos. Not surprisingly, when Macaulay organized his own party, the Nigerian National Democratic party, his candidates won the first elections to the legislative council in Lagos and Calabar and to the municipal council of Lagos. But despite Macaulay's support among the people—or perhaps because of it—and although most issues of political discussion were also those important in Lagos, the bitterness between Macaulay and the educated group in Lagos largely stultified political activity during the 1920s.

The feud between the governor and Macaulay also lasted throughout the twenties; Macaulay himself was twice sent to jail. But when the king whom he had consistently supported was eventually returned to the throne, in 1931, relations changed. When Cameron became governor in 1931, Macaulay became a frequent visitor to Government House, and the governor even consulted his party. Like the congress, the Democratic party came to accept the colonial establishment, participating in its social life and operating its political system. It is symptomatic of the reactions of the small political community of Lagos that in 1933 only seven hundred of the three thousand eligible voters actually went to the polls.

Political opinion in Nigeria during the 1920s was also affected by the Negro movement started by Marcus Garvey. Branches of Garvey's Universal Negro Improvement Association were organized in west Africa, and although his movement collapsed when he was accused of misusing its funds, imprisoned in America, and deported, his words caught the imagination of many. Like Blyden's attitudes, although Garvey's rhetoric was often extravagant, the mood Garvey expressed appealed to many Africans seeking to restore their pride, and his ideas of Negro renaissance in a free and independent Africa lingered long after his eclipse. Inevitably, these ideas were considered dangerous by the colonial government: Garvey's journal, the *Negro World,* was banned and seized in the mail; it was declared illegal to possess it. The Lagos branch of his association was allowed to exist, but in other parts of the country branches had to be formed secretly, naturally raising the political temperature.

Political organization in Nigeria during the 1920s was, therefore, not very impressive. Largely based on Lagos, it often was committed to local infighting and mainly was concerned to secure greater advantages for its elitist members. The accent was on removing discrimination within the colonial structure and thus gaining better jobs, opportunities, and status for the educated minority, and this attitude was to persist to the present and often to fix a gulf between the advantaged few and the many who continued to live a rural, largely subsistence life. Outside this confined circle, however, other groups began to form, thus providing further experience, which later played some part in political efforts, in community organization. Tribal associations, based on the self-help principle in social affairs, trade unions, professional associations, and a variety of cultural groups were formed. Some of the organizations had little connection with modern politics, but they did provide experience in organization. Unfortunately, they often displayed a tribal, ethnic, or communal character that, again, was to be significant later.

The Ibibio Union, which was formed in 1928, aimed originally to provide scholarships for young members of that community. The Ibo Union of Lagos, which was created just before World War II, and the pan-Yoruba movement, the Sons of the Society of Oduduwa, betrayed their closed outlook in their titles; they were to be the forerunners of similarly limited political parties after World War II. On the other hand, bodies such as the Lagos Fishermen's Association, the Palm Wine Sellers' Organization, the Southern Nigerian Civil Servants' Union, the Mechanics' Union, and the Teachers' Union showed that some Nigerians were seeking combination to improve their standards as communities of workers. Certain cultural groups also were being formed among people anxious to create forums of discussion; the Young Man's Literary Association was typical of these. Each group provided experience in organization, in debate and discussion, in association with others, all of which represented a preparation for future political action. And each group increased awareness that Africans were combining for common purposes.

Perhaps the most significant of all interwar associations were those that developed among the young men. (Apart from market women, few women participated in public activity at this time.) Many of the most politically conscious youth were abroad during the twenties. Whether they became aware of political issues through living in other societies or went abroad because of their particular personalities is a moot point. But in London and Paris and, to a lesser degree, the United States, west African students began to develop a concern for the future of their countries. This gave them an intercommunal sense of common purpose rare among their people, and some of them were to take an active part in public life on their return home.

As early as 1917 the first student organization for west Africans was formed, in London. The organization grew from small beginnings and never became very large. In 1925, however, the West African Students' Union was founded and was to become a much more serious body. The force behind the union was a Nigerian, called Ladipo Solanke, who played one of the most important roles in the development of west African consciousness. Solanke canvassed funds and support in most west African towns. His success was remarkable: he persuaded leading figures such as Nana Afori Atta of the Gold Coast and the alake of Abeokuta and the emir of Kano in Nigeria to become patrons of the union. Marcus Garvey gave the union a hostel, and it published its own journal, which enabled many west Africans to express their ideas in print for the first time. The union was not a political party, but it supplied a much greater need at this time: it was a forum where west Africans from different countries could meet each other for the first time, exchange ideas and experiences, see themselves as individuals in a much wider context of political thought and struggle than they had previously recognized in their own localized communities. It also provided them with a sense of security in a strange, foreign environment and sometimes introduced them to Europeans with political ideas that broadened their horizons. In the years after World War II, when many more west African students were in London or other British cities and when branches of west African parties were being formed among these temporary émigrés, the union offered a common meeting place in which differing political ideas could be expressed and debated. Although political differences were constantly voiced within the walls of the union, there also developed among some of its members a sense of national community, at times even of west African unity. By providing the focus for such feelings among students from various Nigerian and west African communities, the union played no small part in fostering a nontribal, national, and international sentiment among many Africans who had been students abroad after they returned home.

It was not surprising that a similar spirit arose among young people at home. By the 1930s many of them were disillusioned with the older politicians and professional men, who seemed more concerned with their own places in the colonial structure and in maneuvering for personal advantage than in the future of the country that the younger people would have to inherit. In 1932 a Nigerian Youth League was founded in Calabar by Eyo Ita to foster the cause of educational reform. Two years later a similar body, the Lagos Youth Movement, was formed in the capital. Its main sponsors were Ernest Ikoli, a journalist and follower of Garvey, H. O. Davies, a lawyer, and a doctor, J. C. Vaughan. Many professional young men, perhaps remembering their student enthusiasm, joined the league, as did some Ibo workers whose life in Lagos had largely severed them from their communal home ties. The concepts of the movement appealed widely, and it began to attract adherents from outside Lagos.

The next move was to change its name to the Nigerian Youth Movement, an important sign of burgeoning national consciousness. Then an influential paper, the *Daily Service,* began to support the movement.

In 1937 Nnamdi Azikiwe returned home after studying in America, where he had become a prominent figure on the campuses of Storer College, West Virginia, Howard University, Washington, D. C., and Lincoln University, Pennsylvania. He had also spent three years in Accra, where he had collaborated with Wallace-Johnson in running a newspaper. Azikiwe soon demonstrated his belief in the power of the press by establishing the *West African Pilot* as a medium for his views and began to attack not just the low educational standards offered to Africans but colonial rule itself. Azikiwe demanded, in place of reformist measures, independence and autonomy for Nigeria within the British Empire. When he joined the Youth Movement he brought to it a radicalism, a base among the Ibo and Ibibio, and the interest of urban workers it had previously lacked. Unfortunately, it was not long before his membership also provoked jealousy and communal consciousness. His newspaper was seen as a rival to Ikoli's *Daily Service;* his Ibo support raised opposition from other communities; his radicalism caused suspicions among the Yoruba middle class of Lagos and the west. The movement assumed a broader, more national posture under Azikiwe's influence, but it also showed signs of the factionalism that was to appear just below the surface of so many Nigerian organizations in the future.

Thus, by the time World War II broke out, significant, if tentative, signs of a change in the political temper of Nigeria were beginning to appear. The press, which had been active in west Africa since the nineteenth century, was, though always in a financially precarious position, taking more assertive attitudes. In particular, it had begun to criticize the colonial administration directly, rather than simply putting the case for reforms. The Italian invasion of Ethiopia had shown that there were Africans who cared about fellow Africans two thousand miles away; in their protests against the Italians, Africans were beginning to identify all European, white imperialism as part of the same conspiracy against African freedom. The younger people were showing signs of political consciousness, as the Nigerian Youth Movement showed. The Youth Movement's wide appeal in Nigeria was demonstrated in 1938 when it won the three Lagos seats in the legislative council and all the elective seats in the capital's town council.

The emergence of young people into political activity was of special significance in Africa; for, although in certain communities—for example, among the Ibo—the younger age groups had been allowed representation in decision-making activities, theirs had always been a subordinate position. In most societies respect for elders was a first principle of social and political life, with little opportunity for the younger elements to express themselves. The assertion of youth in the political movements of the immediate prewar years in fact presaged rebellion, not only against the discriminatory policies of the colonial government, but equally against the traditional authorities in their own African societies and their reformist attitude toward the European rulers.

The war was to act as a catalyst for all these budding forces of protest. It transformed what had so far been almost entirely a claim for improved conditions into anti-colonial agitation based on the ambition of Africanism—the transfer of authority from European to African.

13

THE CRISIS: ACT ONE

IF NIGERIA is regarded as a single entity, it has been in a state of crisis throughout its history; for its experience has always been one of contending ethnic communities. The communities have never been entirely static, constant cultural contact with each other and external groups continually changing their character and personnel, albeit slowly. Ironically, the communities might have evolved into nation states if left to their natural development without outside interference. By the nineteenth century, indeed, the larger communities had certainly approached the status of nations —of cultural entities marked by common language, religion, and custom—and when one recalls that so many tiny societies have achieved statehood since the middle of the twentieth century, there is no reason to believe that this development could not also have occurred among the various Nigerian groups.

As it was, it was Britain that decided, without any reference to Nigerian views, that all the communities should suddenly be combined into a single political unit. That their history did not fit them for this fate is self-evident. The experience of other nation states, not least that of Britain itself, shows that the amalgamation of several ethnic units into a single political system requires much time. Nigerians were never given that time; it was simply decided in the Colonial Office that they should become one unit under British rule. At the time of the decision, whether it is taken to be 1885, 1900, or 1914, the various Nigerian communities shared little in common, other than government by Britain.

To a considerable degree the Nigerians accepted this *fait accompli* when they began to interest themselves in modern politics. With the single exception of the civil war of 1967–1970, no serious attempt has been made to reverse the decision taken by the British. They accepted the responsibility of transforming themselves from a set of separate and disparate ethnic communities into a single nation state.

Yet by the time Nigerians themselves were able to apply their minds to this task, further British policies had raised still greater barriers. In 1900 it was decided that the country would be governed as three units; in 1906 as two; and in 1914 a single Nigerian entity was created. Yet at all stages different areas of the country had been governed according to contrasting principles. The northern emirates, the pagan societies of the middle belt, Yoruba towns, Ibo village clans, the delta ports, and Lagos had all experienced varying dispensations under their respective British rulers.

It can certainly be argued that the creation of a skeleton communications network and the consequent expansion of trade, together with the educational opportunities—supplied mainly by missionaries—had increased mobility between the communities. Yet if these factors are examined closely, they will be seen to have aggravated rather than assuaged intercommunal suspicions. Economic and social growth had been markedly uneven, leading to gross regional imbalance, which, in turn, had resulted in the enjoyment of most of the socioeconomic benefits by comparatively rich areas, such as the

Yoruba west, while poorer regions, such as the Ibo east and the pagan center, had sought to compensate for their weaknesses by sending many of their people to other areas to find employment and the large mass of the north had remained almost stationary. Because of the absence of a single national sentiment and the conflict between religious and social traditions, the emigrants did not seek to transmit their knowledge or skills to the peoples among whom they settled. Their main object was to gain the salaries or trading profits unobtainable at home. They therefore remained largely an alien element, enjoying but slight cultural exchange and sometimes bitterly resented by their neighbors.

The fundamental Nigerian crisis can best be dated from 1914. With greater forethought or imagination the crisis might have been averted in 1885 or 1900, but after the decisions of 1914 it became inevitable. Once the Colonial Office approved the philosophy of Lugard, rather than that of his critics—Bell, Temple, and Morel—who proposed smaller units, British administrative policies inevitably resulted in an ossification of regional separation. Growth of a common political consciousness could only have been achieved through lowering the barriers between ethnic groups.

The effects of the 1914 decision have been tragically evident ever since. Yet it would be unctuously patronizing to suggest that the Nigerian crisis has been thrust upon helpless Africans by Britain. Many Nigerians share responsibility. African missionaries, traders, and other professionals urged the British government to take control of their country in the late nineteenth century. None of them had the foresight to see that only the establishment of separate states, or a deliberate policy of amalgamating administrations and increasing contact between ethnic groups, could avoid a conflict of nations within the single state system. Nor have Nigerians caught up in this crisis been able to summon up the intellectual honesty needed to recognize the reality of the situation they have inherited and, surmounting ethnic allegiances, meet the challenge of choosing either separate nations or a genuine multinational state.

Nineteen-fourteen saw the opening of the first scene; the years immediately following the end of World War II marked the second scene of the crisis drama, though perhaps it is more accurate to characterize the period as a second phase or a crisis within a crisis. It can even be argued that in the late 1940s it was still not too late to begin the process of bringing some unity into the story, of knitting together the skeins of a nation. Yet if it was not too late, the eleventh hour had certainly struck—and the sounds were ignored. By 1945 not only had the framework of British policy hardened, but most African opinion in Nigeria accepted the shape of the structure erected. Hostility between the two major southern groups, the Ibo and the Yoruba, had deepened into bitterness; the gulf between the south and the north was rapidly widening. Certainly the late 1940s saw the last moment at which danger might have been averted; it was lost by both British and Nigerians.

Tribal or communal emotions were bound to spread like an epidemic into politics once modern political organization began to develop within a society in which the communities had no common purpose. The occasions for conflict were many. When the Ibo and Ibibio sought to improve their lot, for palm production could not maintain all of them on scarce land under constant pressure from rapid population increase, they saw that education was their only key to advance under British rule. By their own efforts they provided increasing numbers of their community with educational opportunities, but the effort itself tended to bind them closer together. Since the Ibo also lived among their own people in Yoruba towns and in the *sabon garis,* the strangers' districts, of the northern towns, the traditional extended family was used as economic and social protection and communal cohesion was again strengthened. Meanwhile, however, the Yoruba and the peoples of Lagos, most of whom were also Yoruba, had gained a long lead, in terms of organization and wealth, over the other groups, as a result of their advantageous commercial position, their state systems, and their early association with the British. The contribution of the immigrants from Sierra Leone came to full fruition under British rule, for it provided many Yoruba with European education and gave them the techniques with which to consolidate their earlier economic advantages. The Yoruba were determined to maintain their advantage, although as often feuding among each other. Yet even Yoruba quarrels seemed to emphasize the same trend toward self-protection, for when attempts were made by the Ibo to gain an ally among a dissident Yoruba group, the attempt only drew the Yoruba closer together to repulse the strangers. As Ibo and Yoruba sparred, the emirates of the north remained firmly within their old-fashioned form of Islamic world, almost untouched by the growth of a modern economy or European education, therefore becoming even more dependent on outsiders as the source—especially Ibo or pagans from the middle belt—of the skills needed in their society. Even then, residential and social segregation was added to the lack of comprehension between the modernistic-minded strangers and the traditionalist Hausa-Fulani, again aggravating separation between the communities. What is commonly termed "tribalism," therefore, had both social and economic bases; it was also promoted by the policies of the colonial administration.

These features of tribal, communal, or ethnic conflict became most dangerous when they appeared as factors in politics, as they did in serious proportions during World War II, shattering the hopes raised during the 1930s by the student communities that a greater nationalism than had been experienced by their fathers would be achieved. A major break occurred in 1941, when Azikiwe quarreled with older members of the Youth Movement about the nomination of a candidate for the legislative council elections. He resigned from the movement, and most Ibo members left with him, leaving the rump of the movement almost solely in Yoruba hands. Not only did the movement's influence virtually disappear, but Azikiwe's break marked the beginnings of fragmentation of political circles into communal groups. The Youth Movement remained influential only in Ibadan, where it was to be used as one of the bases of the Action Group formed ten years later. In any case, a Yoruba personality, Chief Obafemi Awolowo, had arisen to challenge Azikiwe; it was he who inherited the movement as a largely Yoruba organization.

Ethnic hostility intensified during the course of the war. Later, Awolowo was to write, in retrospect, that as early as 1940 "It seemed clear to me that [Azikiwe's] policy was to corrode the self-respect of the Yoruba people as a group; to build up the Ibo as a master race." At times Azikiwe made statements that lent credence to this view. On one occasion, for instance, he asserted that "the God of Africa has created the Ibo nation to lead the children of Africa from the bondage of ages." All politicians make rhetorical statements, but when these statements are dressed in tribal clothes, they can hypnotize their hearers with a glitter that makes them dangerously blind to reality.

It was symptomatic of the escalating communal consciousness that before the war ended an Ibibio State Union and a Pan-Ibo Federal Union had been formed. These groups could be considered as basically cultural associations, designed to protect the existence of particular communal cultures. As such they would have been legitimate, even constructive, maintaining cultural diversity within political unity. But the political unity had not been created; consequently, the Ibo groups took on a particularist, separatist nature. Inevitably, they turned to politics, with the result that cultural preservation was transformed into political separatism. In many ways, the groups closely resembled the activities of the Afrikaners in South Africa, similarly creating communal laagers.

In turn, the initiative taken by the Ibo was met by counter-action from their Yoruba neighbors. Yoruba students in London took the lead, forming their own cultural organization in 1945. The London association's activities were soon introduced into Yorubaland itself, its first conference, in 1948, being held symbolically at Ile Ife, the Yoruba spiritual home. Equally significantly, the organization took the name Egbe Omo Oduduwa, "The Society of the descendants of Oduduwa." Its central objective was to promote the concept of a Yoruba nationalism, aiming for Nigerian unity only through a federation of similar associations.

Until the end of World War II northerners were sufficiently isolated from the south as to remain unthreatened by the rise of Ibo and Yoruba nationalism. Yet a few northerners also felt a need to assert cultural and social claims. In 1943, this group, composed of some of the few northerners who had gained a European education and including names that were to become significant, such as Abubakar Tafawa Balewa and Aminu Kano, formed the Bauchi Improvement Association—again a cultural, social organization, but, like the others, later destined to play a political role.

The ethnic or communal trend of Nigerian attitudes at this time has been stressed before the effects of the war itself are dealt with because these strong undercurrents swept the impulses stirred by the war into special channels. All the influences bearing on west Africans during World War I were apparent again in World War II, only to exaggerated degrees. This time there were no German colonies as neighbors, for both the Cameroons and Togoland had been taken from Germany at the end of World War I. (The Cameroons had been divided between Britain and France as mandated territories under the League of Nations, the British portion being administered as part of Nigeria.) But Nigerians still joined the British armed forces. Once again there was no apparent inclination to take advantage of British embarrassment to throw off the colonial yoke. The Nigerian Regiment, augmented by voluntary recruits, raised fifteen battalions and served in the campaign against Italy to restore Ethiopia to its emperor, in Burma against the Japanese, and in the Middle East. The soldiers, therefore, not only learned to kill Europeans but witnessed the restoration of an African ruler to a throne usurped by Europeans and the defeat of European powers by non-Europeans, in the Far East.

While the Mediterranean route was closed to anti-Axis shipping, west Africa assumed a new importance as a line of communication to the Middle and Far East. Navies assembled there, convoys were seen, torpedoing occurred, airports were extended and new ones built, and many aircraft with their service personnel passed through Nigeria. Once again Nigerian produce—palm oil, groundnuts, tin, and rubber—were in great demand because of wartime shortages, and efforts were made to increase their production. Meanwhile, the ideological nature of the war did not escape the Africans. They heard much talk about "freedom"; they saw their neighbors in the French territories torn between Vichy and De Gaulle's Free French; they read of the Nazis' and Fascists' racist philosophies; and they wondered how the ideas bruited around in Europe applied to them at the center of interracial realities.

The impact of the war inevitably stimulated political thought and discussion. Many thousands of soldiers who served abroad could not close their eyes and ears to the different societies and opinions that surrounded them. At home the appearance and behavior of thousands of ordinary European soldiers, sailors, and airmen contrasted sharply with the conduct that Africans had been led by colonial officers to believe was the European norm. Moreover, many European serving men had radical views on colonialism and did not hesitate to express them; in Asia opinions about imperial rule among the forces and local populations were even more radical.

As production increased for war purposes and some small

factories were built to supply goods that could no longer be imported, economic forces also stimulated political interest. The Colonial Development and Welfare Act, passed at Westminster during the period of Dunkirk, 1940, offered a new approach from British economic aid; for the first time it allowed social-service expenditure from British funds in the colonies. The small initial amount was to be greatly increased after the war, but the expectations of the educated and the ex-servicemen among Africans were likely to be even larger—and frustrated expectations implied political activity.

Influences arising from wartime experience were common to the whole of west Africa and were seen especially in the Gold Coast. They left the postwar scene a ferment of discontent, ideologies, and expectation. In the Gold Coast, in many French territories, and, to some extent, in Sierra Leone, they led directly to the conclusion that political organization, usually the result of the educated and especially those with experience abroad, was essential to ensure that the expectations were fulfilled.

Despite the fact that certain overtones of communal jealousy appeared, in the main in the rest of west Africa the paramount need for unity in face of the colonial power resulted in communal considerations' being subordinated to the common purpose. Nigeria was the exception. There, with a much greater population and a history of deeper cultural division among larger state systems, Nigerian unity seemed of less importance than communal advantage.

Azikiwe was the only prominent leader to try and resist this communalism. He had shown a weakness when he resigned from the Youth Movement on account of a communal quarrel. But in the following year, 1942, he founded a study group to try and prepare to meet the problems of the postwar world. In the next year he traveled to London to submit a memorandum entitled "The Atlantic Charter and British West Africa." In this document Azikiwe demonstrated the change that had taken place among the more radical political thinkers since the war began. His memorandum still maintained the criticism of administrative discrimination against Africans; it demanded the immediate Africanization of the civil service. But its political aims went far beyond the objectives of prewar years. Azikiwe laid down an evolutionary policy that was to be largely paralleled by the events that were actually to take place, though in 1942 his suggestions seemed wildly revolutionary, for he insisted that Britain forthwith terminate Nigeria's Crown Colony status and replace it with ten years of representative government, five years of responsible government, and, finally, independence. Since the British Labour party leader, Clement Attlee, had just previously assured African students in London that the freedoms proclaimed in the Atlantic Charter should apply to their continent, Azikiwe could quote good authority. But Winston Churchill would have none of such ideas. He always maintained that the Atlantic Charter did not apply to the British Empire, despite Roosevelt's insistence that it must do so. And Churchill was prime minister, while Attlee was only his deputy.

Although Azikiwe's 1942 venture had no practical success, it did show that he was thinking nationally. In 1944 he tried to put his concept into organized political form. Encouraged by the demands made by the younger generation of politically conscious Nigerians for a coherent national leadership, Azikiwe took the chief part in organizing a conference, from which emerged a new party, the National Council of Nigeria and the Cameroons (later renamed the National Congress of Nigerian Citizens). Like many early African parties, the NCNC was a confederation of various organizations—trade unions, market women, professional, tribal, social, and youth groups, along with surviving sections of the Nigerian Youth Movement and the Nigerian Democratic party—all of which agreed to pool their efforts. Herbert Macaulay became the new party's first president, with Azikiwe as secretary-general; on Macaulay's death in 1946 Azikiwe assumed the presidency.

For a time the appearance of what seemed to be a national party aiming at national freedom and social equality made a widespread appeal. And because the southern communities were more politically conscious than those of the north, it was from among them that it first attracted massive support. But the NCNC also achieved some popularity in the north.

The year that saw the end of the war was also the pivotal year for Nigeria's future, for it saw two domestic events of crucial significance—the publication of a new constitution and a general strike—and one of international importance—the Manchester Pan-African conference. Reactions to all three events from various sections of Nigerian society were to determine, to a critical extent, the political channels into which the country's future would flow.

Azikiwe's political sagacity was immediately revealed when he linked together the two domestic issues, despite the fact that they had little connection with each other. And Azikiwe's success was to represent the highest point in his attempt to stake a claim as the dominant national leader; afterward both his national reputation and the cause of national unity itself declined steadily.

The proposals for a new constitution were published by the governor, Sir Arthur Richards, in March, 1945. They contained a number of measures destined to introduce a greater degree of unified administration. For the first time the north was to participate in the legislative council. Representation in the council was to be greatly broadened by making use of the Native Authorities, Nigerian officials at the local level, in the selection of its members. Although the administration was to be divided between three regions, each with its own assembly, the central direction of policy remained with the secretariat in Lagos.

Objections to the proposals and to the manner of the proposals' introduction far outweighed their attractions. The proposals had been compiled unilaterally by the government, without any consultation with African representatives. They retained the unrepresentative character of the legislature, for the only elective seats were those already existing in Lagos and Calabar (and even in those cities universal suffrage was not proposed, qualifications only being reduced from $240 to $120 gross annual income). Although the new council was to have a majority of unofficial members—twenty-eight to sixteen officials—with the exception of the four members from Lagos and Calabar they would all be either indirectly elected or nominated, and the method of selection of the unofficial members seemed to ensure that most would come from the traditionalist, conservative elements of the country. Above all, the executive council, with only an advisory capacity to the governor, was to remain all-European unless the governor decided to nominate his own African choices to it.

Some commentators have dated the regionalization of Nigeria from the Richards constitution, but that criticism is misdirected. The country had been administered in three sections since 1939, when separate western and eastern administrations, based on Ibadan and Enugu, had been established in the south. It was actually a move toward unification to include the north in the legislature; the central danger in the constitution was the perpetuation of division in the south through the creation of two regional assemblies. In 1945 the menace of rivalry between Ibo and Yoruba was much greater than that between north and south; it was to prove fatal to the cause of national consciousness. In 1945 it might just have been possible to create a nation through linked separate regions in north and south. Much more hopeful would have been Azikiwe's earlier suggestion for a federation of eight states, so that the gross divergence in size and population between north and south should not become a political factor, but at the time it was not regionalization that concerned the critics. Both Azikiwe and Awolowo had already tentatively made regional proposals, and the regional structure only became dangerous when it was used by Nigerians themselves for schismatic political purposes.

The Richards proposals provided excellent material around which to center a political campaign of the nature that was shortly to be seen in the mobilization of national sentiment in the Gold Coast. But the real political fodder the constitution offered its critics was the lack of consultation in devising it and its unrepresentative nature. At a time when many Nigerians had seen the temper of nationalism in India and many others had read or heard about it, when the war was supposed to have been fought for "freedom" and the Atlantic Charter had proclaimed the right of self-government, when neighboring Africans in French territories were preparing to participate in devising a new French constitution, it was ludicrous to expect Nigerians to accept a constitution devised in Government House and the Colonial Office. Moreover, the selection by Native Authorities of members to the regional assemblies, which were to act as electoral colleges for the central legislature, was just as anachronistic. In the 1920s or 1930s the constitutional provisions might have been considered a step toward popular representation. By 1945, as a result of the drive to employ indirect rule, there were 114 principal Native Authorities and many more minor ones, and though they therefore had wide contact with the people, they were an integral part of government, so their nominees could hardly be considered "unofficial." The Native Authorities were also largely composed of illiterates and traditionalists; they could not measure up to the demands of the young progressively minded Nigerians of 1945.

Since the introduction of the constitution was accompanied by a number of ordinances that vested mineral rights and public land in the Crown and gave the colonial government powers to appoint or depose chiefs, another issue of major concern was offered to the critics. Azikiwe immediately saw the sociopolitical implications of the measure, for it would give to the government control over the chiefs, who were popularly linked with land allocation. As everywhere in Africa, land rights had a deep spiritual significance as well as an economic value to Nigerians, and the suggestion of interference by the colonial government immediately raised intense emotions.

In the summer of 1945 the resentment provoked by the Richards constitution was compounded by economic discontents. During the war prices had risen steeply, shortages had become severe, and many more Nigerians had become wage-earners. It had been the policy of the government, influenced from London, especially by Ernest Bevin, to encourage the growth of trade unions. From a handful of unions at the start of the war, the number had grown by 1944 to eighty-five, with about thirty thousand members and a recognized Trade Union Congress. To the young Nigerian with European education or war service it appeared intolerable that almost every high-ranking job should be reserved for a European expatriate, and that while European salaries were raised as the cost of living increased, he should be left to see his standard of living deteriorate. In the event, the workers on the railways, in the ports, and in telecommunications decided to call a strike, paralyzing the vital services of the country. When Azikiwe's newspapers, which supported the strike, were banned, he immediately became a martyred hero. Since cost of living allowances were granted after the strike, Azikiwe was seen to be a successful champion of the workers against employers and colonial government. He toured the country triumphantly, collecting money to send a delegation of protest to London.

The successful strike was the high-water mark of Azikiwe as a national leader. However, partly because of his treatment by others and partly because of his own failings, he never took the opportunity presented to achieve charismatic stature. In this context, it was perhaps unfortunate that he did not attend the Manchester Pan-African conference in October, 1945, for it was there that the strategy of attack on colonial rule was thrashed out. The Richards proposals would have presented an excellent opportunity for thorough discussion on the practical issues arising from colonial policy, but Azikiwe sent only a deputy, though both H. O. Davies and S. L. Akintola also attended. The absence of Azikiwe left vacant the chair for the potential leader of a united Nigeria that, in 1945, only he could have filled.

Then, when he took his delegation to London in 1947, although he was accompanied by representatives from every region and had a firm mandate from Nigerians to demand self-government, Azikiwe did not secure the sympathetic reception that he might have expected from the Labour government's Colonial Secretary, Arthur Creech Jones. Indeed, Jones demonstrated to Azikiwe and his colleagues the same misunderstanding of west African political temper as he exhibited toward the Burns constitution for the Gold Coast. Because many more Africans were to sit in the legislative council and the proposals had been approved by the existing council, Jones assumed that genuine African demands were being met by the Richards constitution. He did not realize that by 1947 educated Africans and ex-servicemen were seeking not simply more black faces in positions of authority but representatives elected by popular vote. As it was, Jones did no more than advise the delegation to return to Nigeria and work through the constitution. This myopia toward the political realities provoked further resentment, raised dissension among the delegates, and denied Azikiwe the success that might have consolidated his position as a national leader. In fact, the return of the delegation to Nigeria was an anticlimax, aggravating tensions within the local political world.

When Azikiwe returned, the situation in Nigeria, and particularly in Lagos, was becoming dangerously volatile. The three Lagos legislative council seats had been won in 1946 by Macaulay's old Democratic party, with the backing of the NCNC, on a platform of repealing the Richards constitution. The snub administered to Azikiwe's London delegation roused the tempers of the young, and it was followed by the NCNC decision to open its doors to individual membership in place of its original group federation. In its turn this move led to the formation of a "Zikist Movement," designed to gain self-government by direct action, protect Azikiwe from attacks, and agitate for a more radical policy. Meanwhile, members of the Youth Movement, who had resigned from the NCNC in opposition to its decision to send the delegation to London, began to provide a body of Yoruba criticism of Azikiwe and his Ibo supporters.

The degree of unity attained in the London delegation soon disappeared, with delegates from different ethnic groups exhibiting personal bitterness toward each other. Since Nigeria, like the rest of west Africa, was suffering from postwar shortages and widespread unemployment, with the streets of Lagos filled with men seeking work, an element of revolt was visible. It was not insignificant that in 1948 similar conditions led to a violent outburst in the Gold Coast, where the revolt was used by the nationalist movement to seek increased concessions and to build a radical national political movement. In Nigeria, by contrast, the pressures seemed to exacerbate intercommunal conflicts, diluting the small degree of national unity that had previously been achieved.

There was to be one last effort to build a unified movement. In November, 1949, a strike among the coal miners at Enugu led to police shooting. Twenty-one miners were killed. The news of this massacre horrified Nigerians and set off chain reactions, resulting in riots in Aba, Calabar, Onitsha, and Port Harcourt. A National Emergency Committee was formed to represent the case of the miners before a commission of inquiry, and it was hoped that this body would then hold together to present a united front in the campaign for self-government. The committee did not do so. Soon after it had presented its case, it dissolved, and Nigeria returned to communal politics.

By late 1949 Richards had been replaced as governor by a much more liberally minded man, Sir John Macpherson. Like his colleague, Sir Charles Arden-Clarke, in the Gold Coast, Macpherson realized that he was responsible for a society that was perched on political dynamite. Unlike Arden-Clarke, he did not have an Nkrumah or a Convention Peoples' party with whom to collaborate. Nevertheless, he quickly made it clear that he was prepared to revise the Richards constitution, consult with African opinion, introduce Africans into the higher civil service, and improve the facilities for higher education. In 1948, indeed, one powerful emotive resentment of educated Africans was removed, when the Yaba Higher College, which was below university standard, was closed and Ibadan University College opened.

Macpherson made it plain that Nigerian representatives would be given the responsibility of advising as to how the constitution should be changed. A select committee of the legislature was established in 1949, and, at its suggestion, discussions and conferences were held at village, district, provincial, and regional levels to make recommendations on the constitutional future. Many Nigerians in the political world were convinced that Britain seriously intended eventually to offer self-government. Already committees of unofficial members from the regional assemblies were cooperating with civil service heads of departments, thus participating in executive government. It seemed to many that those who were agitating for the abdication of colonial government were pushing an open door; the real issue was what character self-government was to take and what was to be the timetable for independence.

With hindsight, it might even be argued that Britain allowed Nigerians to assume too early that self-government was assured, for they reached this conclusion even before Nkrumah and his colleagues in the Gold Coast. In any case, the single focus of national agitation, which, if it had lived a little longer, might have produced some degree of national unity, was removed. It would be expecting an impossible degree of Machiavellian subtlety to suggest that Macpherson and the Colonial Office recognized this possibility. In fact, it seems likely that Creech Jones had been influenced toward granting representative powers by Azikiwe's delegation more than he admitted at the time; he was also swayed by his own Fabian Colonial Bureau and pressures within the Labour party to secure democratic rights within the colonies.

What does seem certain is that the offer of a new constitution and the wide-ranging discussions over its nature were used by the Nigerians to seek communal and regional advantage rather than to envision the creation of a single nation state and forge the means of building it. The whole debate on the new constitution was based on the issue of what form of regional federation should be recommended—not on the question as to whether regionalism and federation might aggravate centrifugal and communal tendencies. The constitutional conferences held in each of the three regions all proposed a federal system based on the existing regions. They agreed that each region should be given certain executive and legislative authority, with an increase in the proportion of elected members. Differences, however, arose between the two southern regions and the northern region over the extent of the authority that should remain in colonial hands. The consequences of insulating the north against modern ideas were now apparent. Whereas the southerners were determined that Africans should attain majority control of the executives, operating on a ministerial system, the north preferred to retain the British commissioners as executive authorities with the power to appoint their own executives, who would remain solely in an advisory capacity.

When the general conference assembled in Ibadan at the beginning of 1950, the major issues were the character of the executives and the distribution of regional representation in the central or federal legislature. The major influences in the country no longer questioned the necessity for a federal system, yet there were those who still refused to ignore the danger signals in this concept. A minority report to the proposals submitted by the drafting committee, signed by Eyo Ita, vice-president of the NCNC, and Mazi Mbonu Ojike, revived the older proposal that in place of the existing three regions a larger number of states should be created, based as far as possible on ethnic considerations. The report also proposed universal suffrage instead of an electoral college system.

The dangers inherent in the federated regional system were recognized by many younger Nigerians. Various groups of young Nigerians submitted resolutions suggesting alternatives to the general conference. A particularly perceptive resolution came from the Nigeria Society, formed by students in London, a frequent source of postwar political initiatives. The students, agreeing with the minority report, proposed that the various ethnic groups should be given control over their domestic affairs without prejudice to the government of the country as a whole. They suggested that Nigeria be divided into nine administrative units, so that none of them would be large enough to threaten the authority of the central government, and that loyalty to Nigeria "must transcend all local attachments and sectarian alignments." These young Nigerians had seen the dangers that their elders refused to recognize or to accept as being more vital than their own immediate interest. It is significant, and perhaps hopeful, to note that a number of the Nigeria Society signatories were prominent in Nigeria's public life at the end of the civil war in 1970.

These warnings, however, went virtually unheeded at the Ibadan conference. From it, and from subsequent discussions with the Colonial Secretary, a constitution emerged that provided a form of parliamentary government in each of the three regions and at the center. The federal executive represented a compromise between the northern and southern viewpoints. Twelve Africans were to sit on it, four from each region, along with six officials and the governor. The Africans were to be called ministers, but they were not to head any government departments, simply to be responsible for groups of subjects to be discussed in the legislature.

The legislature, to be called the House of Representatives, was to be composed of 136 Africans (of 142 members), to be elected by the regional houses, with 34 from each southern region and 68 from the north. In each region there were to be executives and Houses of Assembly, with elections conducted through electoral colleges based ultimately on primary elections in which all male taxpayers were enfranchised. In both the north and west there were also to be Houses of Chiefs.

The division of powers between the center and the regions was somewhat vaguely defined, but the regions could make laws governing local social services, courts, taxation, agriculture, education, and various local economic matters, subject to the governor's final authority.

It was the political implications rather than the constitutional details of the new constitution that were, however, of major significance. What had not been anticipated was that political parties would be formed to contest the elections. The Colonial Office—as well as the Nigerians who dominated the Ibadan conference—seems to have been blind to this elementary facet of political life. London might have learned the lesson of the Gold Coast, where they had made the same miscalculation, yet it was still assumed that no group in Nigeria would be strong enough to organize on a serious political basis.

In fact, there arose a dominant political party in each region. The NCNC somewhat reluctantly abandoned its national role and concentrated on the east. In the west Awolowo, who had been the main organizer of Egbe Omo Oduduwa when he was a law student in London, founded the Action Group on the foundations of the Egbe and remnants of the Youth Movement in Ibadan. In the north the Northern Peoples' Congress had been established in 1949, with Balewa as its main originator. At first, the NPC was a cultural body; it also had some radical members, but it was soon dominated by traditionalist rulers. Consequently, in 1950 Aminu Kano led a group away from the NPC to establish his Northern Elements Progressive Union (NEPU). However, the success of this body in the Kano primaries in 1951 provoked the traditionalists to reorganize the NPC as a political party in which Ahmadu Bello, Sardauna of Sokoto, the northern region premier, quickly became the dominant figure, with the support of the emirs.

The first elections under the new constitution made it evident that, unless some massive groundswell caused a revolt against the dominant trend, the future of Nigeria would be characterized by a balancing of interests and strengths between the three regional parties, by rivalry between north and south, and by conflict between majority and minority ethnic groups within each region. Those Nigerians in a position to influence the course of their country's history appeared to have accepted the underlying implications of the Lugard doctrine: the major ethnic communities were to regard themselves as separate political entities. How they could simultaneously create a Nigerian nation state, or avoid provoking a constant clash of interests within the Nigerian framework, were questions that they seemed to avoid as sedulously as Lugard and the Colonial Office had avoided them in the past.

14

THE CRISIS: ACT TWO

THE CURTAIN rose on the second act of Nigeria's latent crisis not at independence, as might be expected, but with the acceptance of the Macpherson constitution. By this time there could be little doubt that constitutional development would eventually bring independence; indeed, when the constitution came into force, it was expressly stated that it should be considered as a step toward further constitutional progress. Both Nigeria and the Gold Coast were firmly and clearly established in the road to independence, a road that would be marked by a progressive withdrawal of colonial authority.

It was, therefore, not agitation for independence that would dominate the political scene after the Macpherson constitution had come into effect; rather, it was the execution of the separatist, multinational policies first propounded by Lugard and since accepted by leading Nigerians that would most significantly characterize the future of Nigeria. Within this context the attainment of independence and even the civil war represented merely phases of a continuing crisis. Indeed, their real significance can only be understood through this perspective.

The separatist paths chosen by the Ibadan conference and incorporated into the Macpherson constitution were immediately evident when the first elections were held in 1951–1952. The major parties—the NPC, the Action Group, and the NCNC—each concentrated their efforts in the region where they could expect most support. Because each region was dominated by one large ethnic community—Hausa-Fulani, Yoruba, and Ibo, respectively—this necessitated every party's seeking most of its support from a particular ethnic group. The parties, therefore, soon became virtually communal parties, each controlled by a major community. Each party gained overwhelming majorities in its own region, and since the regional houses elected members to the central legislature, representation in the federal house also became largely communal. Equally important was the fact that the majority party in each region selected the ministers of its regional executive and nominated its four ministers to the federal executive. In both bodies the ministers were expected to represent the interests of their respective parties. In fact, the governments of regions and federation alike were composed of communal delegates, who, despite their mutual antagonisms, were supposed to work as cooperative teams.

It was anticipated that the Macpherson constitution would provide the means for the Nigerian people as a whole to elect and select the best men in the country to guide Nigeria, under British tutelage, toward self-government. The British simply did not realize that deep communal emotions divided Nigeria, or that these and other factors had caused differing political opinions to arise. They thought of Nigerians—indeed, of west Africans as a whole—as monolithic communities of black people anxious to see black men in positions of authority. Nor did the Nigerians, who were given the opportunity at the Ibadan conference to devise their own system, see any farther than the British. Consequently, no provision was made in the constitution for political parties or opposition.

Thus it came about that the most prominent national figure of the time, Azikiwe, was excluded from any office after the first elections. He won a seat in Lagos, which was then a part of the western region, but since the Action Group had a majority in the western house and was hostile to Azikiwe, he was neither given a place in the regional executive nor nominated as a federal minister.

Moreover, Azikiwe's absence from the east weakened discipline in his own party, as was demonstrated in 1953, when the NCNC parliamentary party clashed with its selected ministers, causing paralysis of government business. The house itself had to be dissolved.

In 1953, also, the Action Group made a bold attempt to claim for itself the role of national leadership, possibly hoping to take advantage of the confusion into which the NCNC had thrown itself. It tabled a motion in the federal house asserting that self-government by 1956 was the primary political objective. However, the northerners interpreted this move as a direct attack on themselves. They did not feel that they would be ready to assume authority from Britain as soon as 1956, believed that the southerners realized this, and so considered that the move was intended to portray them as reactionaries, tied to British apron strings.

The opposition of the north decided members from the west and east to walk out of the house; as northern members left they were jeered by the crowd of spectators. Southerners in politics and press used the event to discredit the northerners, causing deep resentment in the northern region. Attacks on the emirs, who had a religious as well as a political position, and on prominent northern politicians were bitterly resented. Six weeks later violence broke out in Kano, where southerners had lived unmolested for generations. Mobs of northerners and southerners attacked each other violently, burned and looted each other's houses and stores, mutilated their murdered opponents. A wave of intercommunal violence swept the city; by the end at least thirty-six people had lost their lives. The dreadful dangers of communal separatism introduced into the politics of a single state structure could hardly have been more brutally demonstrated. It appeared that a constitutional breakdown was imminent. The east was in confusion, the north in turmoil, and the federal house bitterly divided.

Finally, another conference was called to London, in the summer of 1953, but again both north-south and east-west rivalries were apparent. The two southern regions agreed to demand self-government by 1956, reviving northern fears; the west demanded that Lagos be retained within its region so vehemently that Awolowo threatened secession if it were removed; the east thought that the capital should become federal territory. Both east and west were agreed on a federal structure, but the north introduced a confederal plan in which no more than customs dues and defense would be administered by the center.

After much bargaining, which again revealed the extent to which political interest was concentrated in the regions, a compromise was agreed, but the compromise increased still further the regionalization of the country: all officials were to withdraw from the eastern and western executives, which would now be entirely composed of members appointed by the majority party. The way was thus open to domestic self-government for both east and west, with communalism entrenched in each. In the federal executive, to be termed the Council of Ministers, only three officials would remain, the other ten members being appointed by those parties that won the federal election in the regions, three being nominated by each region and one from the Cameroons. Federal elections were to be held separately from those for the regional houses. This stipulation might have been thought to encourage some sense of federal or national sentiment, but any chances of this sentiment's emerging were dissipated by the provision that federal members be appointed on a regional basis, thereby encouraging each communal-regional party to fight for control of its regional nominees to the central executive. Further strengthening this regional attitude were the provisions for the regionalization of the civil and judicial services, the tying of revenue allocation to its region of derivation, the removal of federal authority over regional legislation, and the reduction in the list of federal subjects. Thus regional or communal emphasis had become rampant; the extension of the franchise, which was to be based on universal suffrage in the east and male taxpayers in the west, which might have increased popular participation in national decision-making, was thus directed into regional channels. The dispute over Lagos was settled in favor of the east, with the capital becoming a federal territory, a kind of tiny fourth region.

As was to be expected, in the next regional elections each major party retained control of its own region. The heavy emphasis placed on regional politics was illustrated by the fact that the three main party leaders—Ahmadu Bello, Awolowo, and Azikiwe—all chose to take ministerial positions in their own regions, rather than participate in the federal government. But a surprise occurred when federal elections were held. The NCNC won a majority, not only in the east, but also in the west, therefore acquiring power to nominate six of the ten federal ministers. Thus, instead of the federal government's becoming a coalition of the three main parties and regions, the NCNC and the NPC formed a coalition with the Action Group taking the role of opposition.

This development again foreshadowed future conflict and intensified bitterness. It provoked the Action Group to concentrate on maneuvers to defeat its rival, led to disputes within the party between the various Yoruba factions, reviving their historical conflicts, and resulted in talk of dividing the west in order to amputate the Ibo areas. By embittering relations between west and east, the electoral results destroyed any future possibility of tripartite government at the center. Regional rivalries continued to dominate the federal house and government, in addition to the friction caused by their competition in the regions for their own interests and advantage.

The situation was such that the three leaders who could command any substantial following were all prime ministers in their own regions, supported in the main by their own ethnic communities. At the center the NPC and NCNC formed a coalition government, despite the fact that the NCNC had participated in an electoral pact with the opponents of the NPC in the northern federal elections. Balewa, a Hausa of the Jere community near Bauchi, an ex-teacher educated at Katsina College and in London, was leader of the largest group, the northerners, in the federal assembly; he became the first federal prime minister in 1958. Balewa was one of the few politicians genuinely devoted to Nigerian unity, but his task of balancing regional influences and personalities was impossible. Because of the rigors of his job he had little time or effort to spare to initiate any decisive policy of his own. He also had the disadvantage of being considered by some as a puppet of the Sardauna. Ahmadu Bello, who had also been at Katsina and in London, was a Fulani who could trace his ancestry back to Fodio, was a nephew of the sultan, and certainly the most powerful man in the north.

The elements of division and conflict in this situation are obvious, but they were not such as to hinder the attainment of independence. At further conferences in 1957 and 1958 the details were ironed out. The two southern regions were granted internal self-government in 1957, the north in 1959. Elections for the parliament that was to request independence were held at the end of 1959. None of the details agreed upon were important to the basic crisis, except, perhaps, that a single police force was to be established for the whole country.

What was far more important was the issue that was prominently aired at the 1957 conference. As has been seen, in each of the three regions the majority party that formed the government represented mainly one ethnic community. But there were many smaller communities in each region. Because of the monolithic character of the major parties it seemed as though the minorities were doomed to permanent opposition. This in itself was highly dangerous, for it was an open invitation to subversion, to attempts to secure, by violence or intrigue, what could never be gained from legitimate political activity. But, in addition, some of the minorities feared that once British authority was withdrawn and the party governments left in sole control, the interests and even the safety of minority communities would be in jeopardy. They therefore demanded the creation of new regions, just as the students had done in 1949 and Azikiwe before that. As a result of their representations a Minorities Commission was set up at the conference.

The commission admitted that many of the fears expressed by the minorities were genuine, but it did not consider that they should be allayed by dividing the existing regions into smaller units. Instead, it proposed that a human-rights clause should be inserted in the independence constitution, listing the rights guaranteed to every citizen, and that provision be made to foster economic and social progress in minority areas. These recommendations did not satisfy many minority groups, but they had to await a more propitious time to pursue their aims: yet one more divisive factor was added to the accumulating list on the eve of independence.

The 1959 elections repeated the already familiar story. Of the 312 seats in the federal house, 174 were allocated to the north, 73 to the east, 62 to the west, and 3 to Lagos. Adult suffrage applied everywhere except in the Muslim-dominated north, where females were refused the franchise. The senate was composed of twelve members from each region, plus four members from Lagos and four appointed at the discretion of the prime minister. The election gave 142 seats to the

NPC, 89 to the electoral coalition of NCNC and NEPU, 73 to the Action Group, and 8 to independents.

Although a few inroads had been made into the northern domination of the NPC, they were too slight to threaten its control; no party had sufficient numbers to form a government on its own. After intense bargaining and maneuvering, the NPC and NCNC resumed their coalition; Balewa was reappointed prime minister and included in his cabinet ten members of the NPC, seven of the NCNC, and two independent members from the senate. Azikiwe refused to join the cabinet and became president of the senate until he was appointed governor-general at independence; Awolowo, who had tried, but failed, to form a coalition with either rival party, found himself leader of the opposition.

The new legislature duly requested independence from the British government; the parliament at Westminster thereupon passed an independence act on the basis of the constitution that Nigerians themselves had approved. In October, 1960, Nigeria became an independent state and shortly afterward was accepted as a member of the United Nations.

The era of British rule had lasted less than a century, even if dated from the colonization of Lagos; direct colonial rule over the country as a whole had existed for just sixty years. During that time nothing had been fundamentally altered, except that—crucially—the multifarious societies of a large country had become a single political unit. The societies themselves had remained basically unaltered, retaining almost all their languages, religions, and traditions, though adapting them to modern conditions.

The event of independence was hardly momentous, if judged by its effect on the lives of the people. It was another incident in the great drama of crisis over whether different societies and communities could learn to live together or part and form separate nation states. Independence had no bearing on this central issue; it did no more than hand over complete responsibility for dealing with the issues involved to Nigerians; the issues remained the same before and after October, 1960.

There was yet another aspect of independence that held the seeds of future conflict. The period since World War II had been one of massive growth. Government revenue had been increased six times, imports five times, exports three times; many new motor roads had been built, though of the thirty-seven thousand miles of motor road in the country only about four thousand were paved; schools and universities had greatly multiplied; electricity and water supplies had been expanded; urban populations had grown rapidly—Lagos from 230,000 in 1950 to 675,000 soon after independence, Enugu from 15,000 in 1939 to over 60,000 during the 1950s. Some faint signs of industrialization had become visible: factories producing mainly consumer goods, such as textiles, tobacco, beer, soft drinks. Demand for such goods had begun to grow as urban populations increased, though this demand was accompanied by large-scale unemployment in the same towns.

Yet these developments bore very unevenly on Nigeria's peoples. In social amenities the stark, regional contrasts were still apparent. In the year of independence the north, with over half the total population, still possessed only 41 secondary schools out of the nation's 883. Morever, whereas in the country as a whole between 3 and 3.5 million children were in primary schools—perhaps 80 percent of the school-age population in the east and west—and between 300,000 and 400,000 were leaving primary school each year, the vast majority of leavers were unable to obtain any post-primary education and therefore were being thrown onto the labor market with few skills beyond literacy. At the same time, there were only about a thousand students at the university, though soon four new universities were to be created, ominously through communal inspiration in each region, in Ife, Zaria, Nsukka, and Lagos, with a corresponding increase in the student population.

The vast majority of Nigerians remained tied to the land,

which itself produced 85 percent of the country's exports. The per capita income of the whole was around $80 a year. The stratification of society had become obvious: students, professionals, public men living in luxury; peasants on subsistence. And societal tensions were being exacerbated by regional imbalance and by urban-rural jealousies.

The danger of conflicts arising from the above causes was aggravated by two primary factors. First, in the north and east single-crop economies left both regions more vulnerable to world price fluctuations than the more diversified west. The north depended almost entirely on groundnuts; the east on palm products. In the west cocoa, which formed the main staple and was also subject to wild fluctuations, was supplemented by palm oil, rubber, and timber. And although the marketing board system, which had been introduced during World War II, was supposed to cushion price changes for the producers, it had actually become little more than a form of taxation, the returns of which were spent in many ways—not all of them honest—but were rarely returned to the farmers in times of low prices. Thus the seeds of economic resentment on a regional basis were added to political rivalries.

Second, by the time of independence the Nigerian economy had come under powerful external control. Three great companies—the United Africa Company (a subsidiary of Unilever), the Compagnie Française de l'Afrique Occidentale, and the Société Commerciale de l'Ouest Africain, dominated commercial life. During the 1950s, contrary to popular belief, these giants had not resisted the removal of colonial rule or the march toward independence. Much more intelligently, they had shifted their activities and sought to identify the rulers of the future. The United Africa Company, in particular, deliberately changed its functions from retail trading to consumer production. At the end of the war the UAC controlled over a third of the exports from Ghana and Nigeria, the three companies together between one-half and four-fifths of the two countries' export trade. By 1963, moreover, UAC had invested some $31 million in projects such as cold-storage and vehicle-assembly plants, breweries, mineral-water manufacture, cement production. These foreign companies' previous role, that of buying produce in exchange for consumer goods in the rural areas, had been handed over to Africans—or to Syrians and Lebanese.

Three major dangers arose from the domination of Nigerian economy by alien concerns. First, foreign domination prevented Nigerian governments from controlling their own economic policies. Second, it often inhibited the growth of local manufactures and industries through nationally planned labor and productive channels, substituting consideration for European shareholders. Third, it often encouraged graft, corruption, and bribery, which undermined honest government and led to decisions' being taken according to personal rather than to public interest.

All these dangers were enormously aggravated when oil was discovered in the delta area during the 1950s. Production spiraled spectacularly. In 1950, 800 tons were produced; in 1966, 19 million tons; despite the civil war, it was anticipated that over 50 million tons would be produced in 1970. Shell alone invested some $312 million in prospecting, wells, pipelines, and a small refinery, a sum that represented 85 percent of all new net foreign investment during the period and exceeded the total investment in Nigerian manufacturing industry. In April, 1970, Shell-BP announced that it would invest a further $160 million in expansion, and there are other companies with oil concessions.

The danger of this oil boom was not only that, since most of the operation consisted of the export of crude oil, Nigeria was deprived of the added value of manufacture. The major effect was that the boom left the Nigerian economy even more dependent on outside control. Oil revenues played an important part in the conflict leading to the civil war; it seemed probable that Nigerian government would become increasingly dependent on the revenues gained from the oil companies, with all the consequences to national economic policy.

Underlying the whole of the economic situation, however, ran the poisoned stream of gross social inequality. Before, during, and after independence the contrast between those who had secured the fruits of office and the mass of ordinary rural peasants or urban unemployed constantly foreshadowed a revolt against visible injustice. Many of the measures of economic development—some uncompleted or grossly mismanaged—offered large rewards to those concerned in them. Few schemes changed the lives of the rural subsistence peasants or urban poor. The ostentation and luxury displayed by certain public figures only drew greater attention to the contrasts. It was made abundantly obvious that public office offered rich rewards, so the fight for office was intensified and adulterated. The battles before independence had been bitter enough; once the restraining hand of Britain was removed inhibitions in political war entirely disappeared.

The first stark fact that the new Nigeria had to face was that the chances of a tripartite federal government remained extremely slim because of the hostility that had developed over the past decade. At least one party, and therefore one ethnic community, would always be excluded from office at the center and therefore debarred from the fruits in patronage and rewards. Yet each party could gain these dividends in its region. One of the consequences of this situation was that agitation broke out in each of the regions to create new units so that smaller communities could break away from the domination of the major group; in the west non-Yoruba worked for a Mid-West Region; in the east, many peoples of the delta, such as the Ibibio, Efik, and Ijaw, sought escape from Ibo rule, more particularly since most of the oil was discovered in their areas. The elections of 1960–1961, in which each major party gained large majorities in its region, made the escape seem even more attractive.

It was not long before dissension arose within the Nigerian political emporium. Not surprisingly, it first appeared in an area that was particularly subject to quarrels because its party was excluded from the federal government: the west, where Yoruba factionalism had been endemic for generations. The party leader, Awolowo, and the regional prime minister, Akintola, began to quarrel publicly. At the beginning of 1962 the party executive decided to remove Akintola from office, the governor concurred, and a supporter of Awolowo, Alhaji Adegbenro, was asked to replace him. When the regional house met, however, uproar ensued, with Akintola's followers and NCNC members attacking the supporters of the new prime minister. The riot became so severe that the police were called and had to use tear gas. This action suited the purpose of the Akintola faction, for it allowed the federal government to intervene and, with approval from the federal house, to declare a state of emergency and appoint an administrator with executive powers. Paradoxically, six months later a new party formed by Chief Samuel Akintola, the United Peoples' party, was installed as the government in a conservative-radical coalition with the NCNC.

The Akintola incident not only illustrates the labyrinthine nature of Nigerian politics but indicates the further divisions that had already begun to crack the body politic. Awolowo was a member of the Ijebu clan, often resented among other Yoruba for its enterprise; he had also become increasingly radical because of his position as opposition leader in the federal house; and he had always been challenged by recalcitrant factors in his attempt to unify the various elements of Yoruba opinion. Akintola was from the northern division of Oshun and tended toward conservatism, and Awolowo had strength in parts of the west. Yet Awolowo had sent Action Group candidates to fight seats in the north when the northerners in the federal government, led by the federal prime minister, Balewa, were in a position to intervene in the west in support of their potential allies, Akintola and his followers. Akintola could also count on the support of the NCNC, a party that not only was a partner in the federal coalition but had ambitions to control the west and thereby the whole south. Finally, the intervention of the federal government on behalf of Akintola deepened the division within Yoruba society, as was to become apparent even during the civil war.

A further development arose out of the crisis in the west. In 1963 the schism in Yoruba politics was seen as an opportunity to divide the region. The NCNC recognized its chance to control two regions, for it had always been strong in the non-Yoruba areas of the west. A referendum was therefore held, with the NCNC campaigning for separation and gaining the support of western Ibo, the Bini, Itsekiri, Urhobo, and other communities centered on Benin. The supporters of a new region won the referendum, a fourth region, the Mid-West Region, was formed, and the NCNC won the ensuing election. Ultimately, then, the NCNC thus controlled two of the four regions, the East and Mid-West.

Meanwhile, in September, 1962, the country was startled by the news that Awolowo and thirty of his supporters had been arrested and were to be charged with plotting to overthrow the federal government by force. This is not the place to comment on the conduct of the trial, though it should be mentioned that the chosen lawyers of both Awolowo and his lieutenant, Chief Anthony Enahoro, were refused entry to the country. (Enahoro was also the subject of a *cause célèbre* in Britain, from where he was eventually repatriated after his case had gone to the House of Lords and had been the subject of passionate debate in Parliament.)

Both Awolowo and Enahoro were convicted and sentenced to imprisonment. But the significance of the trial was neither its conduct nor its verdict. First, it was generally regarded in Nigeria as a political trial in which the opponents of Awolowo, particularly those in the federal government, were determined to ruin him and remove him from public life. Second, whatever one believed or disbelieved about the evidence produced, the trial lifted the lid off the appalling state of bribery and violence that had become a commonplace in Nigerian politics. And, third, Awolowo himself revealed that in 1961 he had been trying to arrange a coalition with the NCNC, and especially with its militant wing, to "take over power at the federal level." In other words, Awolowo had been attempting to organize southern control of the federal government to the exclusion of the north, whereas Akintola had been attempting to link with the north against the east. The machinations of the politicians, apparently without regard for principle or policy but bent only on power, together with the revelation of the enormous sums being spent by the parties and the use of violence for this purpose, added to the disenchantment with politics and politicians rapidly spreading throughout Nigeria.

The next revolt against the establishment came from a different source. It illustrated the resentment caused by social injustice mentioned above and, for a moment, seemed as though it might unexpectedly introduce one element of national unity on a particular plane of society.

In 1964 a general strike was called. The trade unions had hardly played an heroic role in Nigerian history. Unionists were fervent nationalists just after World War II, but later the unions suffered from the fact that they could organize only a small number of regular wage-earners, while the large number of unemployed, together with ethnic schisms and personal quarrels, weakened their bargaining power. As elsewhere in Africa, these divisions were reflected in the adherence of different trade union centers to either the International Confederation of Free Trade Unions, usually associated with American domination, or to the World Federation of Trade Unions, thought of as a communist body, or to the all-African center, based in Ghana. In 1964, however, all the Nigerian unions managed to work in harness for a short time.

The rapidly rising cost of living inevitably caused greatest suffering among the lowest paid workers and the unemployed, resulting in a gross disparity in living standards that was accentuated by success differences between the elite, professional and political, who received salaries based on British standards, and the "ordinary" worker, whose average per capita income was under $80, a twelfth of that in Britain.

Under pressure from the discontented, the Morgan Commission was appointed in 1963 to examine wages and conditions. It reported that a man with a wife and two children living in Lagos needed $40 per month to live decently; at the same time minimum wages paid to government employees were $18. The commission recommended that the wages be immediately raised to $29, but the federal government delayed publishing the report and was reluctant to implement its findings. The result was that a Joint Action Committee, led by union veteran Michael Imoudou, organized a strike that brought out eight hundred thousand men. It immediately became clear that it was not only wages that caused deep resentment; the corruption, ostentatious luxury, and inefficiency of public life formed a second target. Thus when Prime Minister Balewa tried to treat the strikers high-handedly and then to bully them, he simply provoked greater solidarity. The strike continued for two weeks, and at the end the government agreed to a $24 minimum salary. Once again warning signals of discontent with the establishment had flashed; unfortunately, the unity that had been forged between the unions did not long survive the strike settlement.

It was not only in the south that signs of revolt appeared. In the same year as the strike, 1964, the Tiv community in the Benue province of the middle belt in the northern region rebelled against what they considered to be neglect by the regional government. The Tiv, the mainstay of the movement to create a separate region in the middle belt, were a tough, short, mainly pagan, and very fierce people who traditionally found employment in the army. In the revolt of 1964 over three hundred lives were lost, and the army had to be sent in to control the area. One more thread of the web of discontent had become apparent: a minority of some 1.5 million people was seen to be rebelling against the domination of the major community over its regional government and all the perquisites that it was thought to be supplying in unfair proportions to its own people.

In the middle 1960s politics in Nigeria resembled Chicago politics of the 1920s. Caught in a web of continual crisis the country lurched continually toward disaster. Each new constitutional issue that arose represented merely another milestone along the way. In 1962 a census was held, and a census was politically crucial because on its figures would be based the parliamentary seats for the next election. The central issue was whether the north had a larger population than that of the three regions of the south combined. It was rumored that the census showed the southern population to be equal to the north, though the British official in charge admitted that southern figures were false. In any case, the census findings were never published. Instead, a second census was held, in 1963, this time under the personal supervision of the prime minister. It showed the north to be inhabited by 29.8 million, the east by 12.4 million, the west, mid-west, and Lagos combined by 13.4 million. This gave the north a comfortable majority over the south, but, of course, the figures were passionately contested and were rejected by most southern politicians.

Federal elections were due in the following year, 1964, and they were seen as the final opportunity for those without office to break the increasingly dominant hold of the forces in control of the federal government. These politicians were not thought of simply as federal ministers; even more importantly they were held to be the northern establishment centered around the Sardauna, together with his allies in the west. This division in the power game was reflected in new alliances formed six months before the elections. The NPC and Akintola's group, now called the Nigerian National Democratic party, established the Nigerian National Alliance (NNA); significantly, it was not the federal prime minister who was chosen to head the new coalition but Bello, the Sardauna, premier of the north. To oppose this grouping the NCNC, despite its role as federal partner of the north, formed an alliance with the Action Group, in the wilderness in both western and federal houses and with its two main leaders in jail: the United Progressive Grand Alliance (UPGA). Dr. Okpara, premier of the east, was to be its leader, for Azikiwe, after serving as governor-general, had become nonpolitical president when Nigeria had become a republic in 1963. The two main opposition parties in the north, NEPU and the United Middle Belt Congress, also joined together in the Northern Progressive Front and were supported by the UPGA. On paper, the northern alliance was conservative and the southern more progressive, but by 1964 political bodies had little relationship to policies.

The abuse, violence, bribery, and viciousness of the election campaign were so outrageous that President Azikiwe warned the country that it was heading for "troubles worse than the Congo." As the Nigerian army had performed with fine discipline and dignity in the Congo crisis, and thus seen at first hand the dangers there, the warning was particularly apposite.

The election itself was a tragic farce. The president and federal prime minister disagreed about the necessity for postponing it; it was alleged that many of the candidates were unopposed because returning officers refused to accept nominations from their opponents; the UGPA decided to boycott the poll, though halfway through polling day the premier of the mid-west changed his mind; Michael Imoudou, who had formed a Labour party, tried to call a general strike to get the election postponed, and the railway and port workers actually came out; the electoral commission was divided, and its chairman broadcast that the election would take place while his colleagues were still debating. On election day there were no elections in the east, and few went to the polls in Lagos—which only made it easier for the NNA to secure its majority. But while Balewa waited for the president to ask him to form another government, it became apparent that Azikiwe was strongly disinclined to do so. For several days the two men remained deadlocked in a trial of strength. Azikiwe, however, had to recognize that his powers under the constitution were minimal, even over the armed forces, so, with the help of the eastern and federal chief justices, a compromise was reached. A national government was to be formed, the legality of the elections were to be tested in the courts, the constitution was to be reviewed, and elections were to be held in the western region. In the elections held later in the east the NCNC was victorious again. Balewa interpreted his part of the bargain by selecting a government drawn from all the parties in power in the regions, but this meant that once again the Action Group was excluded.

Though the plans of the "progressive" UGPA were defeated, the real losers were the principles and practices of parliamentary democracy in Nigeria; for the parliamentary system of government depends essentially on an honest belief on the part of everyone concerned that a genuine measurement of the people's will and the acceptance of the popular verdict by the losers is more important than the achievement of power. The concept had been flagrantly thrown aside in the 1964 election; without it the parliamentary system loses its legitimacy before and after an election. After the events of the last days of 1964 no one could expect the Nigerian people to retain any respect for their system of government. Symbolically, during the campaign, Dr. Okpara, the NCNC premier of the east, was heard to threaten that the east would secede from the federation, and the threat of secession was the natural reaction of those who were disgusted with the conduct of federal politics and believed that they could manage their affairs better within their own community.

Only one further demonstration of the collapse of political morality was necessary to end the life of Nigeria's dying body politic. In November, 1965, elections were held in the west. Akintola's government was now thoroughly discredited. It was clear to most observers that if genuine elections were held, Akintola would be defeated. The UGPA saw its opportunity to add the west to the east and mid-west that they already controlled, giving them command of the whole south and thus a majority in the senate, which could restrain government business. Success in the west would give the UGPA a strong bargaining position to face the NPC from the north; for in such a confrontation it could well have been that the middle belt and Kano province would have defected from the north and given the UGPA control of the federal house.

Events were not allowed to take their course. No one will ever know the result of that election, except that it finally assassinated parliamentary democracy. When nominations were refused, electoral officers were kidnapped or dismissed, ballot papers and returns falsified, candidates with a minority of votes declared elected, officers and agents shot, the whole process was reduced to a tragic farce. Even the UGPA pact between the Action Group and the NCNC was flimsy; in thirteen seats their respective candidates fought each other. After the "election" was complete, the leaders of both parties, Akintola and Adegbenro, claimed the right to form a government. The latter was arrested. Demonstrations were held in the east, while in the west itself terror ruled, with riots, arson, and murders. It was later estimated that two thousand people lost their lives during and after the election. Tragically significant for the future was the fact that some of the killed were Hausa from the north, while many of the troops sent to quell the riots were sympathizers with the UGPA, who increased the tension. At the very time that leaders of Commonwealth countries from all over the world were arriving in Lagos for a conference about the Rhodesian crisis, murderous riots were in process a mile from the airport.

There is every reason to suppose, from all knowledge of his character, that Balewa was trying to prevent a collapse into chaos. But since he had declared a state of emergency in 1962 over scuffles in the western house, why did he not repeat his act in the much more serious situation of January, 1966? The fact that Akintola was, at this latter time, in office, whereas in the earlier incident it had been Adegbenro who was premier, cannot be ignored; nor can the fact that Akintola flew to Kaduna for discussions with Bello. Both pieces of evidence point to the determination of the forces centered on the Sardauna to prevent at all costs the Action Group–NCNC alliance from capturing the west. It has been reported that Bello, Akintola, and Balewa discussed a plan to arrest all the pro-UGPA supporters in the west, disband those units of the army suspected of UGPA sympathies, and send General Ironsi, the military commander, also under suspicion of similar sympathies, on leave.

Whether there was such a plan or not, it was now too late. The first Nigerian republic was on its deathbed, poisoned by the reckless thirst for power and wealth of its own parents. For some time there had been intimations of impending military intervention, but they had been discounted even by Balewa on the assurances of special branch police. During the night following Akintola's conference with Bello the coup was executed. By next morning the three main actors were dead. Balewa and his minister of finance, Chief Festus, for long one of the main targets for critics of ostentatious luxury, were taken from their neighboring homes and killed. Akintola tried to defend himself with an automatic rifle in his lodge in Ibadan; he was mortally wounded. In Kaduna the premier's lodge was seized by troops, and the Sardauna was killed. A number of northern army officers also were assassinated. In Benin and Enugu troops surrounded the premiers' houses, but neither premier was attacked. Meanwhile, General Ironsi was trying to restore order in the army and succeeded in preventing its occupying Lagos.

In the capital the remainder of the cabinet met on the Saturday and Sunday, but President Azikiwe was away in London. There was some dispute as to whether another prime minister could be appointed in an acting capacity (it was not yet known whether or not Balewa was alive) in the absence of the president. There was also doubt as to whether an easterner or another northerner should be appointed. General Ironsi was himself an Ibo, and it had been Ibo officers who had led the coup. Eventually the general told the cabinet that he would have to assume power himself. A military government was formed under him, consisting of the heads of the military services and the military governors who were appointed over each region. It was quickly stressed that the military had only taken over temporarily, that a new constitution would be sought, and that civilian government would be restored as soon as possible. The main object was to stamp out corruption and dishonesty in public life. Over much of the country the coup was welcomed as a relief from the political chicanery and ostentatious high living that had so disfigured Nigerian life; even in the north, which had suffered the greatest political and personal blows, there was an inclination to await developments.

Yet the poison-letting was not finished. General Ironsi was essentially a soldier, not a politician. He made numerous mistakes, probably under the influence of his advisers, who tended to be mainly Ibo, and these mistakes dissipated much of the goodwill that had greeted his advent to power. The military government had to take some action to try and resolve the crisis that had been undermining the morale of the people for twenty years. Yet the military administrators had inherited the bitter passions of their predecessors. When Francis Nwokedi, a leading Ibo public servant, was appointed as sole commissioner to report on the possibility of unifying regional public services, northerners became suspicious; the promulgation of a decree abolishing the regions and the federation, unifying the administration, and creating a group of provinces confirmed their suspicions. They recalled that it was mainly northerners, together with a few Yoruba, who had been killed in the coup, that the eastern premier had not been harmed, that Ibo officers had led the revolt.

Ironsi was in an impossible position. His regime had tried to initiate some reforms, rooting out corruption and patronage so deeply embedded in Nigerian society. But the cost of living rose astronomically, and with the widespread dislocation inevitable after a revolution there was little chance of halting it. At the same time Ironsi was being pressed from two opposite sides. The north expected him to put the rebel majors on trial; southern radicals regarded them as national heroes. Nigeria as a country lives on rumor. The idea that the coup was part of a plot to impose Ibo, or southern, domination over the whole country began to gain ground, particularly in the north. The appointment of every Ibo to government office fed the rumor. More dangerous still, the action of a few Ibo in boasting to the northerners about the killing of the Sardauna, Balewa, and the others stoked the fires of resentment rising in the north.

A few days after the publication of the unification decree in May, 1966, the suspicious resentment exploded in the north. Demonstrations quickly turned into riots aimed at the Ibo and other easterners. As in 1953, the rioters in Kano raced out of the old city into the *sabon gari,* killing, burning, and looting. The epidemic spread to other towns in the north. To the northerners the day for revenge had arrived, and there was already open talk of secession.

The northern governor, Colonel Katsina, tried desperately

to restore order; Ironsi attempted to modify the impact of his decree by insisting that its purpose was no more than to allow the military government to carry on the administration, and that it did not affect territorial divisions; the military governor of the east, Colonel Ojukwu, urged those Ibo who had fled back to the east to return to their homes—advice that he was to regret bitterly later.

It was clear to all by May that the first coup had solved nothing, serving only to remove corrupt politicians—and honest ones, too—but that its nature might well provoke counteraction. Further coups were widely expected, though there was doubt as to whether they would come from the north or south. In July this question was answered. While Ironsi was staying in Ibadan, he was seized by northern soldiers, taken outside the town, and, with the governor, shot. Once again the army, which had been the most consistent stronghold of discipline and national unity, was seen to be torn between ethnic factions. Easterners were killed in several barracks, and this time the mutineers were northerners. Brigadier Ogundipe, now the senior officer and a Yoruba, tried to quell the mutiny and was asked by Ojukwu to take over as supreme commander. Ogundipe was reluctant to do so; there was even louder talk about secession; and at this moment Colonel Yakubu Gowon, then army chief of staff, was sent to negotiate with the mutineers. After three days of chaos Gowon emerged as the new supreme commander and immediately repealed the contentious unification decree.

Gowon was thirty-one when this dreadful responsibility fell on his shoulders. He was a northerner, but an unusual northerner; for he was a Christian—his father being an evangelist—from the plateau province of the middle belt. Gowon had been in the army since leaving school and had had several spells of training in Britain, including one at the army staff college at Sandhurst. He had also served in the Nigerian army with the United Nations in the Congo. His obvious sincerity, modesty, and shyness made him one of the most unusual figures to hold such high office in any state. Yet he became accepted as the only symbol of unity in Nigeria.

Gowon's first task was to stop the killings in the army. He had some success in this by posting the soldiers to barracks within their regions of origin. But there was one flaw in this solution. There were very few Yoruba in the army; consequently, since troops had to be kept in the west, most of them were northerners, often appearing to be an army of occupation.

Gowon then turned to constitutional review, genuinely anxious to find a way to restore civilian government without risking the disasters of the past. A conference was called of "leaders of thought," from the regions, now restored to their previous position. At first the north and the east favored a loose association, while the west proposed the creation of more states. Northerners even at first suggested that regions should have the right to secede, but they quickly changed their minds—and in a significant manner. The north soon began insisting that there should be a strong central government without any right of secession, with agreement in principle to increase the number of states. It was clear that a new factor had entered the debate: the minorities were beginning to assert themselves; Gowon himself was from such a minority group. The minorities were determined not to submit to the degree of domination previously imposed by the major communities. And this applied not only to people such as the middle-belt groups in the north but also to the river communities in the east: the Ijaw, Ibibio, and Efik.

At this stage of the conference the ulcers of poisoned emotions in Nigerian society suddenly burst. A second massacre of easterners began in the north; this time it was much more ferocious, hysterical, paranoiac than before. Resentment against Ibo economic, educational, and technical superiority had simmered for years. It was the familiar case of an alien minority economically dominating a larger community beside which it is living. On this occasion, the fury was fanned by reports that northerners were being killed in the east, though it has never been established which killing started first. The pogrom in the north, whatever its immediate cause, produced a trauma that will affect Nigerian life for a generation. It has been variously estimated that between ten thousand and thirty thousand Ibo and other easterners lost their lives during the holocaust of September, 1966; perhaps another million fled back to the eastern region. Despite the restraining efforts of Colonel Hassan, soldiers joined in the massacre, again tainting the army with communalism. The killings were accompanied by mass looting as the northerners gave vent to their jealousy of Ibo wealth. The regional government of the north tried its best to halt the riots and gave shelter and food to what victims it could; many Ibo found succor in the palace of the emir of Kano; but nothing could halt the northern fury.

The catastrophe represented the logical consequence of the failure by either the British or the Nigerians to make a firm choice between separate communal statehood and strong centralized government; it was aggravated also by the deliberate insulation of the northerners from modernization until a wide gap had appeared between them and southern Nigerians. Thus when the well of envy that had been filled from the superior skills of the easterners spilled over, there was no state security to protect them. The uncontrolled passions loosed in September, 1966, on both sides were soon to release a dimension of violence in the Nigerian crisis that had never before been experienced.

The events in the north and east rendered constitutional talks academic. Ojukwu, faced with the mammoth task of caring for the flood of refugees who streamed into the east, ordered all non-easterners to leave his region for their own safety. He refused to attend any further discussions or meetings in Lagos until his personal safety was assured. The east increasingly felt itself to be a beleaguered state, and clamor for secession grew louder.

No one had the authority or the personality to overcome the inexorable logic of the years of crisis; it is to be doubted whether such a superhuman has ever existed. The situation was worsened by the fact that Ojukwu saw no reason to recognize Gowon's authority. Ojukwu had been to Nigeria's prestigious school, King's College, and to Oxford. He had proved himself intellectually—which tended to make him arrogant towards others. He did not recognize Gowon as a superior officer and had tried to get Ogundipe to assume command on the death of Ironsi. Yet while he could see no reason to bow to Gowon, Ojukwu had inherited a large fortune, most of it in Lagos, and, consequently, his personal interest lay in remaining within the federation. Nevertheless, Ojukwu was being steadily pressed toward secession, especially by a group of high civil servants who had left Lagos to return to Enugu. Moreover, the situation worsened as an open arms race developed between the east and the federal military government.

In an effort to avert what appeared an inevitable rush toward disaster, General Ankrah, head of Ghana's military government, with fellow-feeling for his military colleagues in Nigeria, persuaded them to meet at Aburi, just outside Accra, in January, 1967. The meeting was dominated by Ojukwu, who guided his less astute officer rivals into agreeing to create a kind of confederation in which each region would have control of its own internal affairs and the central government would be subject to a veto from any region on matters affecting either a region or the whole country. Once this agreement was studied in Lagos, it was evident that it could not be implemented without destroying the federation and raising the probability of national disintegration, and the agreement was repudiated. However, the military government made one last attempt to satisfy Ojukwu, by decreeing that legislative and executive powers should be vested in a Supreme Military Council, which would be subject on every important matter to unanimity among all military governors, with senior appointments approved by every region. But Ojukwu was not satisfied, pointing to the powers still vested in the federal government to interfere in regional affairs and at the end of March, 1967, he appropriated all federal revenues collected in his region.

It was clear to all that Nigeria was again on the verge of disintegration. Not only was the east moving inexorably toward secession, Awolowo—released from prison the previous year together with Enahoro—now declared that if the east were to secede, the west would follow suit. However, a reprieve came from an unexpected source. The north had always been the strongest opponent of increasing the number of regions or states, fearing that it would thereby lose its dominant position, but in 1967 the northern emirs, faced with an imminent collapse of the whole federation and with discontent among the Tiv and middle-belt peoples, called on the federal government to divide the north into several states —whatever happened in the other regions. This move persuaded Awolowo that he could discard his long-standing fears of northern domination, and he agreed to become commissioner for finance and deputy chairman in the federal government, now to be a mixed group of military men and civilians. Enahoro also agreed to join the new government.

Thus, at the eleventh hour, a stronger team was assembled at the center than ever before, and for the first time Nigeria would face the intransigence of Ojukwu with confidence. But if Nigeria had stronger leaders, the crisis was becoming more severe. In retaliation against Ojukwu's appropriation of revenues, a postal blockade was declared against the east, and despite one last attempt to prevent an irretrievable confrontation—when Awolowo and the chief justice visited Ojukwu and the federal government announced acceptance of his demands

—it seemed that the race toward disaster had gained too great a momentum. When Ojukwu met his Ibo consultative assembly on May 26, he offered them three alternatives: accepting the terms proposed by Gowon, continuing the existing stalemate, or asserting autonomy. The assembly passed a resolution giving Ojukwu authority to declare the eastern region "a free, sovereign and independent state by the name and title of the Republic of Biafra. And I do declare that all political ties between us and the Federal Republic of Nigeria are hereby totally dissolved."

Gowon immediately declared a state of emergency and reimposed the blockade on the east. In the same broadcast he also announced the momentous news that Nigeria would now be divided into twelve states, six in the north, three in the east, Lagos, mid-west, and west. Four days later, on May 30, Ojukwu declared that his region "shall henceforth be an independent sovereign state of the name and title, the Republic of Biafra." War between the east and the rest of the federation was now inevitable.

This is not the place for a military history of the war; no doubt it will be written sooner or later, though the confusion in which the war was fought will make the task unusually difficult. It is more important to note its significant consequences. The first shots were fired on July 6, 1967; on January 12, 1970, General Effiong, who had assumed the leadership of Biafra when Colonel Ojukwu left the country a few days earlier, ordered his men to lay down their arms and sought an armistice. The war thus lasted for two and a half years. During most of this time the federal forces were pressing the Biafrans into a gradually shrinking enclave. By the end of the war Biafran territory had shrunk to less than one-tenth of the area Biafra had controlled at its beginning. In January, 1970, Biafra was also entirely landlocked, and all supplies had to be brought in by air. Inevitably, therefore, starvation and disease had become rampant. The total number of deaths from starvation and kwashiorkor will never be known; nor will the casualties in battle or from bombing. But they certainly run into millions, another deep scar on Nigerian consciousness the consequences of which no one can predict.

The war was fought at first between forces that, until the outbreak of hostilities, had been part of the same army. Because of their superior education, many of the Nigerian army officers had been Ibo—which may partially explain the early successes of the Biafran forces the Ibo officers were now leading. In September, 1967, it had even seemed that by bold tactics the Biafrans might reach Lagos. They had advanced into the mid-west, seized its capital, Benin, and reached Ore, only about one hundred miles from the capital, before they had been thrown back. But after Biafra's initial successes there was little threat to the rest of Nigeria. Biafran forces retreated.

Almost from the beginning of the war the federal air force had control in the air, though various sorties made by the handful of makeshift Biafran planes caused some damage throughout the war. Indeed, the main problem facing federal commanders was the training and deploying of a greatly expanded army. When the war began, they had about 9,000 troops; by the end of the war there were 120,000. The loss of many Ibo officers inevitably handicapped the Nigerian army's task. Moreover, the necessity to promote officers rapidly during the expansion led to inefficiency. Nor did war bring an end to the endemic Nigerian habits of personal rivalry, corruption, and ambition for power; indeed, the tremendous expansion of the army, and the large contracts and provisioning entailed, opened the way for corruption to become as much a part of military activity as it had been of political life.

In Biafra itself conditions were somewhat different. To most of the inhabitants the war seemed to be a people's war, as well as a battle for survival. The Biafran leaders convinced many of their people that the federal forces—particularly the northerners—were bent on genocide, the annihilation of all easterners. The people therefore believed that they must either fight or be massacred. Only toward the end of the war, when news began to percolate through about the numbers of Ibo living in federal territory unmolested and in peace, did conviction waver. And, while there doubtless were cases of corruption and intimidation within Biafra, there must also have been discipline, cooperation, and a sense of national purpose uncommon in Nigerian history. Some hope that the Biafran morale will still serve to strengthen the Nigerian nation.

As the war progressed, gradually yet steadily the federal forces pushed the frontiers of Biafra inward, from the south, west, and north. The loss of the oil centers—Bonny, Port Harcourt, Calabar—dealt severe blows to Biafra's economic prospects. By 1969 only one town, Owerri, remained in Biafran hands, and it was clear that Biafra could not win, unless some upheaval occurred within the federation. Biafra could only hold on.

When Biafra's fate became clear, in 1968, the argument over relief grew most bitter. Since the outbreak of the war, the federal government had, remarkably, allowed food and medicines to be sent to its enemies, but it feared that the Biafrans were using the aid that flowed from many international sources as a cover for supplies of arms. The Nigerians were therefore prepared to facilitate a daylight airlift but refused to countenance night flights, which could be used to reinforce the Biafran army.

The aid question was only one part of the paradoxical international involvement in the war. The federal government was always recognized as the legitimate government of Nigeria. As a member of the Commonwealth, the federal government was entitled to obtain arms from Britain, with which nation Nigeria also had a defense pact. Arms were also bought from the Soviet Union, which took the Leninist line that national self-determination involved recognition of one legitimate government. On the Biafran side, arms were bought quietly wherever they could be obtained. Almost as important, with the help of a first-rate public-relations firm in Switzerland, the Biafrans secured widespread international sympathy, particularly over the harrowing pictures of starving children that were frequently distributed.

Despite Biafra's outside help, by August, 1968, the federal government really believed that it was on the point of winning the war. However, it was then that the French began to supply Biafra with substantial quantities of arms, largely through the Ivory Coast and Gabon, ex-French colonies that had recognized Biafra. At the same time, it was believed that the Portuguese and South Africans were supplying arms to Biafra on the basis of their policy of "divide and rule." The war therefore went on.

Meanwhile, the African countries were very unhappy. Secession is a very dangerous concept in postindependence Africa. The frontiers of all states are artificial, drawn by their former European rulers. Africans are well aware that such frontiers enclose many communities that have had histories of conflict. Once an ethnic community had demonstrated the possibility of successful secession, the epidemic could spread to every African state. Consequently, the Organization of African Unity regularly preached unity and tried to mediate between Gowon and Ojukwu under the leadership of its senior member, the emperor of Ethiopia. The OAU efforts were as unsuccessful as were those of other bodies, including the papacy, the Commonwealth secretariat, and the British government. Finally, after nine months of fighting, President Nyerere of Tanzania and President Kaunda of Zambia both recognized Biafra, stating that although they believed in unity, people could not be driven into it by force, and hoping that their gesture would help to end the war. Tanzania and Zambia and the two ex-French countries were the only African states to recognize the rebel state. In any case, Nyerere and Kaunda were mistaken in their hopes and unfortunately antagonized Lagos, although their motives were undoubtedly humane.

Another factor that certainly played some part in international reactions was concern with the oil interests. Britain, Holland, and the United States were particularly involved in oil in Nigeria. For some time it was a matter of doubt whether Biafra would continue to control the oil installations or whether they were bound to fall into federal hands. Moreover, when federal forces did capture them, the installations still remained vulnerable to Biafran attacks and much damage was done to them by air raids. Consequently, the oil situation remained constantly uncertain, with corresponding effects on foreign policy. However, to what extent the oil companies influenced diplomatic attitudes remains unclear.

Toward the end of 1969 the federal forces had brought some coordination into their command and had accumulated sufficient firepower to give them a definite expectation of victory. It is therefore significant at this juncture that General Gowon again showed his sincere desire to end the rebellion without so antagonizing his opponents that their reintegration into the federation would be impossible. He did not aim to secure a complete military victory; he believed that this might well entail bitter fighting through the Iboland forests, probably followed by years of guerrilla warfare. Gowon's object was to bring sufficient military pressure on Ojukwu to persuade him that he could not win the war and that his best choice was to negotiate peace. If Ojukwu would not be persuaded, Gowon hoped that other Ibo leaders would recognize reality and overthrow Ojukwu in order to negotiate. Peace talks were actually scheduled for mid-December, Siaka Stevens of Sierra Leone acting as honest broker. At the last moment, however, the talks were postponed.

Ojukwu, making a last feeble effort to persuade the world

that he was willing to talk but that the federals had refused, did send a delegation to Addis Ababa, where the talks were scheduled, but stated that the talks were to be held under the emperor of Ethiopia in his capacity as head of his country, not as chairman of the OAU conciliation commission. The point of this maneuver was to escape from the unification policy that had always been the basis of OAU mediation. The ploy did not work; in fact, the emperor had asked the federal government to postpone the talks, and it seems as though, after all, the federals were not quite ready.

After Christmas, 1969, the military situation changed rapidly and radically. Federal forces met much less resistance than they expected: the Biafrans were worn out and debilitated; Owerri was taken; and the one remaining airfield at Uli came within shelling range. At the end of the first week in January Ojukwu left the country for the Ivory Coast and Effiong was left to sue for peace. He and his colleagues were greeted in Lagos by Gowon as brothers returning home. The war was over, and the mammoth tasks of creating peace had to be faced. Gowon's policy of negotiation in place of military victory never reached fruition—which left him with the massive problems that he had hoped to avoid.

The issues facing Nigerians at the end of the war may be divided into three categories: the immediate, the mid-term, and the long-term. Immediately, food, medicine, and relief had to be mobilized, transported to the rebel enclave, and distributed. This process was complicated by the fact that many of the relief organizations that had been working in Biafra were considered in Lagos to be hostile and dangerous to the federation. In any case, the outside world tended to regard Nigeria as a country in which alien organizations could take unilateral actions, whereas the whole purpose of the federal military action had been to prove that the central government could provide security and peaceful conditions for all its citizens.

Thus there was confusion, anger, and a great deal of misunderstanding in the early days of peace. The government insisted that it was the only responsible body and organized the relief effort under the Nigerian Red Cross and its own relief organization, led by a senior civil servant. Death and suffering certainly continued among the Ibo population after the end of the war, aggravated by the fact that the Biafran currency became worthless and that planting for the next harvest was bound to be terribly difficult in the immediate aftermath of war. Still, by its actions the federal government proved that it would make every effort to succor those it still considered to be Nigerians.

Second, the rebel Ibo had to be reintegrated into the Nigerian community, while the whole swollen apparatus of war had to be dismantled. Fortunately, an Ibo administration had already been assembled in Enugu under the leadership of Tony Asika and was ready to move into the stricken area, though the continued presence of troops and the danger of Biafran pockets of resistance in the bush might make its task hazardous. The rebel area, the East-Central State, was much smaller than the old eastern region and was therefore more easily handled; moreover, Ibo had been accustomed to live and work throughout the country. The problem was how to keep the core of Ibo living in the attenuated East-Central State employed and fed.

Most of the jobs Ibo had previously held, especially in the oil companies in Port Harcourt and surrounding districts, had been filled by other workers. There could be no question of dismissing the newcomers to accommodate the rebel Ibo, and it would take time before expansion had reached the point at which all former employees could be reemployed. Yet the federal government would be judged by its ability to fulfill its claim to reinstate and reintegrate the Ibo people.

Meanwhile, the federal government was faced with the awesome task of dealing with its swollen army. It would obviously be highly dangerous to demobilize too quickly, allowing trained soldiers, with arms and money but probably unemployed, to roam the country. Yet the cost and dislocation of economic life consequent on maintaining such large military forces in peacetime could not be borne for long. Either way, there were dangers ahead.

But these problems, daunting though they were, paled into insignificance beside the fundamental, long-term issues facing Nigeria's 50 million people. The war can be seen as one mountain across the path of Nigeria's twenty-year march toward a solution to its basic crisis. Nigeria climbed it, but the climb exhausted the country, and there were many more mountains ahead. An attempt had been made by the Ibo to essay the solution of separation; the attempt had failed, and to the extent that it was seen to fail, one path was closed as too dangerous to explore again. However, the attempt left deep scars and provoked heightened tensions among those seeking a solution. Yet, as the most famous Nigerian psychiatrist told the author, positive action can only arise from struggle. Some believed that the civil war would prove a salutary experience for Nigerians.

The Nigeria that emerged from the war was a vastly different society from the one that entered it. Local administration was divided between twelve states. This new division represented another path toward the solution of the basic dilemma of seeking a system that provided local autonomy for ethnic communities within a central authority capable of promoting national interests, but it was an expensive system. Before the military coups the federal government was composed of eighty members costing the country nearly $2.4 million yearly out of an annual government expenditure of some $206 million (there were also 160 members of regional governments along with about 1,000 members of parliaments). The twelve states were bound to increase this public expenditure considerably, and there were demands that some states be further subdivided.

Yet there were also some signs that local state loyalties had begun to develop, a change that could be healthier than the previous attitude to large regions in which many communities felt underprivileged. Certainly the minority groups felt more content, especially in the north, where it was thought that the Hausa-Fulani domination had been broken, and in the rivers area, where the Ibibio, Efik, and Ijaw showed no desire to return to Ibo rule. But the relationship between these states and the form of central government necessary for a strong Nigeria remained undecided. But then, this is not a specifically Nigerian problem; it is to be seen in many different states in the world, with India and the United States as prominent examples.

The local-central relationships issue seemed likely to be further complicated by the personalities involved. It was significant that at the end of the war several of the most prominent public men came from minority communities: Gowon himself, Effiong, Enahoro, and Tarka. Several of the army commanders also seemed to have political ambitions. And what was the future of the older politicians? Azikiwe had played a curious role during the war. At first he had represented Biafra, being partially instrumental in securing recognition for the regime by the four African states that were prepared to entertain the idea. Then he changed sides, coming out publicly for the federal case of a united Nigeria. Meanwhile, Awolowo, although a prominent member of the federal government, had kept out of the limelight, but within his western region Yoruba factional in-fighting had never ceased, sometimes breaking out into ugly violence. The dangers of a recurrence of the political intrigue, corruption, and thuggery that had disfigured precoup Nigeria were obvious for all to see.

Meanwhile, as the war came to an end, Africa was watching to see how its giant was to use its strength in continental affairs. Under Balewa, Nigeria had been one of the leaders of the "moderate" faction, a member of the Monrovia group that opposed the Casablanca radicals. Yet Nigeria had always tried to bridge the gap between the two groups and had played an important role in the creation of the OAU. It was the policy of South Africa's Vorster government, in line with its attitude to Malawi, Swaziland, and Lesotho, to seek influence through support of Biafra, not only to divide black Africa's most powerful state, but to entice it into the economic and diplomatic web that it hoped to spin throughout the continent. It would have suited this purpose well for secession to succeed and to be followed by further fragmentation of African states, leaving small units capable of being dominated by South African economic strength. This policy with regard to Nigeria had failed, but where would Nigeria stand in the major battle against the white supremacists of South Africa, Rhodesia, and the Portuguese territories?

Likewise, the rest of the world would watch the posture of the new Nigeria in foreign policy with interest, and, no doubt, it would be subject to many counter-pressures. The Russians had actively helped the federal government to win the war, while the Americans had remained neutral. Britain remained Nigeria's closest friend and ally, though its patronizing attitude and frequent parliamentary debates on Nigerian affairs constantly irritated Nigerians. Which way Nigeria would turn would remain important.

Fundamentally, though, it was economic policy that would most strongly influence Nigeria's future at home and abroad. The war had brought conflicting consequences. It had been disastrously expensive in resources, yet the economy remained basically strong. As always, war had stimulated industrial development, which, in turn, had assuaged the problem of unemployment and increased the gross national income. Yet industrial development also had aggravated the imbalance between rural and urban standards, between agriculture and industry, an imbalance that was partially offset by import controls, which had made the country almost self-sufficient in food production, whereas before the war 10 percent of foreign exchange had to be spent on food imports. Moreover, as the momentum of oil production picked up speed once more as hostilities ended, the accent on industrialization seemed bound to increase. Was Nigeria to become another oil client state, or could the oil wealth be controlled in such a way as to build a progressive state based on social justice?

It was the answer to this fundamental question that seemed likely to determine whether the young shoots of Nigerian nationalism that had tentatively pushed their heads above the ground during the war were to flower or wither. The history of Nigerians left a legacy of market-minded, competitive, individualistic, often venal characteristics. Nation-building demands austerity, probity, public honesty, and social justice. It was the clash of these two sets of values that had provoked the military coups and prepared the ground for the civil war. That traumatic experience revealed that the country had a civil service that could keep the state afloat through all storms and produced a captain in General Gowon who symbolized national brotherhood, honesty, modesty, and compassion. He offered his countrymen a national purpose to which all could contribute and in which all could share. The future resolution of the fundamental crisis would depend on whether Gowon's values or the debased standards of most previous public men were to prevail in postwar Nigeria.

SELECT BIBLIOGRAPHY

The bibliography, though extensive, is necessarily selective; a complete list of books touching on the subject matter would fill a book in itself. In my selection I have tried to refer readers, not only to the most important books, but also to those books that contain their own wide bibliographies. In particular, anthologies such as Hodgkin's *Nigerian Perspectives* and Davidson's *The African Past* supply invaluable references to source material from previous centuries, and it is unnecessary to duplicate materials listed in such books in this bibliography.

Modern books are now being published in so many different editions, often by various publishers, that to identify each publisher is becoming confusing. Consequently, references are confined to date and place of publication; details of publishers can easily be obtained from booksellers' lists.

CHINUA ACHEBE. *A Man of the People*. London, 1966; New York, 1966.

________. *No Longer At Ease*. London, 1960; New York, 1961.

________. *Things Fall Apart*. New York, 1959; London, 1958.

J. E. ADE AJAYI. *Christian Missions in Nigeria, 1841–1891.* Evanston, 1965.

_______. *Milestones in Modern Nigerian History.* Ibadan, 1962.

_______ & IAN ESPIE (eds.). *A Thousand Years of West African History.* London, 1965.

_______ & ROBERT SMITH. *Yoruba Warfare in the Nineteenth Century.* London, 1964.

WOGU ANANABA. *The Trade Union Movement in Nigeria.* London, 1969.

J. C. ANENE. *Southern Nigeria in Transition, 1885–1906.* New York, 1965; London, 1965.

OKOI ARIKPO. *Development of Modern Nigeria.* London, 1967; Baltimore, 1967.

OBAFEMI AWOLOWO. *Path to Nigerian Freedom.* London, 1966.

_______. *Thoughts on the Nigerian Constitution.* London, 1966; New York, 1966.

E. A. AYANDELE. *The Missionary Impact on Modern Nigeria, 1842–1914.* London, 1966; New York, 1967.

NNAMDI AZIKIWE. *Zik, a Selection from the Speeches of Dr. Nnamdi Azikiwe.* London, 1961; New York, 1961.

AHMADU BELLO. *My Life.* London, 1962; New York, 1962.

S. O. BIOBAKU. *The Egba and Their Neighbours.* London, 1957.

_______. *The Origin of the Yorubas.* Lagos, 1955.

J. W. BLAKE. *European Beginnings in West Africa, 1451–1578.* London, 1937.

_______. *Europeans in West Africa, 1450–1560.* London, 1942.

A. ADU BOAHEN. *Britain, the Sahara and the Western Sudan, 1788–1861.* London, 1964.

W. BOSMAN. *A New and Accurate Description of the Coast of Guinea.* 1701. Ed. J. R. Willis, J. D. Fage, R. E. Bradbury. London, 1967.

E. W. BOVILL & ROBIN HALLETT. *The Golden Trade of the Moors.* London, 1968.

R. E. BRADBURY. *The Kingdom of Benin.* London, 1957.

L. CABOT BRIGGS. *Tribes of the Sahara.* London, 1960.

R. L. BUELL. *The Native Problem in Africa.* London, 1928.

ALAN BURNS. *History of Nigeria.* 6th edition. London, 1963; New York, 1963.

JAMES S. COLEMAN. Nigeria: Background to Nationalism. London, 1958; New York, 1958.

MICHAEL CROWDER. *The Story of Nigeria.* Revised edition. London, 1966; New York, 1966.

SYBIL E. CROWE. *The Berlin West Africa Conference.* London, 1942.

PHILIP D. CURTIN. *Dimensions of the Atlantic Slave Trade.* London, 1969.

_______. *The Image of Africa.* London, 1964.

O. DAPPER. *Description of Africa.* In Dutch. 1688.

BASIL DAVIDSON. *The African Past.* London, 1964; Baltimore, 1964.

_______. *Black Mother.* London, 1961; New York, 1961.

_______. *A History of West Africa to the Nineteenth Century.* New York, 1966.

H. O. DAVIES. *Nigeria: The Prospects for Democracy.* London, 1961.

K. G. DAVIES. *The Royal African Company.* London, 1957.

HARM J. DE BLIJ. *A Geography of Subsaharan Africa.* Chicago, 1964.

M. DELAFOSSE. *The Negroes of Africa.* London, 1931.

K. ONWUKA DIKE. *Trade and Politics in the Niger Delta, 1830–1885.* London, 1956.

ELIZABETH DONNAN. *Documents Illustrative of the Slave Trade to America.* (4 vols.) New York, 1965.

MARY DOUGLAS & PHYLLIS M. KABERRY (ed.). *Man in Africa.* London, 1969.

RENÉ DUMONT. *False Start in Africa.* London; New York, 1966.

PAUL EDWARDS. *Equiano's Travels.* London, 1967.

JACOB U. EGHAREVBA. *A Short History of Benin.* Lagos, 1936.

CYPRIAN EKWENSI. *Jaguar Nana.* London, 1963; Evanston, 1963.

_______. *People of the City.* London, 1963.

ANTHONY ENAHORO. *Fugitive Offender*. London, 1965; New York, 1965.

J. D. FAGE. *A History of West Africa*. 4th edition. London, 1969; New York, 1969.

WILLIAM FAGG. *Nigerian Images*. London, 1963.

J. E. FLINT. *Ghana and Nigeria*. London, 1967.

———. *Sir George Goldie and the Making of Nigeria*. London, 1960.

BARRY FLOYD. *Eastern Nigeria*. London, 1969; New York, 1969; Toronto, 1969.

DARYLL FORDE (ed.). *Efik Traders of Old Calabar*. London, 1956; New York, 1968.

———. *The Yoruba-Speaking Peoples of South-Western Nigeria*. London, 1955.

——— & G. I. JONES. *The Ibo and Ibibio-Speaking Peoples of Southeastern Nigeria*. London, 1950.

——— & P. M. KABERRY (eds.). *West African Kingdoms in the Nineteenth Century*. London, 1967.

——— *et al. Peoples of the Niger-Benue Confluence*. London, 1955.

——— & R. SCOTT. *Native Economy of Nigeria*. London, 1964.

PAUL FORDHAM. *The Geography of African Affairs*. London, 1965; Baltimore, 1965.

MEYER FORTES & E. E. EVANS-PRITCHARD. *African Political Systems*. London, 1940.

S. H. FRANKEL. *Capital Investment in Africa*. London, 1938.

L. H. GANN & PETER DUIGAN (eds.). *Colonialism in Africa, 1870–1960*. Cambridge, 1969.

PROSSOR GIFFORD & W. ROGER LOUIS (eds.). *Britain and Germany in Africa*. London, 1967.

R. H. GREEN & ANN SEIDMAN. *Unity or Poverty?* London, 1968; Baltimore, 1968.

C. P. GROVES. *The Planting of Christianity in Africa*. London, 1948.

LORD HAILEY. *An African Survey*, revised edition. London, 1956.

———. *Native Administration in British African Territories*. (5 vols.) London, 1951.

ROBIN HALLETT. *The Penetration of Africa up to 1815.* London, 1965.

JOHN HARGREAVES. *Prelude to the Partition of West Africa.* London, 1963.

JOHN HATCH. *The History of Britain in Africa.* London, 1969; New York, 1969.

_______. *A History of Post-War Africa.* London, 1965; New York, 1965.

THOMAS HODGKIN. *Nationalism in Colonial Africa.* London, 1956.

_______. *Nigerian Perspectives.* London, 1960; New York, 1960.

S. J. HOGBEN & A. H. M. KIRK-GREENE. *The Emirates of Northern Nigeria.* London, 1966.

J. A. HORTON. *West African Countries and Peoples.* Edinburgh, 1969.

C. HOWARD & J. H. PLUMB. *West African Explorers.* London, 1951.

L. K. JAKANDE. *The Trial of Obafemi Awolowo.* London, 1966; Lagos, 1966.

H. A. S. JOHNSTON. *The Fulani Empire of Sokoto.* London, 1967; New York, 1967.

SIR HARRY H. JOHNSTON. *A History of the Colonialization of Africa by Alien Races.* Cambridge, 1930.

SAMUEL JOHNSTON. *History of the Yorubas.* Lagos, 1921.

G. I. JONES. *The Trading States of the Oil Rivers.* London, 1963.

K. A. B. JONES-QUARTEY. *A Life of Azikiwe.* London, 1965; Baltimore, 1965.

ROBERT S. JORDAN. *Government & Power in West Africa.* London, 1969.

ANDREW M. KAMARCK. *The Economics of African Development.* London, 1967.

A. W. LAWRENCE. *Fortified Trade-Posts. The English in West Africa, 1645–1822.* London, 1969.

_______. *Trade Castles and Forts of West Africa.* London, 1963.

J. M. LEE. *African Armies and Civil Order.* London, 1969.

_______. *Colonial Development and Good Government.* London, 1967.

I. M. Lewis (ed.). *Islam in Tropical Africa.* London, 1966.

Liverpool and Slavery. Published, 1884; reprinted, Newcastle upon Tyne, 1969.

P. C. Lloyd. *Africa in Social Change.* Baltimore, 1967; London, 1967.

Hollis R. Lynch. *Edward W. Blyden, Pan-Negro Patriot.* London, 1967; New York, 1967.

J. P. Mackintosh, *et al. Nigerian Government and Politics.* London, 1966; Evanston, 1966.

Evelyn C. Martin. *The British West African Settlements, 1750–1821.*

Gerald Moore & Ulli Beier, *Modern Poetry from Africa.* London, 1963; Baltimore, 1963.

W. B. Morgan & J. C. Pugh. *West Africa.* London, 1969.

G. P. Murdock. *Africa, Its Peoples and Their Cultural History.* New York, 1959.

C. W. Newbury. *British Policy Towards West Africa, 1786–1874.* London, 1965.

________. *The Western Slave Coast and Its Rulers.* London, 1961.

I. F. Nicolson. *The Administration of Nigeria, 1900 to 1960.* Oxford, 1970.

Obarogie Ohonbamu. *The Psychology of the Nigerian Revolution.* London, 1969.

C. Odumegwu Ojukwu. *Biafra (Vol. I).* New York, 1966; London, 1966.

________. *Biafra (Vol. II).* New York, 1969; London, 1969.

P. N. Okigbo. *Nigerian Public Finance.* Evanston, 1965; London, 1966.

Roland Oliver. *Sir Harry Johnston and the Scramble for Africa.* London, 1957.

S. K. Panter-Brick. *Nigerian Politics and Military Rule: Prelude to the Civil War.* London, 1970.

Margery Perham. *Lugard.* (2 vols.) London, 1960.

________. *Native Administration in Nigeria.* London, 1937.

BERNARD PORTER. *Critics of Empire*. London, 1968.

K. W. J. POST. *The Nigerian Federal Elections of 1959*. London, 1963; New York, 1963.

KEN POST. *The New States of West Africa*. Baltimore, 1964; London, 1964.

R. E. ROBINSON & JOHN GALLAGHER. *Africa and the Victorians*. London, 1961.

THE ROYAL INSTITUTE OF INTERNATIONAL AFFAIRS. *Nigeria: the Political and Economic Background*. London, 1960.

L. H. SCHÄTZL. *Petroleum in Nigeria*. London, 1970.

WALTER SCHWARZ. *Nigeria*. London, 1968.

RICHARD SKLAR. *Nigerian Political Parties*. Princeton, 1963.

SIR BRYAN SHARWOOD SMITH. *But Always as Friends. Northern Nigeria and the Cameroons, 1921–1957*. London, 1970.

M. SMITH. *Baba of Karo*. London, 1964; New York, 1964.

M. G. SMITH. *Government in Zazzau*. London, 1960.

ROBERT SMITH. *Kingdoms of the Yoruba*. London, 1969.

WOLE SOYINKA. *Kongi's Harvest*. London, 1967; New York, 1967.

_______. "The Lion and the Jewel," "The Trials of Brother Jero," "The Road" in *Five Plays*. London, 1964; New York, 1964.

A. P. THORNTON. *Doctrines of Imperialism*. New York, 1965; London, 1965; Sydney, 1965.

_______. *The Imperial Idea and Its Enemies*. London, 1963; New York, 1963.

ROBERT O. TILMAN & TAYLOR COLE (eds.). *The Nigerian Political Scene*. Durham, 1962.

J. S. TRIMINGHAM. *A History of Islam in West Africa*. London, 1962.

Y. URVOY. *Histoire de l'Empire du Bornu*. 1949.

JAMES R. WEBSTER & A. BOAHEN. *The Growth of African Civilization*. London, 1967.

JOAN WHEARE. *The Nigerian Legislative Council.* London, 1950.
FRANK WILLET. *Ife in the History of West African Art.* London, 1967.
ERIC WILLIAMS. *Capitalism and Slavery.* London, 1944.
H. S. WILSON. *Origins of West African Nationalism.* London, 1970.
RONALD WRAITH. *Local Government in West Africa.* London, 1964; New York, 1964.
_______ & EDGAR SIMKINS. *Corruption in Developing Countries.* London, 1963; New York, 1964.

INDEX